A General Theory of Exploitation and Class

John E. Roemer

A General Theory of Exploitation and Class

Harvard University Press
Cambridge, Massachusetts, and London, England
1982

Printed in the United States of America

Library of Congress Cataloging in Publication Data

Roemer, John E.
A general theory of exploitation and class.

Bibliography: p.
Includes index.
1. Marxian economics. 2. Historical materialism.
3. Social classes. 4. Communist countries—Economic conditions.
5. Communist countries—Social conditions. I. Title.
HB97.5.R6163 305.5 81-13329
ISBN 0-674-34440-5 AACR2

To Carla
and to the memory of my grandmother
Sarah Rostow Rosenbaum—
two women for whom these matters
are, and were always, more than academic

Preface

This book has developed, to some extent, independently of the will of its author. The question which originally provoked the study was: How can Marxism explain the apparent class phenomena and political behavior of socialist countries? This question has been posed by many; for me, it has been an issue since the late 1960s, but became particularly compelling with the war between Vietnam and China in 1979. These two countries both pass various tests for qualifying as socialist states, such as having fought long wars against capitalist and imperialist antagonists, led in each case by a communist party. But it is extremely difficult to understand how two socialist states can fight a war against each other, according to the received theory. There is, of course, a certain Ptolemaic approach which constructs epicycles on the old theory to explain ex post each aberration. But I think any honest appraisal must conclude that, within the Marxian tradition, a quite radically new application of historical materialist methods must be made to provide useful and convincing analysis of the economic and political behavior of socialist states. Without such a development, Marxism will atrophy as a science of society, taking its place as an exhibit in the history of thought, a corner to which it has already been relegated by much of Western social science.

My approach to the question has not been historical but theoretical, if such a distinction may be allowed. Marx imposed great clarity on the workings of capitalist economy by making certain highly stylized abstractions and proposing a theory of exploitation. That theory is the foundation from which Marxian political theory is developed. The natural approach for confronting the problem of modern socialism would seem to be to embed the Marxian theory of exploitation in a more general theory of exploitation which will be capable of specializing to cases other than capitalism—in particular, to socialism. One can that way perhaps propose a theory of exploitation and class for socialism which can provide a basis for a materialist political theory of socialism. This book presents such a general theory, although it is only the economic foundation. There is no attempt to develop its corollary political theory.

But once such a program is embarked upon, other questions arise. By embedding the Marxian theory in a more general environment, answers to many classical questions appear in a natural way. These questions concern the labor theory of value, the relative importance of various institutions for the presence of exploitation, the comparative ethics of bourgeois and Marxian ideology, the formation of classes, the claims of historical materialism. Thus, in the final product, only one chapter deals with the motivating question (Chapter 8), while the other nine chapters are necessary to report the answers to the other questions. For those who are not especially interested in existing socialist society, I hope the rest of the book will show the usefulness of the theory. For that usefulness can be demonstrated either by showing the theory's capacity to pose new questions and answer them, or by showing its capacity to answer old questions in a new and perhaps better way.

This said, I must add the book has weaknesses, which flow principally from its nonhistorical approach. There will be a charge that I have missed the correct explanation of contemporary socialist society by abstracting from the historical specificity of the birth of socialism in the first half of the twentieth century: in opposition to fascism, in poor and largely peasant societies. Readers must render a verdict on this. I present Part III more tentatively than Parts I and II. In the first two parts, the interpretation can be challenged, but the main argumentation is in the form of theorems, which are (I hope) not contestable. Part III, however, has a higher ratio of interpretation to theorems, and is therefore more open to question.

I have imposed on many friends to read the manuscript, and their comments and discussion have been the cause of substantial revisions. I am indebted to G. A. Cohen and Jon Elster for commenting upon the book with the precision and ruthless standards which they bring to their own work. Their intellectual comradeship has been invaluable. In Copenhagen, Birgit Grodal, Christian Groth, Hans Jacobsen, and Carsten Koch read the manuscript and simplified the proofs of several theorems in Part I. During a year spent at the Cowles foundation, I talked frequently with Roger Howe, always a ready listener; his support is only partially reflected in the several footnotes which credit him. Paul Rhode, in his capacity as research assistant, solved several problems with ingenuity and has been a valuable colleague. I am indebted to Zvi Adar, Wlodzimierz Brus, Paul Cantor, Hasan Ersel, Victor Goldberg, Leif Johansen, Serge-Christophe Kolm, Amartya Sen, George Silver, Laura D'Andrea Tyson, and Erik Wright. Each of them read parts or all of the manuscript and provided important comments and argument. In addition, I thank the many people who have commented on parts of this work as it has been presented in seminars.

Support for this project came from fellowships from the National Science Foundation and the John Simon Guggenheim Memorial Foundation, to whom I am grateful. (Of course, they cannot be held responsible for the views expressed.) The Cowles Foundation at Yale provided partial support and a stimulating environment for a year. I thank them, and especially William Brainard and Herbert Scarf, for their hospitality.

The manuscript was typed impeccably and cheerfully in various versions by Lydia Zimmerman and Marguerite Crown, who made the production of the physical commodity a carefree experience for me. And finally, I have appreciated the enthusiasm and skill of editors Michael Aronson and Katarina Rice of Harvard University Press.

Davis, California
September 1981

Contents

A General Theory of Exploitation and Class

Introduction

Two tasks are undertaken in this book, one urgent and practical for Marxism, the other more scholastic and theoretical. The practical problem is to classify modern socialist states in the taxonomy of historical materialism. The methodology chosen to accomplish this is to construct a general theory of exploitation—general in the sense that it has, as one special case, the Marxian theory of exploitation under capitalism. Other special cases will be feudal exploitation, neoclassical exploitation, and a new construct, socialist exploitation. As one consequence of the general theory, new insights are gained into classical debates in the Marxian theory of value. The general theory provides perspective on why Marxists identify capitalist exploitation with the expropriation of surplus value. As well as answering queries about the proper scope for the Marxian surplus labor theory of exploitation, I link the theory of exploitation with the theory of historical materialism in a precise way so that we can understand the sense in which historical materialism predicts an evolution in the forms of exploitation as history progresses. A theory of the formation of classes is also presented, together with a statement of the relationship between class and exploitation.

Thus, the original practical question concerning modern socialist societies leads to an embedding of the Marxian theory of exploitation into a more general theory, which in turn exposes the link between two great contributions of nineteenth-century Marxian thought: the economic theory of value and exploitation, and the theory of historical materialism. A preview is provided here so that those readers who do not share my interest in the practical problem of classifying modern socialism, and are therefore not motivated to read on by the following section, will perhaps be interested in the general theory of exploitation both in its own right and as a technique to shed light on the differing historical interpretations and values which lie beneath competing economic ideologies.

1. A crisis in Marxism

There is a crisis in Marxian theory, evidenced by its lack of success in explaining the behavior of and developments in modern socialist countries. The political behavior and to some extent the economic performance of these states appear to many late twentieth-century Marxists as a set of anomalies not predicted by the classical theory of scientific socialism of Marx and Engels. Concerning internal political behavior, lack of democracy appears to be, if not ubiquitous in modern socialism, at least sufficiently prevalent that the phenomenon cannot be dismissed as an aberration in a historical experience which was otherwise correctly predicted by Marxism. Concerning external politics, there are few Marxist commentators who approve of the foreign policy of both the Soviet Union and China. If Soviet policy in Eastern Europe is not considered imperialist, then Chinese policy toward South Africa and Pinochet's Chile is opportunist, and conversely. And how can Marxism explain the China-Vietnam war and the Vietnam-Cambodia war? Certainly one aspect of the classical Marxian legacy is that the basis for war is dissolved with the advent of socialism.

From the vantage point of classical Marxism there are also a number of riddles within the strictly economic realm, although perhaps these are not so puzzling as the political riddles. China's leaders are currently claiming that there has been no modernization in China in twenty years, that GNP per capita remained constant for a decade. In the Soviet Union and Eastern European countries, there are tremendous inefficiencies and problems of incentives. The conservative belief that human nature is unchangeable seems to gain credence, for if it is possible to create a socialist human nature, should not substantial progress in that direction have been made in two generations in the Soviet Union and one generation in China? All socialist countries, from Cuba to China to Hungary, seem to be putting increasing stress on the use of material incentives. Privilege and inequality are certainly not eliminated in modern socialist society.

Perhaps these phenomena are not all bad, or, more to the point, perhaps they are unavoidable and therefore to be expected. The question posed here is this: Has classical Marxism prepared us to expect what we see in modern socialism? I believe not, and the consequence is a theoretical disarray of modern Marxism in attempting to understand the laws of motion of socialism. The general expectation of Marxists had been that the annihilation of an economic system based on private ownership of the means of production would bring about a society which would be an unqualified improvement over capitalism. Few, however, would support that position today. How many Western Marxists can point to any socialist country as one which they would recommend that the proletariat in their country emulate?

With the problem stated, a terminological note is now appropriate. Since a purpose of this book is to classify certain modern states in the taxonomy of historical materialism, it is clearly premature to claim that China, the Soviet Union, the Eastern European countries, North Korea, Vietnam, and Cuba are or are not socialist, not to speak of other countries which are variously claimed to be socialist either by their own governments or by others. For the sake of definition I will call the above-named countries socialist. The main index of socialism, for my purpose, is nationalization of the means of production. My discussion of socialism will be at an abstract level, and will not enable us immediately to pass judgment on the precise classification of these particular societies. The hope is, of course, that the theory provided will lay the groundwork for a more painstaking and empirically tractable formulation of the problem.

Since the task here is to understand, at a certain theoretical level, the genesis of these aspects of modern socialist society, I do not believe it is necessary to rehearse extensively the good aspects of modern socialist states, of which there are many. Yet mention should be made of some of these, lest readers receive the mistaken impression that I believe modern socialism is an unmitigated degeneration when compared to capitalism. The growth rate of certain socialist countries during certain periods has been phenomenal. Most notable is Soviet industrialization, which played a large part in the destruction of Hitler. There can be no doubt of the exceptional performance of the Chinese economy when it is compared to India's. Socialist countries have, it appears, made progress in eliminating business cycles. There is an endemic shortage of labor in these countries, rather than unemployment. More specifically, labor power is not a commodity; the worker's survival and security does not depend on his ability to sell his services in the market. While this has given rise on the one hand to incentive problems, it also has ended many of the worst consequences of capitalism: abject poverty, much disease, and economic insecurity.

Nevertheless, the behavior of modern socialism constitutes a crisis for Marxism, for unless it can be understood, Marxism cannot claim to succeed in its task to provide a scientific analysis of the laws of motion of modern society. In particular, how can Marxism play a role as revolutionary doctrine, if this problem cannot be resolved? Marxism's revolutionary role is not a postulate, but a corollary of its theory of historical materialism. When nineteenth-century historical materialism came to an understanding that socialism was not only possible but necessary, and even inevitable, the activist role was mandated. It is conceivable that a modern historical materialist re-evaluation will decide that socialism is not possible, or not yet possible, in which case there is then no revolutionary role for the theory—but that, too, would certainly constitute a crisis for Marxism.

There have been attempts by Marxists to come to grips with this set of issues, but they have been mainly unsuccessful, in my opinion. Some circumstantial evidence for this failure is the lack of any consensus on (a) the class nature of socialist societies, (b) the cause of the aberrations in socialist performance, and (c) the dates at which the aberrations began. On the class nature of socialist societies, one can find represented among Marxists at least these positions: that the states in question are socialist, deformed workers' states, bureaucratic workers' states, transitional socialist, capitalist, state capitalist, feudal. The causes cannot be so simply enumerated, but the dates marking the "turning point" from the progressive development of socialism in the Soviet Union to its degeneration are variously reported as: 1917 (the Leninist revolution was a premature error), 1921 (the Kronstadt rebellion), early 1920s (the NEP), late 1920s (the victory of Stalin over Trotsky), 1929 (collectivization), middle 1930s (the purges), 1953 (the death of Stalin), 1956 (the Twentieth Communist Party Congress). Concerning the progress of socialism in China, the most conspicuous note is the disagreement within the Chinese Communist Party itself on the question. During the Cultural Revolution, the capitalist renegades were Liu Shaoqi and Deng Xiaoping; in 1980 the latter is in power at the head of the state, and the former has been rehabilitated as a great revolutionary communist.

Two errors in the method of study of the behavior of socialist countries are prevalent. The first consists of concluding that the society in question cannot be socialist because it displays certain features which are bad. (If two countries are at war with each other, at least one is not socialist; if privilege and inequality are significant, the society cannot be socialist; if a country practices an imperialist foreign policy, it cannot be socialist.) The weakness of this approach is that it explains nothing. "Socialism" is assumed to be a set of consequences, rather than a mode of production, the consequences of which we do not understand with any rigor. To the practitioners of this method, one might pose the question: What is the form of social organization which will give rise to the set of consequences envisaged as socialist? Indeed, the general assumption of nineteenth- and early twentieth-century Marxism was that if capitalism were overthrown by a party of the proletariat which nationalized the means of production and prevented capitalist counterrevolution, then socialism would ensue. This path was followed in a number of countries, yet the consequences were quite different from what Marxism seemed to predict, or from what Marxists expected. The argument for the nonexistence of socialism by unexpected consequences is no argument at all; it is an escape.

A second methodological error, from a *Marxian* vantage point, is to take as an explanation of the phenomenon a description whose terms are political or sociological, rather than economic or materialist. Quite apart from the validity of the charge that capitalism was reestablished in the Soviet Union as a consequence of Stalin's death and the ensuing takeover of the Communist Party by opportunists, such a description is not a Marxist explanation. For Marxism, political phenomena are corollary to economic phenomena. What is the underlying economic basis of such a coup, or of the rise of Stalinism (for a different story)? Even when such descriptions attempt to root the political phenomenon in some more social explanation, the underlying descriptions frequently use primitive sociological terms such as *elite, bureaucracy,* and *control,* rather than economic ones such as *class* and *ownership*. From a materialist viewpoint, one should be obliged to explain what economic phenomena give rise to political-sociological characterizations of elites and bureaucracies and locus of control. That is, the primitive terms in the answer to "why" should be economic ones. If it is not possible to provide such an economically based answer, then one must ask whether Marxism, or historical materialism, is a useful method for understanding the phenomenon.[1]

2. A general theory of exploitation

To understand why I choose to construct a general theory of exploitation to study the problem of modern socialism, one must look back to the problem Marx faced in his study of capitalism. The economic problem for Marx, in examining capitalism, was to explain the persistent accumulation of wealth by one class and the persistent impoverishment of another, in an economic system characterized by voluntary trade. Regarding feudalism, it was perfectly clear where the locus of expropriation (or appropriation) of surplus was, since the ties of bondage of the serf to the lord required the former to perform corvée and demesne labor. To state the point in a slightly more relevant way, it was no surprise that the lords became rich from serf labor, since the institution of labor exchange was a coercive one characterized by bondage. Obviously, the same is true of societies where the institution of labor exchange was slavery. The institutional innovation of capitalism, however, was to render labor exchange noncoercive: wage workers voluntarily trade labor power on the labor market. Perhaps the bargaining power of the two sides is not in balance, but that does not obviate the fact that the institution itself is noncoercive. The riddle for Marx was: How can one explain the systematic expropriation of the surplus product (beyond subsistence requirements of workers) by one class, by one side of the market, when the institution for labor exchange is not coercive? To answer this query, Marx constructed his theory of value and exploitation. The purpose of the value theory was to make the point that exchanges

1. Marxist scholars have made this admission with respect to other historical periods. G. A. Cohen claims that historical materialism cannot explain the "endless nuances" of precapitalist class history—the various forms of social organization in precapitalist class society. All that historical materialism explains, of this epoch, is that when society is capable of producing some surplus, some form of precapitalist class society will ensue; and that when the surplus becomes moderately high, capitalism will ensue. Between so-called Asiatic forms and feudalism, however, historical materialism cannot distinguish. (See Cohen, 1978, p. 200.)

under capitalism are not coercive but competitive; that idea takes the form of insisting that all commodities exchange "at their values." (Coercive exchange would, on the contrary, involve one side being forced to exchange its service for less than its value.) Despite these competitive exchanges in the labor market (and elsewhere), Marx maintains a systematic expropriation of surplus value emerges, which provides the theory of exploitation. A very simple model illustrating this theory is presented in the next section of this chapter.

The institutional culprit in the emergence of Marxian exploitation is the private ownership of means of production, or more accurately, the concentration of such ownership in the hands of a small class. The prediction was that if the means of production were nationalized and put in the control of the working class, then capitalist exploitation would cease. This recipe was not unique to Marxism but was shared by many socialists of the period. The contribution of Marx and Engels was to claim that such a development was possible, perhaps inevitable, and to display the mechanism by which the transformation would occur, a series of claims which were corollary to their theory of historical materialism.

Let me now draw the parallel which we face in studying modern socialism. We understand the locus of surplus expropriation under capitalism, as Marx did of feudalism. In the transition to socialist society, the institutional culprit responsible for capitalist exploitation has been eliminated, the private ownership of the means of production. Nevertheless, we observe certain systematic types of inequality, and certain political behaviors, which are less than ideal—one might wish to think of them as an indication of exploitation (which, of course, is an undefined term in this context). The institutional dimension which we are now required to vary is the one labeled "ownership locus of the means of production," not the one with which Marx was concerned, labeled "coerciveness of the institution of labor exchange." The formal problem, however, has the same abstract structure for us as for Marx. He required a theory of exploitation which was robust even when one relaxed the institutional specification of an economy concerning the coerciveness of its institution of labor exchange; we require a theory of exploitation which is robust even when one relaxes the institutional specification concerning the private locus of ownership of the means of production.

To put the matter still more generally, we would like to ask:

Which institutions of an economy are essential for some conception of exploitation to make sense, and which are incidental? Can we conceive of a theory of exploitation sufficiently general that it permits of definition even under conditions of considerable institutional variation? Presumably, such a theory should entail as one special case the phenomenon of Marxian exploitation, when the institutions are capitalist. Perhaps as another special case it can entail what might be called neoclassical exploitation, the situation prevailing, roughly speaking, when labor is not paid its marginal product. As another special case, the theory—if successful—would entail a notion of socialist exploitation, when the institutions of the economy are socialist.

But to what extent will the formulation of a theory of economic exploitation for socialist society provide an explanation for the political behavior of socialist society? The theory itself will be formulated in economic terms, and will deal, strictly speaking, only with inequality in distribution of the social product. This analysis can be called Marxist precisely because of the historical materialist premise underlying the approach: if we understand economic inequality and the relations of surplus appropriation in a society, then we can deduce political behavior, and the phenomena of the superstructure as corollary. In this book, only the theory of exploitation is provided; the corollary theory of socialist superstructure and politics is not constructed. Certainly one test for the usefulness of the proposed theory would be whether it entails a superstructural theory which appears to describe real socialist practice. Thus, in a certain practical sense the task here is quite narrow, as it provides only a theory of economic exploitation under socialism and does not directly account for some of the motivational material displayed in the first section, such as wars between socialist countries. In another sense the theory is quite broad, as it provides a recipe for cooking up a conception of exploitation for a general specification of an economy, and specifically displays a series of exploitation concepts which fit with the evolution of societies as described by historical materialism.

3. A simple model of Marxian exploitation

Although this book is not elementary, in that it is assumed the reader has some knowledge of Marxian exploitation, a simple model is presented here which illustrates the central concepts of that theory.

Consider a society which consists of many producers, which produces one good: corn. Each producer requires a certain amount of corn in a week to survive—say, one bushel. There are two techniques available for producing corn, and everyone has knowledge of both of them. The first technique is labor intensive (LI); it requires no seed corn as input, but a lot of direct labor. Indeed, it requires six days of labor to produce one bushel of corn using the LI technique. There is also a capital intensive technique (CI) which uses some seed corn (capital) as input. (Neither technique requires land; alternatively, land is in abundance.) Using the CI technique, one bushel of corn can be produced using only three days' labor; that labor also includes the time required to reproduce the seed corn employed. Thus, three days is the *labor embodied* in one bushel of seed corn produced net, using the CI technique. In Marxian language, socially necessary labor time is three days per week, since in that time the producer can produce his subsistence and replace the capital used up in so doing. (Actually, we will see in a moment that socially necessary labor time may be a bit more complicated.)

The problem is that not everyone can operate the CI technique, because it requires possession of seed corn. A producer will starve unless he eats every week. So a producer with no stock of seed corn cannot operate the CI technique; he does not have time in the week to produce, using the LI technique, both his subsistence needs and a stock of seed corn to operate the CI technique next week.

Suppose, now, there is a limited stock of seed corn. By "limited" I mean there is not enough to employ the whole population in the CI technique. There is, perhaps, enough seed corn to employ half the producers in the CI technique. But the stock of seed is not distributed equally among the population; it is all owned by several people. What will happen in a competitive economy? Assume initially that all the propertyless producers operate the LI technique, and work six days a week. (They do not desire to work the seventh day to accumulate some seed corn, or they are too tired to do so.) The few owners of the seed corn cannot possibly use it all by working it by themselves with their own labor, so they offer to hire others to work up some of it for them. They agree to pay, each week, wages in corn equal to the subsistence needs of the employed worker. The variable they set, which is the real wage, is the number of days in the week the employee must supply as labor to get his subsistence. If the work week is set at anything less than six days, the asset holders will be flooded with proletarians banging on their doors, because the alternative for a proletarian is to work six days a week using the LI technique. But there is not sufficient seed corn to employ all the propertyless producers; and so the asset holders will competitively set the length of the work week at six days. Six days is the equilibrium length of the work week in this example. (We assume no special disamenities from working in the CI technique compared to the LI technique. If there are such, the work week in the CI technique will equilibrate at something less than six days.)

But now a marvelous thing has happened. For each worker employed, the asset holder receives, net, two bushels of corn (six days' work on the CI technique) and he only pays out one bushel as a wage. Thus, he realizes as many bushels of corn as *profit* as he employs workers, which number is determined by the size of his capital stock. Each worker is working longer than socially necessary labor time (he produces a surplus over his subsistence needs), but this outcome is not the consequence of any coercion or cheating. It is the competitive outcome of individual optimization facing the given property constraints. It is important to notice that for this example to work, there must be an industrial reserve army—that is, more producers available than seed corn to employ them. For if, instead, seed corn were in excess relative to the labor supply, then the work week in the CI technique would be bid down to three days. Owners of seed corn would compete for workers, rather than the other way around.

What happens if the seed corn, still in short supply, is equally distributed among all the producers? We assume there is just enough to allow half the population to reproduce themselves using the CI technique. Then everyone will work exactly $4\frac{1}{2}$ days a week, assuming no surplus is produced. This can be arranged in various ways. The simplest way is for each producer to work $1\frac{1}{2}$ days a week on the CI technique using up and replacing his seed corn stock, and producing half a bushel of subsistence corn, and to work 3 days a week on the LI technique, producing the other half bushel. Alternatively, the same result can be arranged using either a labor market or a credit market. Using a labor market, some producers will offer to hire others at a real wage of half a bushel of corn for 3 days' labor, in the CI technique. It is easily checked that some producers can spend $4\frac{1}{2}$ days working in the CI technique, earning one bushel of corn, and others will spend $4\frac{1}{2}$ days working in the LI technique, earning a total of one bushel, three-fourths of it from their output in the LI sector and one-fourth of it as profit from the workers they hire on their capital in the CI technique. Thus, there can be an egalitarian but profit-taking society, if the distribution of capital is equal. In this case, one must conceive of socially necessary labor time as $4\frac{1}{2}$ days per week, not 3 days per week as originally claimed, because society must work, on average, $4\frac{1}{2}$ days to reproduce itself, given the scarcity of capital. There is no exploitation in the egalitarian society, since everyone works socially necessary labor time.

Return to the first example, where the propertyless work 6 days, in which they are therefore supplying $1\frac{1}{2}$ days a week of surplus labor, from the social point of view, or 3 days a week of surplus labor from the individual employer's point of view. Society has divided itself into two classes, the capitalists who hire labor and the proletarians who sell it.[2] Surplus value is expropriated from the proletarians by the capitalists. The proletarians work longer than is socially necessary, and this is so precisely because of their lack of access to productive assets. Indeed, the following are requirements for this example to work:

(1) a class of propertyless producers, in relative abundance to the supply of capital which can employ them;
(2) the existence of an inferior technology which can keep the unemployed industrial reserve army alive, so they continue to exert their downward pressure on the real wage next week;
(3) the necessity of time in production, so the propertyless ones cannot instantaneously synthesize seed corn, and, in fact, have no time to accumulate capital on their own, after seeing to their subsistence needs.

(In modern capitalism, (2) can, alternatively, take the form of state payments to the unemployed, or it can be the agricultural periphery from which workers are drawn to the capitalist sector.)

That the propertyless proletarians work longer than is socially necessary is called exploitation. The neoclassical or bourgeois replies to this accusation are various, and include the following. First, the model is not complete. Perhaps there is a reason that some have seed corn assets and others none; perhaps the asset holders worked very

2. More precisely, there is a third class as well, the peasants who stay in the LI technique and work 6 days a week. A question not pursued here: Are the peasants exploited?

hard in the past, and starved themselves, to accumulate their seed stock. Thus the differentiation of the population into asset holders and propertyless, before the model starts, is a consequence of differential rates of time preference on consumption, and not something that, therefore, should lead to consequences called exploitative. A second reply is that the model is incompletely specified in other ways: perhaps there are some special skills which make it possible to operate the CI technology, which only a few people have. The propertyless ones could not operate CI on their own even with the seed stock. (Perhaps anyone could accumulate seed stock, but only the "capitalists" do, since the others do not know how to use it anyway.) The proper interpretation, then, is that the proletarians are trading their "surplus" labor for the exercise of skills by the capitalist, without which CI could not be used. (We can even change the model slightly so that even the proletarians are strictly better off working for the capitalists than they would be partaking of the idiocy of rural life using LI, yet "surplus" labor still passes to the capitalist.) Thus, it is not correct to view the extra work time provided as a surplus, because it is, from the proletarian's viewpoint, a fair trade for the skill of the capitalist. Another scarce skill the capitalist might possess, which the proletarian does not, is risk-taking ability. The "surplus" labor provided by the proletarian is then viewed as his insurance premium against the alternative of having to become a capitalist and take those horrible risks himself.

I will not attempt to reply to these replies at this point. The Marxian contention, in brief, is that no good justification exists for the differential access to the means of production, and the proletarians are exploited precisely because they are denied access to them, under capitalist property relations, for no justifiable reason.[3] The subtleties in the account of this position will occupy us in Part III of the book.

4. A brief outline

In this section an outline of the main line of argument is presented. It is hoped that this section, as well as being a preview, can serve as a

3. Some further discussion is available in Roemer (1981, pp. 83–86).

summary which the reader will refer to after finishing the book, to tie together the argument.[4]

Instead of attempting to formulate a general definition of exploitation from the start, I ask the question: What institutions are necessary to generate the familiar phenomenon of Marxian exploitation? In Part I, models of precapitalist, private ownership, subsistence exchange economies are constructed, and it is shown that Marxian exploitation exists in these models. In the starkest model of this type, displayed in Chapter 1, individual producers are concerned only with producing enough exchange value to purchase their subsistence needs. Since there is trade, an individual need not produce the physical bundle he must consume, but what he produces must be worth as much as his subsistence requirements, at the going prices, so he can trade to acquire his subsistence. Producers differ only in their endowments of stocks of produced goods; this is important because what stocks they possess determine which production activities they can operate, as it is assumed that a producer must lay out the costs of production before production begins. That is, time is essential in production, and a producer cannot borrow against future revenues to finance production today. Thus, wealthier producers have greater production opportunities, and can produce the exchange value they need to purchase subsistence with less labor than poor producers. It is also assumed there is no labor market, nor any institution for labor exchange in this model.

What is perhaps surprising is that although there is no accumulation in this model, and no institution for labor exchange, there is a phenomenon of Marxian-like exploitation. At a reproducible solution of the model (which is the appropriate notion of equilibrium), some producers work longer than is socially necessary, in the Marxian sense, to subsist, and others work less long than is socially necessary. In total, society always works precisely the total socially necessary labor time. Thus, the rich are able to "exploit" the poor despite the absence of *any* institution for labor exchange, whether it is coercive or not, and despite the lack of accumulation of a surplus. Exploitation is mediated entirely through the markets for produced commodities.

This conclusion is interesting in its own right, for it implies that

4. There is also an article summarizing this book in somewhat more detail than this section (Roemer, 1982).

competitive markets and the differential ownership of the means of production are the institutional culprits in producing Marxian exploitation, rather than the key locus of exploitation being at the point of production where labor is directly expropriated by the capitalist from the worker, as is often implied by classical Marxian theory. But our interest in the model, more generally, is that it permits us to conceive of Marxian exploitation as a phenomenon which can exist with considerable institutional variation in the specification of the economic mechanism.

In this first model, producers are divided into exploiters and exploited at an equilibrium, but all producers are of the same *class,* in that they all relate to the means of production in the same way—each has to work for a living, and there is no labor hiring or labor selling. In Chapter 2 we append a labor market to the economy of Chapter 1. The economy is still a subsistence one, where producers are motivated only to produce enough exchange value to subsist, and where they differ only in their endowments of produced assets. Subject to the goal of subsisting, each tries to minimize labor performed. Their options are now broadened, however, with the opening of a labor market. Each can now choose to operate production activities on his own, hire labor to operate them, or sell his labor power for a wage. There are thus three qualitatively different sources of revenues. When a producer optimizes, he will in general engage in some combination of these three types of activity. This defines his *class position.* For instance, if a producer optimizes by hiring labor only, and does not work his own shop at all or hire himself out, he is a "pure capitalist." If he optimizes by selling labor power only he is a "pure proletarian"; if he operates his own shop he is a "petty bourgeois." There are also various combinations of the three pure class positions which producers may choose in order to optimize. Altogether there are five relevant class positions which determine an exhaustive and pairwise disjoint decomposition of society. It is noteworthy that class position is determined endogenously in the model, as a consequence of producers' optimizing behavior facing wealth constraints.

As in Chapter 1, producers in the model with labor market are also decomposed into exploiting and exploited producers at an equilibrium, depending on whether they work less or more than socially necessary labor time. We have now two decompositions of society at an equilibrium: one into exploiters and exploited, the other into the five classes. The key theorem of Chapter 2 relates these two decompositions, and is therefore called the Class Exploitation Correspondence Principle (CECP): it states that every producer who must hire labor power to optimize is an exploiter, and every producer who must sell labor power to optimize is exploited.

This theorem is remarkable because it formally models and verifies a key Marxian insight—that membership in a labor-hiring class is associated with exploiting, and membership in a labor-selling class is associated with being exploited. Such a statement may seem to be a truism and not remarkable, but in this model both exploitation status and class position emerge endogenously as a consequence of individual optimization in the face of a constraint determined by one's ownership of productive assets. Thus, it is not at all obvious that the CECP will be true; its verification can be taken to show that the Marxian theory of class and exploitation can be derived simply from the institutional specification of the subsistence model of Chapter 2. The Class Exploitation Correspondence Principle is the most important analytical result of Part I of the book, and it is used to give new insights into Marxian value theory in Part II.

As a consequence of the model developed in Chapter 1 I am able to say that Marxian exploitation can logically exist even with no institution for labor exchange, a somewhat heretical statement. With the opening of a labor market, however, exploitation is further articulated into a class decomposition of society. Next, in Chapter 3, we pursue the heretical path of Chapter 1 by showing that classes, also, can be produced in an economy without a labor market. Instead of opening a labor market (that is, appending a labor market to the subsistence economy of Chapter 1), we open a credit market. Producers are not allowed to hire and sell labor power; however, they can lend and borrow finance capital from each other at an interest rate. This gives rise to three types of revenue-raising activity in which a producer can engage: he can operate production activities on his own funds, he can operate them on borrowed funds, or he can lend out funds at interest. A class decomposition of society again follows, at equilibrium: the three pure class positions are the pure lenders, the pure borrowers, and those who are neither borrowers nor lenders. There are also mixed class positions, with five relevant classes in all. The key theorem of Chapter 3 relates the class decomposition which obtains in the credit market economy to the one which obtains in labor market economy. It is called the Isomorphism Theorem, as it states that the two class decompositions are identical. Pure capitalists in the labor market economy become pure lenders in the credit market economy, pure proletarians become pure borrowers, and so on. The two markets are functionally equivalent in the sense that they produce precisely the same exploitation and class profiles. A producer with given wealth will work precisely as long in the two economies.

The Isomorphism Theorem informs us that the labor market is not necessary to produce the class phenomenon which we associate with it; in fact, an identical class structure can be induced by a credit market. Thus, not only is a labor market unnecessary to produce Marxian exploitation, it is also unnecessary to produce Marxian classes. The entire orchestration of exploitation and class can be logically mediated simply through a capital market, without the existence of any institution for the direct exchange of labor.

I hasten to emphasize that this is a *logical* construction only, for there are certainly differences between labor and credit markets which are not captured at this level of abstraction, which historically have necessitated the development of labor markets as the locus of capitalist exploitation. My argument, however, is conducted at the level of abstraction which is usual in discussions of Marxian value theory, or neoclassical value theory for that matter. Hence, one conclusion is this: if one wishes to understand the labor market as an institution of capitalism qualitatively different from the credit market in its function vis-à-vis the articulation of exploitation and class, one must proceed to a finer level of concreteness in institutional specification than is customary in these models. But an important conclusion of Part I is that it is the differential ownership of productive assets, rather than what happens in the labor process, that is the key determinant of Marxian exploitation.

In Part II a model of an accumulation economy—a polar opposite of the subsistence economy—is constructed, and a definition of Marxian exploitation in that model is proposed. The methodological program is to verify the CECP in the accumulation model, and along the way we infer some startling facts about Marxian value theory. The first task of Chapter 4 is to propose a definition of Marxian exploitation which makes sense in the accumulation model, when all agents are trying to accumulate as rapidly as possible. Subsistence is now irrelevant. An agent tries to maximize the revenues he can earn, through operating production activities, hiring labor power, and selling it, constrained as before by his access to finance capital. I define a concept of exploitation which is independent both of any subsistence concept and of agents' subjective preferences. The proposal is, briefly, this. An agent is exploited if, no matter how he spends his revenues from production, he cannot possibly purchase a bundle of goods which embodies as much labor as he in fact worked. Similarly, an agent is an exploiter if, no matter how he dispenses his revenues, he cannot help but purchase a bundle of goods which embodies more labor than he worked. Thus, at an equilibrium, society is decomposed into three groups: exploiters, exploited, and a "gray area" of agents who are neither exploited nor exploiting. Because of the definition, this gray area is in general quite significant.

As before, society is also decomposed into classes at an equilibrium, and the question is: Does the Class Exploitation Correspondence Principle still hold? This is a decidedly more difficult question than in Part I, because of the new definition of exploitation and its consequent gray area. Nevertheless, the CECP remains true when production is characterized by a Leontief input-output model, which is proved in Chapter 4. The validity of the CECP may be taken as a verification that our definition of generalized Marxian exploitation, in the accumulation model, is correct, in the sense that it permits the preservation of this fundamental Marxian insight concerning the relation between class and exploitation. We are also able to view the classical transformation problem through the lens of the CECP. It turns out that the existence of the gray area is equivalent to the transformation problem, and the CECP can be viewed as the satisfactory "resolution" of that problem.

In Chapter 5 I tackle the problem of the validity of the CECP in a more general model of production than the Leontief model. I posit only that the production set is a convex cone, which includes, of course, the case of the von Neumann activity analysis technology, which has become a more frequent object of study in Marxian discussions. The Class Exploitation Correspondence Principle would be a rather fragile idea if it were true only for the Leontief technology, and so it is an important result that it remains true when production is specified simply as constant returns to scale, that is, as any convex cone. Proving the CECP for the cone technology, however, involves an important surprise. The first step in setting up the theorem is to propose a definition of labor-embodied in goods, and therefore a notion of Marxian exploitation, when the technology is no longer Leontief. This, however, has been done, by Morishima (1974) for the von

Neumann technology, and generalized in Roemer (1980a) to a general convex technology. The disturbing result is that if we use the received Morishima definition of labor-embodied for the cone technology, the CECP is false.

Is the CECP, then, a fragile idea which is valid only in a very special model of production? This, indeed, would be a blow for the Marxian theory of exploitation and class; in particular, that theory could not be said to be valid in the presence of fixed capital, joint products, substitution between factors, and so on. Or is there a missing piece to the puzzle? The reader will, I hope, forgive my account of this part in detective-story fashion: that genre does capture the nature of my search for the answer to this problem.

The solution is that one requires a new definition of labor-embodied in the cone technology to make the CECP true. The new definition is eminently sensible, and is better than the received Morishima definition in a number of ways; the surprise is that the new definition makes labor-embodied in commodities depend on the market. One cannot define labor-embodied until one knows what equilibrium prices are. This has startling conclusions for a venerable debate in Marxism concerning the logical priority of prices versus labor values. The fundamentalist position maintains that labor value exists logically prior to and independent of prices. The more recent, revisionist position is that prices and values have a common ancestor, but that neither determines the other. The position necessitated by the argument of Chapter 5 is that, if we wish to preserve the Marxian correspondence between exploitation and class, then we must adopt a definition of labor value, in the case of general technology, which renders values dependent on prices.

It is instructive to note the methodological role which the CECP has played in the development of the analysis to this point. We first proved the CECP in a simple model of production. But although the formal appearance of the CECP is as a theorem, its epistemological role is as a postulate; that is, we wish to construct models which verify our intuition that the CECP should be true. (Our models are formal attempts to verify a certain intuitive theory.) In so doing, we are directed to choose certain definitions of the basic concepts of the model, such as labor-embodied and exploitation. Thus, the CECP finally informs our understanding of how basic concepts must be conceived: in particular, *labor value must depend on the market,* in the general case.

In Chapter 6 another aspect of the model is perturbed. Instead of assuming that every agent has the same amount of labor power, I assume a differential endowment of labor power. This is a simple way of approximating the idea that different producers have different skill levels, although the model assumes that the differentially endowed labor power is all of a homogeneous skill level. The CECP is proved for this model, but again there is a surprise. While it remains true that class and exploitation status are correlated in the proper way, as specified by the CECP, it is no longer true as it was before that these statuses are correlated with wealth in the proper way. That is, with differential labor endowment there may be labor sellers who are exploited, but they are rich, and labor hirers who are exploiting, but they are poor. Thus, although the relation between class and exploitation continues to hold, neither class nor exploitation is an indication of welfare, if we take wealth as the proxy for welfare. How useful is a concept of exploitation which has no obvious correlation to welfare? By constructing a model with differential labor endowment, we have pushed the Marxian theory of exploitation to the limits of its credibility. I argue that when labor is assumed to be heterogeneous, the Marxian theory of exploitation is even less tractable.

The anomaly of Chapter 6 will only be resolved with the general theory of exploitation of Part III, when we conclude that the *Marxian* theory of exploitation does not generalize properly to models where agents have differential labor endowments, or where there is heterogeneous labor. Thus, the surplus labor theory of exploitation which we have studied in Parts I and II ceases to give the right answers when labor is no longer equally endowed to all. While problems with Marxian exploitation have long been known to exist when labor is heterogeneous, the usual conclusion has been that, therefore, the Marxian concept of exploitation only applies in a very special situation. But our approach of embedding the Marxian theory of exploitation in a more general theory enables satisfactory resolution of the problem of differential or heterogeneous labor endowments. The resolution, again heretically, will be to redefine Marxian exploitation in language entirely independent of the labor theory of value.

In Part III the general theory of exploitation is proposed. All the models of Parts I and II are of Marxian-like exploitation, and our general theory must be sufficiently flexible to include them as special cases. The general definition of exploitation is proposed and developed in Chapter 7. It is a game-theoretic definition in which property relations, not the labor theory of value, is the central concept. An individual or coalition is considered to be exploited if he (or they) has (have) some alternative which is superior to the present allocation. How we specify the alternative determines the type of exploitation which we conceive of. Formally, we think of the alternative as specified by the characteristic function of a game. If a coalition is receiving less, at a given allocation, than it would receive as its payoff under the characteristic function of the specified game, and if its complementary coalition is receiving more currently than under the alternative, then it is exploited with respect to the conception of exploitation associated with that game.

I then offer different specifications of the alternative which capture notions of feudal, capitalist, and socialist exploitation—that is, three different games. Each game, or characteristic function, is defined by adopting a particular specification of property relations which we conceive of a coalition as being entitled to, if the coalition exercised its option to "withdraw" from the economy and take the payoff assigned to it by the characteristic function.

It turns out that feudal exploitation is equivalent to the neoclassical concept of exploitation: a producer is exploited if he is not being paid his marginal product. The neoclassical statement that an agent is not exploited so long as he receives his marginal product becomes, in our theory, "There is no feudal exploitation under (perfect) capitalism."

Capitalist exploitation turns out to be equivalent (for all practical purposes) to Marxian exploitation, when labor is homogeneous and equally endowed to all. But there is a decided superiority of our formulation of capitalist exploitation in the game-theoretic manner to the Marxian formulation in terms of surplus value: the game-theoretic formulation is independent of the labor theory of value. Indeed, it makes no mention of labor values, but poses the test for exploitation in terms of an alternative specification of property relations—namely, that access to alienable means of production should be equalized for all producers. Because of its independence of the labor theory of value, the game-theoretic notion of capitalist exploitation is also viable when there are differential skills. We are therefore able to finesse all the criticisms of Marxian exploitation which can be made because of its reliance on the labor theory of value. But in addition the game-theoretic formulation is superior in that it makes explicit what ethical presumption lies behind the Marxian theory of exploitation: that presumption is displayed in the assumption of egalitarian property entitlements which poses the alternative against which one evaluates whether a coalition is capitalistically exploited. Indeed, it is clear from the analysis that neoclassical (or feudal) exploitation arises as a consequence of barriers to free trade, and Marxian (or capitalist) exploitation arises from barriers to opportunities which agents face as a consequence of their restricted access to the alienable, nonhuman means of production. Feudal exploitation is that inequality which arises as a consequence of ties of bondage which prevent producers from freely engaging in trade, with their own assets; capitalist exploitation is that inequality which arises as a consequence of the constraints in access to private alienable property, which hinder producers' opportunities in production.

The Marxian surplus labor theory of exploitation, thus, appears as a special instance of a more general theory which is expressed in the language of property relations, not the labor theory of value. Not only is the labor theory of value irrelevant as a theory of equilibrium prices, but it can also be dispensed with, and fruitfully so, in the theory of exploitation. The various arguments for the superiority of the property relations approach over the surplus labor approach are summarized in Chapter 7.

Socialist exploitation, the third variety, arises as a consequence of producers' different endowments of inalienable assets, chiefly skills. The hypothetical alternative against which one tests whether a producer is socialistically exploited is one in which he would have access to his per capita share of society's skills. Thus, feudal exploitation entails a situation where producers have differential access to freedom from bondage; capitalist exploitation exists when they have differential access to alienable productive assets; socialist exploitation exists when inalienable assets are differentially endowed. All three forms of exploitation exist under feudalism; capitalist and socialist exploitation exist under capitalism, but feudal exploitation does not, in principle; and under socialism, only socialist exploitation continues to exist, in principle. Each revolutionary transition has the historical task of eliminating its characteristic associated form of exploitation.

In Chapter 8 I descend from the heights of pure abstraction and apply the theory developed in Chapter 7 to existing socialist countries. To what extent can one classify the inequality which exists in these societies into the various forms of exploitation? This entails a discussion of the literature on the nature of the mode of production in these countries, and I am able to phrase the various positions in terms of the theory. My conclusion is that socialist exploitation certainly exists in these societies, as it should. Moreover, another kind of exploitation exists, which I name status exploitation: it is that inequality which arises as a consequence of unequal access to privileged positions. I argue that both status exploitation and socialist exploitation are prevalent under existing socialism, but that capitalist exploitation is not. In particular, the theory implies that it is incorrect to conceive of these societies as capitalist in any meaningful sense.

The concept of socially necessary exploitation is also introduced in Chapter 8. A form of exploitation is socially necessary if its elimination would alter incentives and institutions in such a way as to render the exploited *worse* off. The concept of socially necessary exploitation entails our relaxation of a ceteris paribus assumption on institutions and incentives. In modern socialism, for example, socialist exploitation takes the form of material incentives to skills—the highly skilled are paid more. If, however, one were to eliminate these payments, those skills might not be developed or offered, with the consequence that everyone would be worse off, including the poorly skilled. That is, there is no way at this point in history of receiving the benefits from those skills unless those benefits are differentially received. If a form of exploitation is socially necessary at a given time in history, it would be utopian to demand that it be eliminated. (In parallel the Rawlsian maximin principle is mentioned.) There is some discussion in Chapter 8 of the social necessity of the forms of exploitation which are present in existing socialism. This discussion is shown to provide some insight into the debate on the plan versus the market in modern socialism.

There is an obvious similarity between the theory of exploitation which has been advanced, of the successive elimination of feudal, capitalist, and perhaps socialist and status exploitation, and the theory of historical materialism. Chapter 9 makes these links explicit. I discuss the relationship between the successive elimination of the various forms of exploitation and the motive force in the theory of historical materialism, the development of the productive forces. To what extent can the development of productive forces drive this successive elimination? We observe that the two dynamics are not quite the same, although they are related. From this we gain some new perspective on Marx's theory of self-actualization of man, the teleological aspect of historical materialism. Why is it good to eliminate exploitation? Finally, we are able to resolve a question which has surfaced at various points: Why is the labor theory of exploitation, and not a corn theory or an energy theory, appropriate for describing capitalism? The answer is of the following qualitative form: although the labor theory of exploitation is not objectively true, as Marxists have often claimed in the past, it is the normative theory of exploitation which must be used to describe the capitalist epoch if one adopts historical materialism as one's view of history. If one adopts a view of the motive force in history as man's struggle against nature, then the labor theory of exploitation is not appropriate. If one takes as a more illuminating historical description the struggle of class against class (albeit perhaps as a consequence of natural scarcity), then the Marxian theory of exploitation is mandated as the corollary ethically appropriate description of the capitalist period. Thus, a conclusion concerning competing theories of value is this: one cannot settle such a debate at the level of value theory per se. The debate must rather be conducted at the level of which historical description is more enlightening, more "correct"; for the competing theories of value derive only as corollaries to their associated conceptions of history.

While starting to build a theory of exploitation capable of shedding light on existing socialist society, I construct a sufficiently general apparatus to resolve various classical debates in Marxian value theory and to permit a schematic representation of historical materialism. The general theory of exploitation, furthermore, facilitates a comparison of Marxian and bourgeois economic ideology, by permitting an explicit representation of the normative presumptions behind their differing conceptions of exploitative economic relations. The theory of historical materialism explains why Marxists subscribe to the view that the transfer of surplus value is exploitative under capitalism, but it also claims, as I understand it, that the relevant form of exploitation evolves as history does.

5. A defense of method

A perhaps unfortunate and certainly sectarian habit within Marxism is to subject any piece of work to a series of tests before it is admitted to the academy of Marxian analysis. What becomes problematical with this practice is the lack of consensus on what the criteria should be. Doubtless this book will be attacked from some quarters as un-Marxian, for at least three reasons: (1) the analysis is not explicitly historical; (2) the concepts are not explicitly from Marx, but are generalizations of Marx's concepts; (3) no exegetical attempt is made to support arguments by reference to Marxian texts. In addition, a number of conclusions such as those reached concerning the labor theory of value will be viewed as heretical within the Marxian tradition. This fourth objection, however, should be reducible to a more basic objection, since if one claims a certain conclusion is un-Marxian, then something in the method or premises must have already been un-Marxian.

To these criticisms, my defense runs briefly as follows. Concerning (1), it is clear that the motivation of this work is to explain an important historical phenomenon. That the work in its present state is not more explicitly historical is due partly to my limitations and partly to time and space limitations. Moreover, the role of abstraction and theory in Marxism requires, I would hope, no more rehearsal. Concerning (3), I have explicitly avoided exegetical reference (except where I cannot resist mentioning an appropriate quotation), because I do not see what bearing Marx's statements could possibly have in passing judgment on the validity of a theory constructed to explain history occurring a century after his death. At best, such exegesis could verify the consistency of the theory with his theory. But concern with consistency often causes one to relax inquiry as to validity, for the goal becomes the demonstration of proper pedigree of the theory, rather than of its usefulness.

Objection (2) is the one against which I am most vehement. That part of Marx's work which I consider the core insight is the doctrine of historical materialism. Marxist economic theory, as such, was the attempt of a nineteenth-century economist to apply the historical materialist method to an analysis of nineteenth-century society. The categories and concepts which were useful for that purpose are not necessarily the ones useful for analyzing late twentieth-century society. Our task cannot be the application of "Marxism" to late twentieth-century conditions, but of the historical materialist hypothesis to those conditions. The product of this method here is a general historical materialist theory of exploitation. If this exercise and others like it cannot produce a theory which makes sense of current reality, then it will be appropriate to question the validity of the hypothesis of historical materialism, a task which is beyond our scope here. If, however, this theory of exploitation does aid us in understanding modern socialist society, that would reinforce the usefulness of a historical materialist approach.

Part I

Exploitation and Class in Subsistence Economies

The experiment of varying the institutions of an economy, to see in what environments a Marxian-like phenomenon of exploitation can take place, begins in Part I. Rather than studying a model of socialist economy, it is prudent to examine a simpler economy than capitalism, to proceed backward in logical time, as it were, and postulate a hypothetical precapitalist, commodity-producing, exchange economy, where each producer is guided simply by the motivation to subsist.

I will examine a series of models of precapitalist, subsistence economies. In the first of these, the subject of Chapter 1, markets exist only for produced commodities, not for labor power. Nevertheless, a phenomenon of exploitation—the systematic expropriation of surplus value—emerges in the economy. Thus, while Marx showed that exploitation could be meaningfully conceived of when the institution for labor exchange was noncoercive, my conclusion is stronger: exploitation, in the Marxian sense, can exist even when there is no institution of labor exchange, no surplus produced, and no accumulation of wealth in the economy. This should indicate that the phenomenon under study is considerably more robust to institutional variation than one might have thought.

In Chapters 2 and 3 I introduce a labor market and then a credit market into the subsistence economy, and examine the consequences for the articulation of the exploitation phenomenon. With the advent of either of these two additional markets, classes, which do not exist in the simpler economy of Chapter 1, will emerge. The key question of these chapters will be the relationship between exploitation and class, both endogenous phenomena of the economies.

1

Exploitation in a Precapitalist Subsistence Economy

1. Two elementary subsistence economies

A. Simple Commodity Production (SCP)

The first model is one of classical simple commodity production. There are N producers (or agents), all identical. Each producer requires for subsistence a certain vector $b \in \mathbb{R}^n_+$, to be thought of as a column vector. Each producer can operate any activity of a certain Leontief input-output technology (A, L), where:

> A is an $n \times n$ commodity input-output matrix of activities
> L is a $1 \times n$ row vector of direct labor coefficients.

That is, there are n goods, and production of one unit of the jth good is accomplished using as commodity inputs A_j, the jth column of A, and L_j units of labor, measured in producer-days.

We assume for the duration of Part I:

Assumption 1.[1] A is indecomposable and $L > 0$.

These assumptions simplify the analysis, and do not qualitatively alter the results.

The subsistence assumption for this economy is captured as follows. There are markets for the n commodities but not for labor power. Facing a commodity price vector $p \in \mathbb{R}^n_+$, each producer will

1. Convention on vector orderings: for two vectors x and y, $x > y$ means $x_i > y_i$ for all components i; $x \geqq y$ means $x_i \geqq y_i$ for all components; $x \geq y$ means $x \geqq y$ and $x \neq y$.

choose technology activity levels to operate which enable him to produce goods whose exchange value is sufficient to purchase his subsistence requirement, b. Subject to this requirement, our typical producer minimizes the labor time he is to expend. That is, producer ν chooses a vector of activity levels x^ν in $\mathbb{R}^n_+$ to

$$\min Lx^\nu$$

subject to

$$p(I - A)x^\nu \geqq pb \tag{1}$$

$$Lx^\nu \leqq 1 \tag{2}$$

Inequality (1) states that the value of net output is sufficient to purchase consumption b; inequality (2) says that ν possesses enough labor power to operate the chosen activities. Let $\mathscr{A}^\nu(p)$ be the set of vectors x solving this program. We shall say vectors in $\mathscr{A}^\nu(p)$ are *individually optimal* (IO); vectors satisfying (1) and (2) are *individually feasible* (IF).

What is the concept of equilibrium prices? A price vector p will be a *reproducible solution* (the equilibrium concept) if, subject to individual optimization, producers will operate the economy in such a way that the net output is sufficient to allow each person to purchase his subsistence needs.

Definition 1.1. p is a reproducible solution (RS) for the SCP economy $\{A, L, N, b\} \Leftrightarrow (\forall \nu)\ (\exists x^\nu \in \mathscr{A}^\nu\ (p))\ ((I - A)x \geqq Nb)$, where $x = \Sigma x^\nu$.

Notice that $(I - A)x$ is the net output of society when producers are each producing at their optimal activity levels x^ν, and the condition $(I - A)x \geqq Nb$ states that the market for consumer demands can clear. Note, however, that the net output of the individual $(I - A)x^\nu$ need not be a nonnegative vector. The individual makes his decision solely in value terms according to his program.

This is a model of Adam Smith's deer-and-beaver economy and Marx's simple commodity production. It is a production and exchange subsistence economy without stocks, where production is instantaneous. Smith and Marx both argued that equilibrium prices would be proportional to embodied labor time in simple commodity production, which we now show.

Theorem 1.1. Let p be a RS for the SCP economy $\{A, L, N, b\}$. Then p is proportional to $\Lambda = L(I - A)^{-1}$, the vector of labor values, or embodied labor times.

Proof. Let $x^1, \ldots, x^N$ be the individually optimal solutions associated with p, and $x = \Sigma_1^N x^\nu$. By the indecomposability of A, $x \geqq (I - A)^{-1}(Nb) > 0$. Let $\hat{x} = (1/N)x$. By reproducibility, $p(I - A)\hat{x} \geqq pb$; since $Lx^i = Lx^j$ for all i, j, it follows that $L\hat{x} = Lx^i$ for all i and so $L\hat{x} \leqq 1$. Hence $\hat{x}$ is individually feasible for any i. Note that $\hat{x} > 0$ since $x > 0$.

Consider the dual program to producer i's program:

$$\text{choose } \gamma \in R \text{ to max } \gamma pb$$

subject to

$$\gamma p(I - A) \leqq L$$

$$\gamma \geqq 0.$$

(Note that we can dispense with the second constraint in the primal program, since the existence of an optimal solution makes the constraint $Lx^\nu \leqq 1$ unnecessary.) Since i possesses a strictly positive IO solution $\hat{x}$, it follows by the complementary slackness conditions of linear programming applied to the dual constraint that:

$$\gamma p(I - A) = L$$

and so

$$\gamma p = L(I - A)^{-1} = \Lambda. \quad \text{QED}$$

This is all there is to be said about simple commodity production. The only price vector capable of reproducing the system is the vector Λ of embodied labor values. Note that since all producers are identical in this economy, they must all have identical solutions to their individual optimization programs; that is, $Lx^i = Lx^j$ for all producers i and j. In this sense, any reproducible solution is *egalitarian*. We shall see that this association of egalitarian equilibria with labor-value pricing continues to hold in more complicated economies, when there are also nonegalitarian solutions.

We can, in fact, deduce how long each producer works at a reproducible solution. First, note that inequality (1) of the producer's optimization program must be binding at an optimal activity plan x^ν, for if not, some positive component of x^ν could be reduced, maintaining feasibility, thereby reducing labor performed, Lx^ν. (We use here the assumption that L is a strictly positive vector.) Hence, at a reproducible solution, where $p = \Lambda$, we have:

$$\begin{aligned} p(I - A)x^\nu &= \Lambda(I - A)x^\nu = L(I - A)^{-1}(I - A)x^\nu = Lx^\nu \\ &= pb \qquad\qquad\qquad\qquad\qquad\qquad\qquad = \Lambda b. \end{aligned}$$

That is, at a reproducible solution, each producer works time Λb. That is what Marx called *socially necessary labor time*, as Λb is the labor embodied in the subsistence vector b. All producers work exactly socially necessary labor time at an equilibrium in the SCP economy, and there is no exploitation.

Finally, note that a key feature of this economy is the absence of time in production. Producers can instantaneously produce the inputs they need to operate activities. That is, to operate a vector of activity levels x^ν, a producer simply synthesizes his net output $(I - A)x^\nu$. We do not require him to have available inputs in amounts Ax^ν before engaging in production. If we did, there could emerge some asymmetry among producers, based on differential access to inputs. We next introduce time into the economy, in the sense we have indicated: stocks must be available to use as inputs today, for production which will deliver outputs tomorrow. First, we take account of time in the simplest possible way.

B. Communal economy with stocks

We assume now that production takes time in this sense: to operate an activity vector x requires an input from stocks Ax, which must have been produced in the past. Production of net output is not instantaneous from a vector of stocks $\omega \in \mathbb{R}^n_+$.

We envisage a communal subsistence economy with stocks, specified by the data $\{A, L, N, b, \omega\}$. The problem for the economy is to operate its technology in such a way as to provide for society's subsistence needs, subject to the limitations on labor and stocks available. This motivates:

Definition 1.2. A communal economy with stocks $\{A, L, N, b, \omega\}$ is *reproducible* $\Leftrightarrow \exists x \geqq 0$ such that:

(1) $Lx \leqq N$ (availability of labor)
(2) $Ax \leqq \omega$ (availability of stocks)
(3) $(I - A)x \geqq Nb$ (reproducibility)

One should note that allocations of goods to producers take place at two points in time. At the beginning of the period, the communal producers are given the stocks they require to operate their activities at the assigned levels; at the end of the period, subsistence goods, the fruits of production, are distributed. This particular dating of investment and consumption shall be remarked upon at a later point. (Note that if we wished to view labor as an input into production requiring fuel in amount b at the beginning of the period, then (2) in Definition 1.2 would be revised: $Ax + Nb \leqq \omega$.)

Theorem 1.2. A communal economy $\{A, L, N, b, \omega\}$ is reproducible $\Leftrightarrow$

(a) $\Lambda b \leqq 1$
(b) $A(I - A)^{-1}(Nb) \leqq \omega$.

Proof.
$\Rightarrow$ Let $\bar{x}$ be a reproducible activity vector. Then $\bar{x} \geqq (I - A)^{-1}(Nb)$, so $L\bar{x} \geqq L(I - A)^{-1}(Nb) = \Lambda(Nb)$. By (1) of Definition 1.2, $1 \geqq \Lambda b$ follows. By (2) of Definition 1.2, $\omega \geqq A\bar{x} \geqq A(I - A)^{-1}(Nb)$.
$\Leftarrow$ Let $\bar{x} \equiv (I - A)^{-1}(Nb)$. QED

The communal economy with stocks is an economy in which there is no private property. The natural way for private property to enter the economy would be in differential ownership of the inputs required for production. Without this differentiation, however, the conditions for communal reproducibility as stated in Theorem 1.2 are rather trivial: the labor time embodied in the subsistence bundle must not exceed one working day, and society must possess enough stocks, in aggregate, to fuel activity levels whose net output is total consumption needs.

The communal reproducible equilibrium of Theorem 1.2 is of no inherent interest. What it provides is a necessary condition on aggregate stocks which any economy must satisfy in order to be able to reproduce. In particular, conditions (a) and (b) of the theorem remain necessary for reproducibility when we introduce private ownership of stocks, in the next section.

2. A private ownership, subsistence, production and exchange economy with stocks

We next introduce both time and private ownership into the economy, through the private and differential ownership of stocks needed as inputs for production. Each producer now owns a vector of stocks $\omega^\nu \in \mathbb{R}^n_+$. Facing prices p, he seeks to produce net outputs sufficient in value to be exchangeable for subsistence needs b. His program is:

choose x^ν to min Lx^ν

subject to

$$p(I - A)x^\nu \geqq pb \tag{2.1}$$

$$pAx^\nu \leqq p\omega^\nu \tag{2.2}$$

$$Lx^\nu \leqq 1 \tag{2.3}$$

$$x^\nu \geqq 0.$$

(2.1) says he insists upon not running down the value of his stocks: $p(I - A)x^\nu$ is the value of his net output, and pb is the value of his consumption. Hence, (2.1) states that the value of his endowment will not be less, next period, than it is now (assuming goods are costlessly storable). Let ω_0^ν be the νth producer's stocks at time 0. Then (2.1) is easily seen to be equivalent to:

$$p\omega_0^\nu - pAx^\nu - pb + px^\nu \geqq p\omega_0^\nu. \tag{2.1$'$}$$

But (2.1′) is a statement that the value of goods held after production and consumption (the left-hand side) should not be less than the value of goods held before production and consumption (the right-hand side). (2.2) states that he must be able to afford to run the chosen activities x^ν with his wealth. He need not possess the endowments in physical form, Ax^ν, that he chooses to use, but he must be able to trade for them before production starts, and (2.2) assures this. In particular, *there is no credit market.* Producer ν must finance his own production out of present endowment.

We shall introduce an abusive notation, and call this economy $\mathscr{E}(p)$, which might be thought of as an abbreviation for $\mathscr{E}(p|A, L, b, \omega^1, \ldots, \omega^N)$. The notation $\mathscr{E}(p)$ should conjure up the vision that markets exist only for the n commodities, whose prices are

p; it is abusive, since the economy does not depend on its prices. In particular, there is no labor market or credit market in this economy.

Definition 1.3. $(\bar{p}; x^1, \ldots, x^N)$ is a reproducible solution (RS) for $\mathscr{E}(p) \Leftrightarrow$

(1) x^ν is IO for ν (that is, $x^\nu \in \mathscr{A}^\nu(\bar{p})$) (optimality)
(2) $(I - A)x \geqq Nb$ where $x = \Sigma x^\nu$ (reproducibility)
(3) $Ax \leqq \omega$ (feasibility)

Thus, a price vector $\bar{p}$ equilibrates the economy if, subject to individual optimization, the economy can feasibly reproduce.

We view markets as operating at two points in time. At the beginning of the period, trades take place on the market for production inputs. Condition (3) of Definition 1.3 assures that supplies can meet demands at going prices in this market. At the end of the period, trades take place on the market for consumption goods. Condition (2) of Definition 1.3 assures that this market equilibrates.

Since time is of the essence in this model, it would be more precise to differentiate between prices today, p_t, and expected prices tomorrow, p^ν_{t+1}, for producer ν. We shall, however, note later that any reproducible solution $\bar{p}$, as defined, can be viewed as a stationary state in this economy. Hence, we may simply ignore the time subscript with the understanding that only stationary states are under discussion.

We proceed to study the reproducible solutions in $\mathscr{E}(p)$. The main goal is to show that a typical phenomenon at a reproducible solution is exploitation—that some producers work more time than is socially necessary in the Marxian sense, Λb, while others work less. Before proceeding to the details, it is useful to outline the sense of what is happening. In the economy $\mathscr{E}(p)$, producers all have access to the same technology (A, L), and all have the same subsistence requirements. They differ, however, in the property they own, ω^ν. According to the optimization programs of individuals, it is clear that if ν is wealthier than μ at prices p, that is, $p\omega^\nu > p\omega^\mu$, then in general ν's subsistence work time at an individually optimal solution is less, that is, $Lx^\nu < Lx^\mu$. Now the hidden hand of the market will see to it that society produces in toto precisely what it needs, at a reproducible solution. (Since every producer is trying just to subsist, it would be inefficient if the market directed them to produce more in toto than social subsistence requirements.) Hence, society will work, at a reproducible solution, $N\Lambda b$, which is total socially necessary labor time. But if wealth is unequally distributed among the N producers, we will expect some to work more than Λb and others less than Λb at an equilibrium. This we will call exploitation, as it has the same form as classical Marxian exploitation under capitalism.

To carry out this program, we require a series of results.

Lemma 1.1. If p is a RS, then $p - pA > 0$.

Proof. Let $x = \Sigma x^\nu$ be the aggregate activity levels associated with p. By indecomposability of A, $x > 0$. Suppose for some sector j,

$$p_j - pA_j \leqq 0 \tag{1}$$

where A_j is the jth column of A. Since $x > 0$, we must have $x_j^\nu > 0$, for some ν. By (1) above, producer ν can reduce this activity level x_j^ν to zero and his new activity vector then formed, $\hat{x}^\nu$, is still individually feasible. Moreover, $L\hat{x}^\nu < Lx^\nu$, since $L > 0$. Consequently, x^ν was not IO. QED

(Lemma 1.1 says that prices can only reproduce the economy if positive profits are generated in all sectors.)

Lemma 1.2. For any price vector p, $x^\nu \in \mathscr{A}^\nu(p) \Rightarrow p(I - A)x^\nu = pb$.

Proof. If $p(I - A)x^\nu > pb$, then components of x^ν can be reduced, preserving feasibility and lowering Lx^ν. QED

Theorem 1.3. $(p; x^1, \ldots, x^N)$ is a RS. Then

(a) $x \equiv \Sigma x^\nu = (I - A)^{-1}Nb$
(b) $Lx = N\Lambda b$.

Proof. By reproducibility, $(I - A)x \geqq (Nb)$. Suppose $(I - A)x \geq (Nb)$. By Lemma 1.1, $p > 0$. Hence $p(I - A)x > p(Nb)$, and so, for some ν, $p(I - A)x^\nu > pb$, which contradicts Lemma 1.2. Hence, (a) follows. (b) follows by premultiplying equation (a) by L. QED

This theorem states that society will produce precisely what it requires for subsistence, at a RS; and that society will work in toto precisely that length of time that Marx would call socially necessary, $N\Lambda b$. This verifies the intuitive notion that a subsistence economy will produce no surplus.

We can note that a RS $\bar{p}$ is a stationary state:

Theorem 1.4. If $\bar{p}$ is a RS this period, $\bar{p}$ is a RS next period.

Proof. Since $\bar{p}(I - A)x^\nu = \bar{p}b$ for all ν, every producer's endowment next period has the same valuation, $\bar{p}\omega^\nu$, as this period's endowment. Moreover, since $x = (I - A)^{-1}(Nb)$ at the RS, society's aggregate endowment remains component-wise identical next period to what it was this period. Hence, each producer's *program* remains the same at prices $\bar{p}$, and the aggregate condition for $\bar{p}$ to be a RS remains the same—even though an individual's endowments may change component-wise. Hence $\bar{p}$ continues to be a RS. QED

This verifies, as remarked previously, that if we wish to view the model as a temporary equilibrium one, then reproducible solutions are stationary temporary equilibria, and hence it is permissible to drop time subscripts from the price vector.

According to Theorem 1.3, average labor time expended at a RS is precisely Λb, the labor value of subsistence. This motivates the following:

Definition 1.4. A RS $(p; x^1, \ldots, x^N)$ is egalitarian $\Leftrightarrow Lx^\nu = \Lambda b$ for all ν. Otherwise, it is inegalitarian.

In the SCP economy, all reproducible solutions were egalitarian. There is no reason to expect that to be the case here, since the programs of producers differ according to their "wealths" $p\omega^\nu$. A generalization of Theorem 1.1, however, holds:

Theorem 1.5. Let $\omega \geq A(I - A)^{-1}(Nb)$. Let p be a RS. Then $p \sim \Lambda \Leftrightarrow$ p is egalitarian. ($p \sim \Lambda$ means p is proportional to Λ.)

Note: By Theorem 1.2 we observe that a reproducible solution cannot exist unless $\omega \geqq A(I - A)^{-1}(Nb)$. Thus the assumption on ω of Theorem 1.5 rules out only the singular case $\omega = A(I - A)^{-1}(Nb)$.

To prove *Theorem 1.5*, we require:

Lemma 1.3. Let p be any price vector. Let ν be a producer who possesses an IO action $x^\nu \in \mathscr{A}^\nu(p)$, $x^\nu > 0$, and $pAx^\nu < p\omega^\nu$. Then $p \sim \Lambda$.

Proof. Since ν possesses an optimal action at which $pAx^\nu < p\omega^\nu$ and $Lx^\nu \leqq 1$, his program can be written, without loss of generality:

$$\min Lx^\nu$$

subject to

$$p(I - A)x^\nu \geqq pb$$
$$x^\nu \geqq 0.$$

The dual program is

$$\max \gamma pb$$

subject to

$$\gamma p(I - A) \leqq L$$
$$\gamma \geqq 0.$$

Since $x^\nu > 0$ is a solution of the primal, it follows from complementary slackness that $\gamma^* p(I - A) = L$. QED

Proof of Theorem 1.5.

$\Rightarrow$ If $p \sim \Lambda$, a producer's program becomes:

$$\min Lx^\nu$$

subject to

$$Lx^\nu \geqq \Lambda b \quad (1)$$
$$\Lambda Ax^\nu \leqq \Lambda\omega^\nu \quad (2)$$
$$Lx^\nu \leqq 1 \quad (3)$$

By Lemma 1.2, constraint (1) holds with equality at an optimum, and so $Lx^\nu = \Lambda b$ for all ν.

$\Leftarrow$ Let $(p; x^1, \ldots, x^N)$ be a RS, and $x = \Sigma x^\nu$. By hypothesis, $Lx^\nu = \Lambda b$ for all ν. By Theorem 1.3, $x = (I - A)^{-1}(Nb)$. Hence, $pAx = pA(I - A)^{-1}(Nb) < p\omega$, by hypothesis on ω, and since $p > 0$ by

Lemma 1.1. Consequently, for some ν, $pA((1/N)x) < p\omega^\nu$ since $\Sigma\omega^\nu \equiv \omega$. Trivially, $p(I - A)((1/N)x) = pb$; and $L((1/N)x) = \Lambda b$. Thus, for the chosen ν, $\hat{x}^\nu \equiv (1/N)x$ is in fact not only individually feasible, but individually optimal. Since $x > 0$, $\hat{x}^\nu > 0$. Hence the solution $\hat{x}^\nu$ fulfills the requirements of Lemma 1.3, and the theorem follows. QED

Theorem 1.5 verifies a claim mentioned earlier. In the model of simple commodity production, it was shown that the only prices capable of reproducing the system were labor value prices, and that all equilibria were egalitarian. Now, with the introduction of private property and time in production, we have the possibility of inegalitarian equilibria. Nevertheless, the latest theorem maintains that the classical association between egalitarianism and labor value pricing is maintained: labor value pricing is in some sense fair pricing—if one believes egalitarian solutions are fair.

We have as yet not shown that economies exist which actually support inegalitarian reproducible solutions, which is the heart of the matter at hand.

Theorem 1.6. There are economies $\mathscr{E}(p|A, L, b, \omega^1, \ldots, \omega^N)$ for which inegalitarian RSs exist.

Before constructing an example to demonstrate Theorem 1.6, the significance of the result should be discussed. At an inegalitarian solution, we can say exploitation is occurring in the Marxian sense. Let $(p; x^1, \ldots, x^N)$ be such a solution. Then for some producers μ, ν: $Lx^\mu > \Lambda b > Lx^\nu$. Producer ν is working less time than is socially necessary to reproduce himself, and producer μ is working longer than is socially necessary. Producer ν is exploiting μ. This comes about because at prices p, ν is wealthier than μ, and is able to use his wealth as leverage through the exchange mechanism to force μ to work "for" him. Producer μ, at prices p, is relatively poor; because of his "capital constraint" ($pAx^\mu \leqq p\omega^\mu$) he must choose labor intensive activities. Since ν is relatively capital-rich, he may concentrate in capital intensive activities.[2]

2. In the appendix to this chapter it is shown explicitly that the wealthy operate capital intensive sectors and the poor operate labor intensive sectors in $\mathscr{E}(p)$. There is a social division of labor.

Why one might wish to call this phenomenon exploitation can be seen by the following. Suppose μ and ν were the only producers in the economy, and ν expropriated μ's endowment and killed him. Producer ν would now be wealthier than before; yet, at any RS for the new economy in which only he is a member, he will have to work time Λb, *longer* than when μ was there. Thus, exploitation is an explicitly social phenomenon: ν can get away with working less than Λb only because there is someone else working more than Λb, to "support" him. Suppose, now that μ kills ν and expropriates the latter's stocks. Then μ can reproduce himself by working precisely Λb labor time, and he is better off than before. After hearing that ν became worse off after dispensing with μ, a skeptic might reply that that was because both ν and μ were benefiting from cooperation (or some sort of scale economies when both were present), and is therefore not evidence of ν's exploitation of μ. But the fact that μ becomes *better* off when he annihilates ν indicates that this is not a correct explanation.

Yet, from the Marxian vantage point, there are several surprises with this construction. First, although there is exploitation, there is no surplus product: each producer consumes the same bundle b, and no one gets richer. (Actually, it is not correct to say each consumes the same bundle, since they consume different amounts of leisure. Nevertheless, there is no surplus product and no accumulation.) Second, and more important, *exploitation occurs even though there is no institution for the exchange of labor*. Exploitation is mediated entirely through the exchange of produced commodities. This is one model of what has been discussed in the Marxian literature as *unequal exchange*.

The existence of exploitation despite the fact that each producer is entirely in control of his own labor in the production process calls into question the Marxian notion that expropriation of surplus value occurs at the point of production. The present example would lead one to this statement: although *production* of surplus value may occur at the point of production, *appropriation* of surplus value or the realization of exploitation can occur at the point of exchange. To the extent that one can accept the somewhat vague notions of "point of production" and "point of exchange" as analytical concepts, one is, therefore, forced to treat the point of exchange as an important locus of exploitation. This is not difficult to accept for those Marxists who are used to thinking of exploitation as emerging from the entire "circuit of capital." It does, however, damage the fundamentalist interpretation which insists upon the point of production as the only relevant site for the origin of exploitation.

Moreover, it should be remarked that this is not a model of capitalism, and hence claims about the locus of exploitation in capitalist economies cannot be rigorously inferred from the results. What the model shows is the logical possibility of exploitation even in the absence of appropriation of surplus value at the point of production.

Proof of Theorem 1.6. An example is constructed for an economy with $n = 2 = N$. We wish to choose A, L, b, ω^1, ω^2 so that the programs of the two producers are solved at points E and G, as illustrated in Figure 1. The feasible set for producer 1 is horizontally hatched and that of producer 2 is vertically hatched. Minimizing Lx leads to the points G and E, which is clearly inegalitarian.

To realize this construction, we start by requiring

$$p(I - A) = (1, 1) \tag{i}$$

$$pA = (1, 2). \tag{ii}$$

This guarantees that the lines $pAx = p\omega^1$, $pAx = p\omega^2$, and $p(I - A)x = pb$ in Figure 1 have their slopes as pictured. (i) and (ii) imply:

$$p = (2, 3). \tag{iii}$$

It is easily verified that the following choice of A satisfies (i) and (ii):

$$A = \begin{pmatrix} .25 & .625 \\ \frac{1}{6} & .25 \end{pmatrix}.$$

A is, furthermore, productive and indecomposable. Choose $L = (2, 1)$ which gives the lines $Lx = k$ the slopes pictured in the figure. Choose a vector b so that $\Lambda b < 1$.

We now choose ω^1 to be huge—in particular, huge enough so that $\omega^1 \geqq A(I - A)^{-1}(2b)$ and so that the line $pAx = p\omega^1$ intersects the x_2 axis above the point G. Hence $\hat{x} \equiv G$ is IO for producer 1 at prices p. This determines the required optimal solution for producer 2 as:

$$\hat{x}^2 = (I - A)^{-1}\,(2b) - \hat{x}^1. \tag{iv}$$

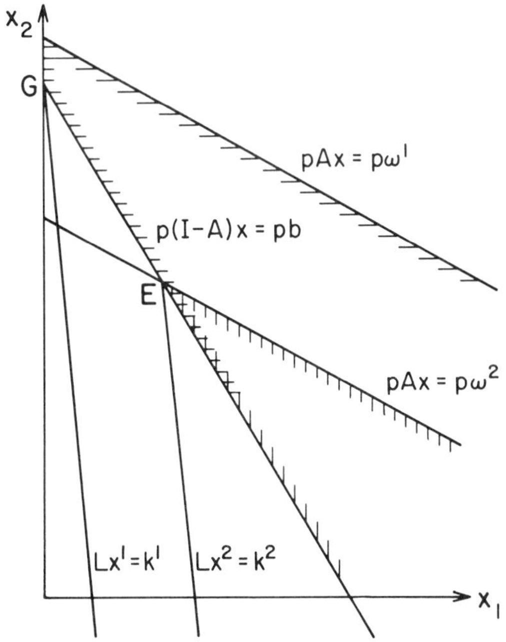

Figure 1 An inegalitarian solution with $n = N = 2$

$\hat{x}^2$ lies by construction on the line $p(I - A)x = pb$. We finally choose ω^2 so that $pA\hat{x}^2 = p\omega^2$. It is easily checked that $(\hat{x}^1, \hat{x}^2)$ is an inegalitarian reproducible solution for the economy constructed. QED

We have shown that a Marxian-like phenomenon of exploitation can emerge in a subsistence exchange economy where there is no institution of labor exchange and no surplus product. There is no attempt to justify, at this point, using the word *exploitation* to describe this phenomenon, other than by reference to the Marxian phenomenon which goes by the same name, and by the short story of murder and expropriation recounted above. Why one might wish to conceive of this transfer of labor as exploitative is a topic that will be discussed in Part III, when the general theory is formulated. At this point, nevertheless, one important conclusion with respect to the institutional robustness of Marxian exploitation is in order. It appears as if Marxian-like exploitation, by which I mean the appropriation of surplus labor time of one agent by another, is possible given only the institutions of private ownership of the means of production and competitive markets. The institutions upon which Marx focused, the accumulation of capital and the labor market, do not exist in our model.[3] Thus, we tend to implicate competitive markets and private ownership as the institutional culprits in bringing about exploitation more sharply than Marx did.

Since exploitation emerges simply from the existence of a market for produced commodities and private ownership of stocks, it is worthwhile to ask: Where does political power enter this model? Are there necessarily any coercive institutions? After all, under capitalism the state is conceived, in Marxian theory, as a coercive institution which maintains the rules of the game; and coercion exists also at the point of production, in the factory, unlike the present model where every producer works for himself. In the present model, why do the exploited not expropriate the exploiters? This leads one to say that if this model is to be viewed as in any sense enforceable and historical, there must be an institution which coerces producers to operate by the rules of the market, and which prevents such expropriation. One might infer that the existence of the market as a socially accepted institution presupposes the solution of the problem of political authority. Coercion is not necessary at the level of the market, because it operates on a prior level, to preserve property relations.

3. In Marxian models of simple reproduction there is exploitation without accumulation. In fact, if capitalists consume only what workers consume but do not work, the subsistence models here can be viewed as simple reproduction models. The more precise phrasing is to say that exploitation is logically conceivable even without surplus production, so long as a surplus is potentially producible.

But one must not go too far in ascribing historical reality to these models. They are not intended as economic anthropology, but as logical exercises to inquire into the function of different institutional and behavioral specifications of economies, with regard to exploitation. For instance, one might reasonably ask of this model, if it were intended as a historical one: Why should an exploited producer maintain the "utility function" of minimizing labor expended today, subject to producing net exchange value in sufficient amount to trade for subsistence? If I observe that I am exploited, perhaps I would decide to work longer than is absolutely necessary today, thereby building up some additional endowment so that in the future I can work less time. In fact, as long as the exploited producers are not working the whole working day just to subsist, and if their utility function is to minimize some discounted valuation of labor expended in all future periods, then under reasonable assumptions exploited producers will build up their endowments so that asymptotically the economy becomes egalitarian. But this is beside the point, which is not to debate what is the reasonable utility function with which to endow our precapitalist agents, but rather to demonstrate the logical possibility of exploitation in the absence of capitalist institutions. One can, however, interpret the behavior giving rise to the individual's program as follows. Each individual lives for one time period. The rule is that he must pass on at least as much finance capital to his replacement as he had. Subject to this constraint and his consuming the necessary amount, he minimizes his effort.

A second ahistoricism of the model is its inability to account for the differential ownership of the means of production. If we all have the same subsistence needs and labor-minimizing utility function, how does the differential distribution of property come to be? If such ahistoricism were leveled as a criticism of the model, I would consider it inadmissable, for the same reason as above. The model does not claim to discuss history; its purpose is to show that differential distribution of property and competitive markets are sufficient institutions to generate an exploitation phenomenon, under the simplest possible assumptions.[4]

4. The point has been raised by G. A. Cohen whether it is appropriate to list the competitive market as an institution. Perhaps, given private property as an institution, competitive markets are logically entailed, in which case it would be sufficient to list private ownership of the means of production.

3. Reswitching

In the so-called Cambridge controversy, one of the qualitative conclusions was that one cannot unambiguously associate profits with a return to capital. It is not my intention to resurrect the debate here; but it is interesting to observe that a reswitching phenomenon exists in the economy $\mathscr{E}(p)$.

Consider a reproducible solution p for a precapitalist subsistence economy $\mathscr{E}(p)$, at which producer μ exploits producer ν. How does it come about that μ can exploit ν? Perhaps it is because μ worked harder in the (prehistorical) past and built up a bigger endowment, so that today he can reap the fruits of his past labor. But suppose there is another reproducible solution $\hat{p}$ for the same economy, at which ν exploits μ. (That is, the same data of an economy are consistent with at least two equilibria, p and $\hat{p}$.) Then we would be forced to maintain that ν must have worked harder in the past, if this is our explanation of the source of exploitation. It is, however, impossible that μ and ν each worked harder in the past than the other. Hence, the exhibiting of such a "reswitching" phenomenon will show that there is no intrinsic property of the producer's behavior, such as working harder in the past, or risk taking, which can be claimed to be responsible for his ability to exploit another.

I will exhibit below an economy which supports just such a reswitching phenomenon. Having argued for its significance, let me now argue for its insignificance. Clearly, reswitching can only occur when neither of the vectors ω^ν and ω^μ dominates the other component-wise. For if $\omega^\nu \geq \omega^\mu$, for example, then at any prices ν is wealthier than μ, and hence μ can never exploit ν. Perhaps the most prevalent example of real exploitation is where some producers have a lot of everything, and others very little of anything, and in this case the reswitching phenomenon cannot occur. Second, we see that reswitching here is a phenomenon of multiple equilibria in a general equilibrium model. We are, as it were, comparing the situation on two identical islands which are supporting different prices; if we heed Joan Robinson's warnings about the inadmissability of such interisland comparisons, then we must view this reswitching as a curiosus. Given these qualifications, I exhibit an example of reswitching.[5]

5. The example is due to Michael Woodford.

The economy consists of $N = 2$ people. The data are:

$$A = \begin{pmatrix} \frac{1}{2} & \frac{1}{4} \\ \frac{1}{4} & \frac{1}{2} \end{pmatrix}; \qquad L = (6, 1); \qquad b = \begin{pmatrix} 22\frac{3}{4} \\ 30\frac{5}{8} \end{pmatrix};$$

$$\omega^1 = \begin{pmatrix} 56 \\ 112 \end{pmatrix}; \qquad \omega^2 = \begin{pmatrix} 101\frac{1}{2} \\ 50\frac{3}{4} \end{pmatrix}$$

Two reproducible solutions are exhibited in Figures 2 and 3. Note that the labor input can be adjusted, by dividing by 1,000, to produce a solution conforming to the requirement that $Lx^\nu \leqq 1$.

There is one special aspect of this example which should be mentioned. It is constructed so that the aggregate endowment $\omega^1 + \omega^2$ is precisely the minimum possible for social reproduction; that is, $\omega = A(I - A)^{-1}(2b)$. This is a singular case, for under this condition there is in fact a whole continuum of price equilibria for the economy, whereas when $\omega \geq A(I - A)^{-1}(Nb)$, the equilibria are always discrete and finite in number. It is the existence of a continuum of equilibria which makes this construction relatively easy. Indeed, in a two-commodity, two-producer model, I have not been able to produce an example of reswitching if there is any "excess capital" in the sense $\omega \geq A(I - A)^{-1}(Nb)$. R. E. Howe and I have examples of "weak reswitching" for such economies, where both an egalitarian and an inegalitarian reproducible solution exist. We believe that in higher dimensions the strong reswitching phenomenon can be exhibited for nonsingular economies (those with some excess capital), although the phenomenon is not sufficiently important, in my opinion, to merit the painstaking work necessary for such a construction.

4. Another characterization of exploitation in $\mathscr{E}(p)$: coalitions and cores

We can define the *private ownership core* of an economy $\mathscr{E}(p)$ as the set of allocations which allow the economy to reproduce, and which no coalition can block, by withdrawing from society with its own endowments and arranging production on its own. This is precisely the usual definition of the core in an exchange market economy. To be precise, we define:

$$p = (3, 2)$$

$$pA = (2, 1\tfrac{3}{4}), \quad p(I-A) = (1, \tfrac{1}{4})$$

$$pb = 129\tfrac{1}{2}, \quad p\omega^1 = 392, \quad p\omega^2 = 406$$

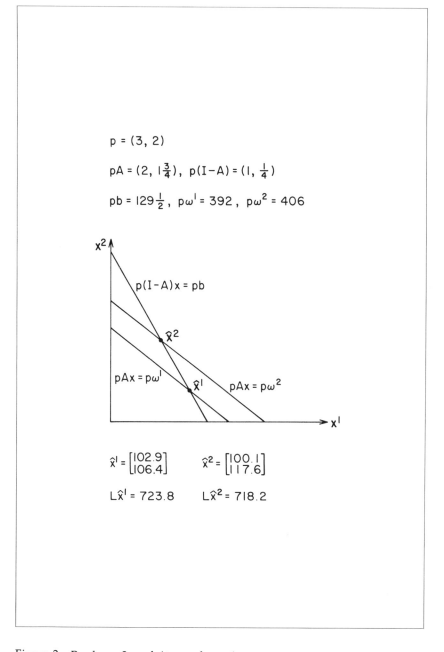

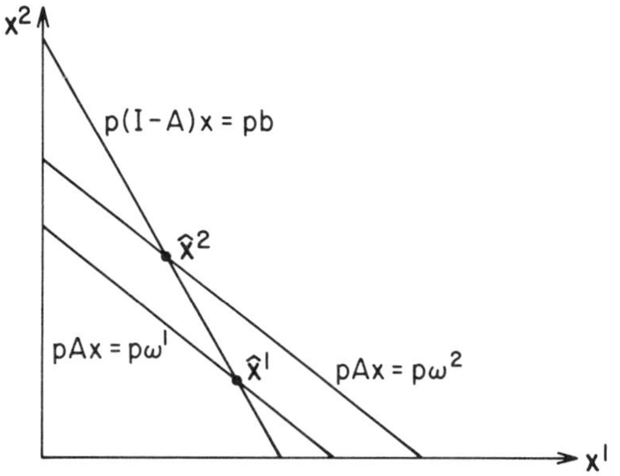

$$\hat{x}^1 = \begin{bmatrix} 102.9 \\ 106.4 \end{bmatrix} \qquad \hat{x}^2 = \begin{bmatrix} 100.1 \\ 117.6 \end{bmatrix}$$

$$L\hat{x}^1 = 723.8 \qquad L\hat{x}^2 = 718.2$$

Figure 2 Producer 2 exploits producer 1

$p = (5, 4)$

$pA = (3\frac{1}{2}, 3\frac{1}{4}), \quad p(I-A) = (1\frac{1}{2}, \frac{3}{4})$

$pb = 236\frac{1}{4}, \quad p\omega^1 = 728, \quad p\omega^2 = (710\frac{1}{2})$

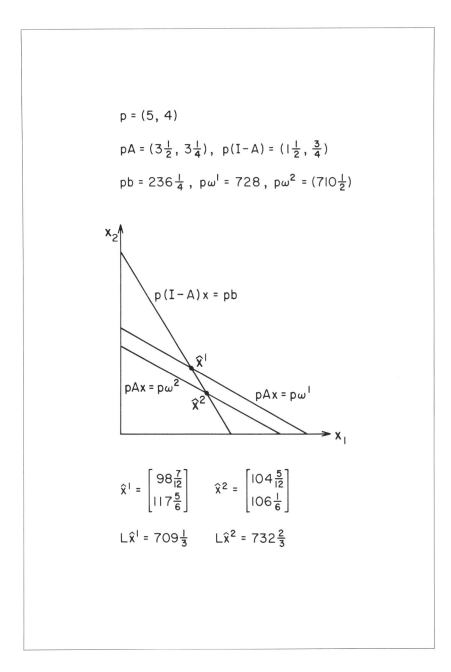

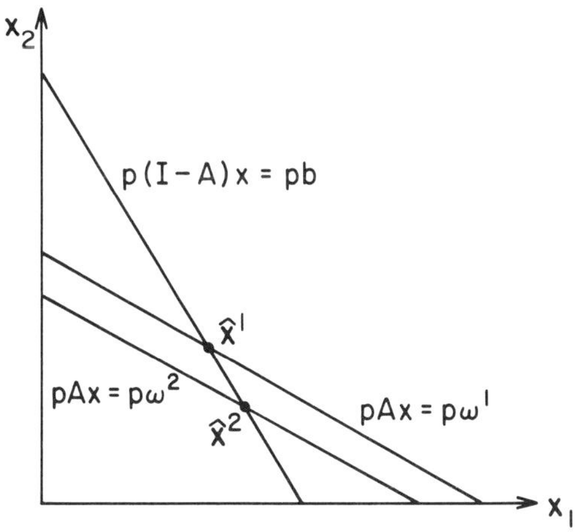

$$\hat{x}^1 = \begin{bmatrix} 98\frac{7}{12} \\ 117\frac{5}{6} \end{bmatrix} \qquad \hat{x}^2 = \begin{bmatrix} 104\frac{5}{12} \\ 106\frac{1}{6} \end{bmatrix}$$

$$L\hat{x}^1 = 709\frac{1}{3} \qquad L\hat{x}^2 = 732\frac{2}{3}$$

Figure 3 Producer 1 exploits producer 2

Definition 1.5. Let $I = \{1, \ldots, N\}$ be the set of producers. Let $J \subseteq I$ be any subset. J is *viable* if

$$\sum_{\nu \in J} \omega^{\nu} \geqq A(I - A)^{-1}(|J|b)$$

where $|J|$ is the cardinality of J.

According to Theorem 1.2, the condition for viability assures the coalition that it can reproduce itself if it withdraws from society, taking its own endowments of property and labor power with it.

Definition 1.6. A *reproducible allocation* is a set of activity levels $(x^1, \ldots, x^N)$ such that:

(1) $Lx^i \leqq 1$ for all i (labor feasibility)
(2) $x = \Sigma x^i$, $Ax \leqq \omega$ (communal feasibility)
(3) $(I - A)x \geqq Nb$ (reproducibility)

Thus a reproducible allocation is any set of activity levels which is communally feasible and reproduces the economy.

We now define blocking. A viable coalition can block a reproducible allocation if it can assure each of its members a reduced worktime by withdrawing with its resources and arranging communal reproduction on its own. We know reproduction requires $M\Lambda b$ in total work time for a coalition of size M, since the coalition must produce net output in amount $(I - A)^{-1}(Mb)$ which requires total labor in amount $L(I - A)^{-1}Mb = M\Lambda b$. We therefore arrive at the following definition of a core allocation:

Definition 1.7. A reproducible allocation $(x^1, \ldots \ldots x^N)$ is in the *private ownership core* of $\mathscr{E}(p) \Leftrightarrow$ for all viable coalitions J, $\Sigma_J Lx^{\nu} \leqq |J|\Lambda b$.

Recall our abusive notation $\mathscr{E}(p)$, which is here misleading: the core is a concept independent of any price vector or any equilibrium. To verify that the definition captures the core accurately, notice first that if, at the reproducible allocation, work time for every viable coalition does not exceed $|J|\Lambda b$, then clearly no viable coalition can arrange to do better on its own, since it must work $|J|\Lambda b$ time on its own to reproduce. Conversely, if there is a viable coalition for which

$\Sigma_J Lx^\nu > |J|\Lambda b$, then the work time for every member can be reduced when the coalition withdraws. This verifies the definition.

We may observe, trivially, that egalitarian RSs are in the private ownership core. Moreover, inegalitarian RSs are stable against blocking by coalitions of the exploited:

Theorem 1.7. Let $(\bar{p}; x^1, \ldots, x^N)$ be an inegalitarian RS. Then no coalition of exploited agents can block it.

Proof. On the contrary, suppose $J = \{1, \ldots, M\}$ were a viable coalition of the exploited: $Lx^\nu > \Lambda b$, for $\nu = 1,M$. By viability, $\Sigma_1^M \omega^\nu \geqq A(I - A)^{-1}(Mb)$. Let $z = (I - A)^{-1}(Mb)$. Then $Az \leqq \Sigma_1^M \omega^\nu$; $pAz \leqq p\Sigma_1^M \omega^\nu$; and so for some $\bar{\nu} \in J$, $pA((1/M)z) \leqq p\omega^{\bar{\nu}}$. Trivially, $p(I - A)((1/M)z) = pb$, and $L((1/M)z) = \Lambda b < 1$, so $(1/M)z$ is individually feasible for $\bar{\nu}$. Hence $x^{\bar{\nu}}$ was not originally optimal for $\bar{\nu}$, since $Lx^{\bar{\nu}} > \Lambda b = L((1/M)z)$. By contradiction, J is not a viable coalition. QED

This tells us that reproducible solutions are stable against noncooperative behavior of the exploited. No coalition of exploited agents can feasibly withdraw, in the sense that no such coalition is viable. Furthermore, reproducible solutions are obviously stable against coalitions of exploiters: for such a coalition, S, works less than $|S|\Lambda b$ at the reproducible solution, whereas its members would have to work $|S|\Lambda b$ in total if they withdrew.[6] However, reproducible solutions are not always in the private ownership core of the economy. In general, viable coalitions consisting of some exploited and some exploiting agents can be constructed and can block a reproducible solution. The reason this occurs is because of the incomplete set of markets in $\mathscr{E}(p)$. Agents in $\mathscr{E}(p)$ cannot trade labor or capital, but when coalitions examine their possibilities with cooperative behavior, they can effectively trade their capital. Hence it is not sur-

6. Assuming the coalition were viable. While coalitions of exploited agents are never viable, it is not true that coalitions of exploiters always are. This is irrelevant to the present concern, but would be relevant if we were to investigate a more aggressive notion of "blocking," in which a coalition considers withdrawal if it can inflict harm on its complement, thus bargaining for a better deal in the original society. Such aggressive blocking will not be considered here.

prising that some market solutions are not in the private ownership core.[7]

We proceed to the example to show that reproducible solutions are not necessarily in the private ownership core. In this economy there are three agents: two exploiters and one exploited.[8] Let

$$A = \begin{pmatrix} \frac{1}{6} & \frac{1}{6} \\ \frac{1}{5} & \frac{2}{5} \end{pmatrix}; \qquad b = \begin{pmatrix} \frac{1}{2} \\ 1 \end{pmatrix}; \qquad L = (\tfrac{3}{10}, \tfrac{1}{10}).$$

Calculate:

$$(I - A)^{-1}b = \begin{pmatrix} 1 \\ 2 \end{pmatrix}, \qquad \Lambda b = \tfrac{1}{2}.$$

Choose:

$$p = (\tfrac{12}{7}, \tfrac{15}{7});$$

then

$$p(I - A) = (1, 1); \qquad pA = (\tfrac{5}{7}, \tfrac{8}{7}).$$

For $N = 3$, the total stock necessary for the existence of a reproducible allocation is:

$$\omega = A(I - A)^{-1}(3b) = \begin{pmatrix} \frac{3}{2} \\ 3 \end{pmatrix}.$$

For a two-person coalition, the endowment needed to reproduce is therefore $\begin{pmatrix} 1 \\ 2 \end{pmatrix}$, whose value at given prices is $\frac{42}{7}$. The choice of p guarantees that the relative slopes of the lines $p(I - A)x = pb$, $pAx = p\omega^\nu$, and $Lx = k$ are as depicted in Figure 4. We may further choose the endowments of agents so that the optimal solutions for them lie at:

$$x^1 = \begin{pmatrix} 3 \\ 0 \end{pmatrix}, \qquad x^2 = x^3 = \begin{pmatrix} 0 \\ 3 \end{pmatrix}.$$

7. This explanation for why reproducible solutions are not generally in the core is due to Paul Rhode. That the insight is correct is proved in Appendix 2.2. There it is shown that when either a labor or credit market is added to $\mathscr{E}(p)$, the reproducible solutions of the new economy always lie in the private ownership core.

8. I thank Paul Rhode for working out this construction.

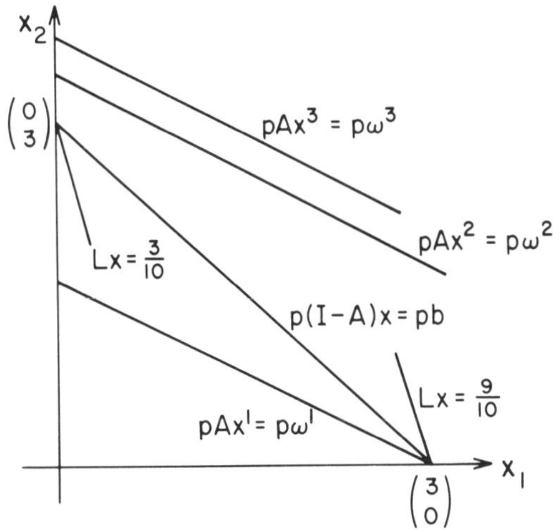

Figure 4 A reproducible solution of $\mathscr{E}(p)$ not in the core

(See Figure 4.) This only requires that:

$$p\omega^1 = pAx^1 = (\tfrac{5}{7}, \tfrac{8}{7}) \begin{pmatrix} 3 \\ 0 \end{pmatrix} = \tfrac{15}{7}$$

and ω^2 and ω^3 each satisfy:

$$p\omega^\nu \geqq pA \begin{pmatrix} 0 \\ 3 \end{pmatrix} = \tfrac{24}{7}.$$

ω^2 and ω^3 may be chosen to be huge. In particular, choose them large enough so that $\omega^3 + \omega^1$ and $\omega^2 + \omega^1$ are each sufficient to make the coalitions {3, 1} and {2, 1} viable. Finally, notice that:

$$\sum x^{\nu} = \begin{pmatrix}3\\0\end{pmatrix} + 2\begin{pmatrix}0\\3\end{pmatrix} = \begin{pmatrix}3\\6\end{pmatrix},$$

and so $(I - A)x = 3b$, as required for a reproducible solution. Note that $Lx^1 = .9$ and $Lx^2 = Lx^3 = .3$, so agent 1 is exploited and agents 2 and 3 are exploiters at the solution. But the coalition {3, 1} works 1.2, while its socially necessary labor time is 1. The same is true for {2, 1}. Hence, each of these coalitions can block the reproducible solution.

We pass now to the alternative characterization of exploitation promised in this section's title. In defining the private ownership core above, the alternative specified for a coalition which is considering a block is to withdraw with its own assets and arrange reproduction using those assets, for its members. Suppose we conceive of a different alternative; that is, we define a different game which specifies the opportunities available to agents and coalitions acting on their own. If a coalition decides to withdraw, it is assigned not its own assets, but its per capita share of aggregate social assets. That is, a coalition J choosing to withdraw gets to take with it assets in amount $(|J|/N)\omega$, plus its own labor. This is a perfectly reasonable specification of a game, and we define the *communal core* as the set of allocations which can be blocked by no coalition, under this withdrawal specification. Notice, first, that all coalitions are viable under this withdrawal option. This follows immediately from the fact that $\omega \geqq A(I - A)^{-1}(Nb)$, the necessary condition for the existence of reproducible allocations for the entire economy. Hence, in the definition of the communal core stated above, there is no need to mention viability of coalitions.

We now can provide the following very simple characterization of exploitation, in terms of the communal game:

Theorem 1.8. The communal core of an economy $\mathscr{E}(p)$ consists precisely of the egalitarian reproducible allocations. A coalition J is exploited at a reproducible allocation if and only if it can communally block the allocation.

Proof. The proof is trivial. If an allocation is not egalitarian, let J be the coalition of the exploited producers. By blocking communally, they receive $(|J|/N)\omega$ in endowment, which allows them to reproduce themselves in an egalitarian fashion, each working Λb, and they are therefore each better off. Conversely, it has already been mentioned that an egalitarian allocation is in the communal core. The second statement in the theorem has the same proof. QED

The advantage of this game-theoretic formulation of exploitation is that it specifies concretely the alternative against which we are hypothetically evaluating a coalition's alternatives when we state that it is "exploited." Presumably, a concept of exploitation should embody some specification of a hypothetical alternative under which the exploited agents would be better off. Note, also, that this characterization of exploitation brings to the fore the institution of property relations, as that is what coalitions are allowed to change when they evaluate their alternative. A glimmer of the distinction between Marxian and neoclassical conceptions of exploitation can be seen at this point by comparing the private ownership core to the communal core. If one conceives of a group of agents as unfairly treated because they could do better by trading among themselves while respecting private property endowments, then the appropriate concept of fair or nonexploitative allocations is the private ownership core. If one conceives, however, of coalitions as exploited because they do not have access to (their share of) the means of production, then the communal core specifies the nonexploitative allocations. The private ownership core allows agents to gain fully from trade and organization, while respecting private property; the communal core annihilates inequalities arising from differential ownership of the means of production.

5. Summary

Although other results could be presented, if one were interested in the economy $\mathscr{E}(p)$ in its own right, they will only be mentioned here, as our use of $\mathscr{E}(p)$ in this book is primarily as a stepping stone to the next model in the hierarchy, which will fill in our understanding of exploitation and class. Several results deserve brief mention.

(1) The group of exploiters always includes at least those producers who are wealthier than average; that is:

$$p\omega^{\nu} > \frac{1}{N} p\omega \Rightarrow Lx^{\nu} < \Lambda b$$

where p is a reproducible solution. This is not surprising.

(2) The study of existence of reproducible solutions is difficult: there does not seem to be a simple condition on the data of an economy which will guarantee the existence of reproducible solutions.[9] For reasons which may become clear later, this has to do with the incomplete set of markets in the economy: if a labor market or a credit market is added on, then existence of equilibria becomes quite tractable. A somewhat interesting fact is that reproducible price vectors in $\mathscr{E}(p)$ do not equalize any sort of profit rate—as will be the case when another market is added on. (See the appendix to this chapter.)

Notice that at a reproducible solution in $\mathscr{E}(p)$, everybody works, although some may work less than others. If a producer has too little endowment, there may be no prices at which he has even a *feasible* solution to his program. An agent who has no endowment (except his labor power) dies in the economy, since he cannot trade his labor power to acquire his subsistence, nor can he borrow capital to operate production himself. This gives rise to the natural addition of a labor market or a credit market to the stark economy $\mathscr{E}(p)$, which is the purpose of the next chapters in Part I.

Notice that although producers are divided into two groups, exploiters and exploited, at an equilibrium, these groups are not *classes* in the Marxian sense. In $\mathscr{E}(p)$, everyone relates to the means of production in the same way: he works for himself. A class is a group of people who share the same social relation to the means of production. Hence, although exploitation has emerged in $\mathscr{E}(p)$, classes have not. The full regalia of Marxian social phenomena are not displayed in $\mathscr{E}(p)$.

The main conclusion of the study of $\mathscr{E}(p)$ is that a phenomenon of Marxian-like exploitation can be logically conceived of, given only competitive markets and differential property ownership. No institution of labor exchange need be posited, nor any accumulation of

9. Consider this proposed sufficient condition for the existence of a RS in $\mathscr{E}(p)$. Call an economy $\{A, L, b; \omega^1, \ldots, \omega^N\}$ *irreducible* if it possesses a reproducible allocation (see Definition 1.6), but no proper subcoalition of agents possesses one. That is, every coalition (with its endowment) is indispensable for the reproducibility of the economy. This appears to be a fairly strong way of postulating that each producer has "enough" endowment, and one might conjecture the market could find a way of organizing the reproduction of the economy. The conjecture is false. Examples of irreducible economies with three agents and two goods can be constructed which support no reproducible solution.

wealth or surplus production. Surplus labor can be expropriated even without the production of a surplus. (It must be possible to produce a surplus, however, for exploitation to exist.) Furthermore, this exploitation can be characterized without specific mention of the transfer of surplus value, by a game-theoretic formulation in which exploitative allocations are precisely those not in the core of the game. This formulation emphasizes property relations as the heart of the exploitation issue and, incidentally, opens up the possibility for redefining the Marxian concept of exploitation without recourse to the labor theory of value, a task which is pursued later on.

Appendix 1.1. $\mathscr{E}(p)$ as a model of unequal exchange between countries

Although there is no labor or capital market $\mathscr{E}(p)$, by examining the dual to the producer's optimization program he can be assigned shadow wage and profit (or interest) rates. We carry out this calculation here, and then interpret $\mathscr{E}(p)$ as a model of exchange between countries, where each agent is thought of as a country.[10]

Consider the producer's program:

$$\min Lx^\nu$$

subject to

$$p(I - A)x^\nu \geqq pb \qquad (\alpha^\nu) \tag{1}$$

$$pAx^\nu \leqq W^\nu \qquad (\beta^\nu) \tag{2}$$

and the dual program:

$$\text{choose } \alpha^\nu,\ \beta^\nu \text{ to max } \alpha^\nu pb - \beta^\nu W^\nu$$

subject to

10. This appendix is best read after reading Chapter 2, as it shows how we can conceive of a shadow labor market in $\mathscr{E}(p)$. For further application of the model to analyzing relations among countries see Roemer (1983b).

$$\alpha^\nu p(I - A) - \beta^\nu pA \leqq L \qquad (x^\nu) \tag{3}$$
$$\alpha^\nu, \beta^\nu \geqq 0$$

where, for each program, the complementary dual variables are written in parentheses next to their respective constraints. By dividing the dual constraint by α^ν, it can be written:

$$p \leqq (1 + (\beta^\nu/\alpha^\nu)pA + (1/\alpha^\nu)L$$

which suggests the following substitution. Let

$$\pi^\nu \equiv (\beta^\nu/\alpha^\nu), \ w^\nu \equiv (1/\alpha^\nu)$$

and the dual program can then be written:

$$\text{choose } \pi^\nu, w^\nu \text{ to max } (pb - \pi^\nu W^\nu)/w^\nu$$

subject to

$$p \leqq (1 + \pi^\nu)pA + w^\nu L \tag{3'}$$
$$\pi^\nu, w^\nu \geqq 0.$$

Observe that the first primal constraint is always binding. The producer always can reduce his optimal work time if the value of subsistence, pb, is reduced; hence $\alpha^\nu > 0$ at the optimum, and so the variables π^ν and w^ν will always be well defined at the solution.

With this transformation of variables, the dual program looks very much like the optimization problem in $\mathscr{E}(p, w)$ (see Chapter 2). In fact, the value of the dual is precisely the formula for optimal work time in $\mathscr{E}(p, w)$ (see Theorem 2.3). The interpretation is this. If π^ν were the profit rate available to producer ν, and w^ν the wage available to him, then the profit revenue from his capital would be $\pi^\nu W^\nu$. The net revenues he would be required to earn from wages would thus be $pb - \pi^\nu W^\nu$, which would require $(pb - \pi^\nu W^\nu)/w^\nu$ hours of labor. At the optimum choice (π^ν, w^ν) for the producer, he will only operate sectors generating the maximal profit rate, that is, sectors for which inequality (3′) is binding, by complementary slackness. (That is, $px^\nu = (1 + \pi^\nu)pAx^\nu + w^\nu Lx^\nu$ at the optimum.) (π^ν, w^ν) is producer ν's shadow profit rate–wage rate pair.

Consider this story which justifies calling (π^ν, w^ν) the shadow "factor" prices. A shadow entrepreneur offers producer ν an interest rate π^ν for his capital and a wage rate w^ν for his labor. The offer guarantees ν at least as much revenue from the deal as he would make by operating each sector on his own, in net revenues, at prices p:

$$p - pA \leqq \pi^\nu pA + w^\nu L.$$

(This is the dual constraint.) Subject to this condition on the offer, what is the profit rate–wage rate pair at which ν is just indifferent between accepting the shadow entrepreneur's offer and not doing so? Answer: the optimal solution to the dual program, for at that choice (π^ν, w^ν) he is working precisely as long as he does when solving his primal problem without the shadow markets.

What is special about $\mathscr{E}(p)$ is the lack of actual labor and capital markets. Hence, different producers will have different shadow factor prices (π^ν, w^ν). We next analyze this. We assume from now on that p is a reproducible solution.

The nature of the solutions (π^ν, w^ν) can be seen graphically in Figure 5. At prices p, for any given wage w, there will be a maximal profit rate $\pi(w)$, defined by:

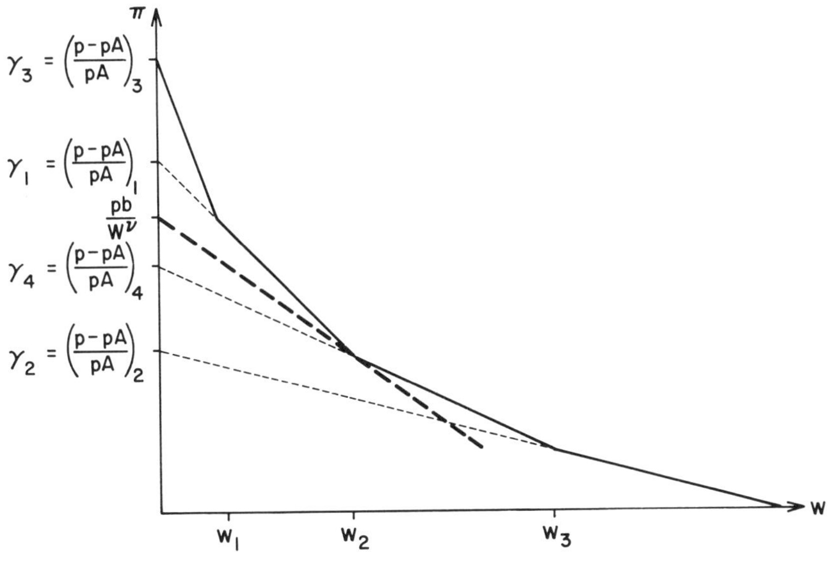

Figure 5 The wage rate-profit rate function in $\mathscr{E}(p)$

$$\pi(w) = \max_j \frac{[p - (pA + wL)]_j}{pA_j}.$$

The curve $\pi(w)$ is graphed as the solid line in Figure 5. The graph represents a four-sector economy, in which the maximal ratio $(p - pA)/pA$ is achieved in sector 3, and so on, as shown. When $0 \leq w < w_1$, sector 3 generates the highest profit rate. At w_1, sector 1 becomes as profitable, and then during the interval $w_1 < w < w_2$, sector 1 is the most profitable; at w_2, sector 4 takes over as the most profitable and remains so in the interval $w_2 < w < w_3$; for $w > w_3$, sector 2 is the most profitable. We will see shortly that at a reproducible solution, the profit rate–wage rate frontier must have this form: specifically, each sector must be maximally profitable for some pair (π, w). Every sector must touch the profit rate–wage rate frontier.

Consider the producer's dual objective function:

$$\max \frac{pb - \pi W^\nu}{w} = k.$$

Writing this as

$$\pi = \frac{pb}{W^\nu} - \frac{wk}{W^\nu},$$

we see the problem for the producer is to choose the line passing through the π-intercept pb/W^ν, having the most negative slope, and intersecting the $\pi - w$ frontier. For instance, if producer ν's value pb/W^ν is as shown in Figure 5, he will choose (π^ν, w^ν) as indicated (at wage w_2). Notice that producer ν will operate only sectors 1 and 4, since they are the only ones generating his shadow profit rate. As W^ν increases, pb/W^ν travels toward the origin on the π-axis; when $pb/W^\nu < \gamma_2$, producer ν will operate only sector 2, and his shadow profit rate will be zero. In particular, we immediately see that the shadow profit rate is monotonically decreasing in wealth (although not strictly) and the shadow wage rate is monotonically increasing. This is sensible: the marginal value of a unit of capital for the rich is less than for the poor.

It can now be seen why every sector must have a maximal profit rate for some w. If there were a sector which did not, no producer would ever operate it, and p would not be a reproducible solution.

Further, it can be seen that

$$\frac{pb}{W^{\nu}} \leqq \left(\frac{p - pA}{pA}\right)_{\max} \qquad \text{for all } \nu$$

at a reproducible solution. (That is, pb/W^{ν} always lies below γ_3 in this picture.) For if, for some ν:

$$\frac{pb}{W^{\nu}} > \left(\frac{p - pA}{pA}\right)_j \qquad \text{for all } j,$$

then there can be no feasible solution to ν's primal program. (Check the two primal constraints.)

We see that in general a producer will operate only two sectors at the optimum. Furthermore, the capital-labor ratio in the sectors operated increases with wealth. Notice that the slopes of the segments of the profit-wage frontier are $-L_j/pA_j$. To see this, write the vector equation from which the frontier is derived as:

$$\pi = \frac{p - pA}{pA} - w\frac{L}{pA}.$$

It is clear from the geometry that L_j/pA_j must decrease as $((p - pA)/pA)_j$ decrease: for if not, the profit-wage frontier for some sector would lie entirely below the aggregate profit-wage frontier, destroying reproducibility. Thus, the richest operate the sector with the highest capital-labor ratio pA_j/L_j, and the poorest operate the one or two least capital intensive sectors.

Specifically, at the equilibrium in Figure 5, we have the division of labor:

—if $0 < pb/W^{\nu} < \gamma_2$, ν has a zero shadow profit rate and operates only sector 2, the sector with the highest capital-labor ratio;

—if $\gamma_2 \leqq pb/W^{\nu} < \gamma_4$, then ν operates indifferently sectors 2 and 4, the two most capital intensive sectors;

—if $\gamma_4 \leqq pb/W^{\nu} < \gamma_1$, then ν operates indifferently sectors 4 and 1;

—if $\gamma_1 \leqq pb/W^{\nu} \leqq \gamma_3$, then ν operates indifferently sectors 1 and 3.

Although this discussion does not provide characterizing conditions for p to be a reproducible solution, we can conclude at least this: at a reproducible solution p, the net revenue-capital ratios $(p - pA)_j/pA_j$ must decrease monotonically with the labor-capital ratios L_j/pA_j.

Finally, we interpret the model in the context of trade between countries. Imagine that each country has available the same technology and labor force, but countries differ in their wealths ω^ν, and hence finance capitals $W^\nu = p\omega^\nu$. There is trade in commodities but not in labor or capital. Thus, each agent in $\mathscr{E}(p)$ is a country, where the *internal* labor and capital markets are suppressed in the model, because there is no international trade on those markets. We assume each country is "subsistent" in the sense of the model—it wishes to purchase the common vector b with the least labor expended. (This is not, perhaps, a very realistic assumption from the point of view of countries.) Then the shadow prices (π^ν, w^ν) represent the profit and wage rates on the internal capital and labor markets in the νth country, at equilibrium prices p. At the equilibrium, there is unequal exchange in the sense that some countries work longer than socially necessary labor time Λb and others less long. As countries get richer, their internal profit rates fall and their wage rates increase. There is an international division of labor: a particular country will operate only one or two sectors, and they will be of similar capital intensities. As countries get richer they operate more capital intensive sectors.

Furthermore, this "unequal exchange" and international division of labor occur even when all countries have the same technological capabilities and labor forces of equal skill. We observe, systematically, the operation of labor intensive sectors in poor countries and capital intensive sectors in rich ones, but that is a consequence of optimizing behavior given the capital constraint, not lack of technological knowledge. There is no extra-economic imperialism necessary to generate this unequal exchange either; that is, the terms of trade need not be politically enforced, as they are the competitive solution to a regime of free trade, given the optimizing behavior of the countries and their differential wealths.

2

The Labor Market and the Emergence of Class

When neither a labor market nor a credit market exists, there is only one way for producers to relate to the means of production: each must work for himself, using his own assets in production. Although exploitation emerges, there is no class differentiation of producers. In the model of this chapter, a labor market is introduced, which opens up the possibility that producers will relate to the means of production in different ways—some may sell labor power as an optimizing strategy, others may hire it, and still others may do neither at the equilibrium, but will work only in their own shops. These are three different types of relations of production, to use the Marxian language, which define three different class positions.

We show below that classes emerge endogenously in a precapitalist subsistence exchange economy with labor market. (There are, in fact, five classes in the model, gotten by forming certain combinations of the three basic relations of production described.) But the central task of the analysis is to study the relationship between a producer's class position and his exploitation status. As in the model of Chapter 1, the exploitation status of producers emerges endogenously from the model. The central theorem is dubbed the Class Exploitation Correspondence Principle (CECP), which states that at an equilibrium every producer who is in a labor-hiring class is an exploiter, and every producer who is in a labor-selling class is exploited. This relationship is often taken as a self-evident truth of Marxism; in my analysis it is not a postulated truth but a theorem. Since both class and exploitation emerge endogenously from the model, as a consequence of the agents' optimizing behavior given their differential ownership of assets, new information is conveyed in proving that a certain relationship exists between the two phenomena.

As has been remarked, the purpose of this modeling is not economic history or anthropology, but an investigation of the institutions which are logically necessary to produce exploitation and now class. The perhaps heretical conclusion of the last chapter was that a Marxian-like exploitation phenomenon could be generated in an economy which lacked any institution for labor exchange. With the addition of a labor market to the model, classes are now generated, and this can perhaps serve as some solace: although an institution for labor exchange is not necessary to generate exploitation, at least exploitation becomes further articulated by a class structure with the advent of that institution. Such solace, however, will be short-lived, as Chapter 3 shows.

Along with the CECP, there are several corollary results of some interest in the history of Marxist doctrine. These concern the transformation problem and the logical requirements for the emergence of prices of production.

1. A subsistence economy with labor market

In the economy $\mathscr{E}(p)$, there are many distributions of endowments for which no reproducible solution exists. In particular, those producers with too little endowment will not be able to reproduce themselves at any prices. In this case, a market for labor power is a natural institution to emerge: those who are well endowed offer to hire the poorly endowed for a wage, thus reducing the former's work time and allowing the latter to survive. With the advent of a labor market, it is convenient to model producer ν's optimization problem as one involving the choice of three vectors, each of which is a vector of activity levels. These are:

$x^\nu \in \mathbb{R}^n_+$: the vector of activity levels ν operates himself;
$y^\nu \in \mathbb{R}^n_+$: the vector of activity levels ν hires others to operate for him;
$x^\nu_0 \in \mathbb{R}_+$: the amount of labor time ν chooses to sell to others, a scalar.

Producer ν's objective is the same as in $\mathscr{E}(p)$. He faces a price vector

(p, w), where prices p are in $\mathbb{R}^n_+$ and wage w is in $\mathbb{R}_+$, and he wishes to minimize the labor he expends in order to end up with a net output worth sufficient exchange value for him to acquire his subsistence needs through trade. His constraints are as before: he must pay for the capital advanced from his current holdings, $p\omega^\nu$, and he faces a labor constraint on his own labor.

Formally, when facing prices (p, w), his program is:

$$\text{choose } x^\nu, y^\nu, x_0^\nu \text{ to min } Lx^\nu + x_0^\nu$$

subject to

$$\left.\begin{aligned} & p(I - A)x^\nu + (p - (pA + wL)y^\nu + wx_0^\nu \geqq pb \\ & \quad \text{(reproducibility)} && \text{(Pi)} \\ & pA(x^\nu + y^\nu) \leqq p\omega^\nu \quad \text{(feasibility)} && \text{(Pii)} \\ & Lx^\nu + x_0^\nu \leqq 1 \quad \text{(length of working day)} && \text{(Piii)} \end{aligned}\right\} \text{(P)}$$

$$x^\nu, y^\nu, x_0^\nu \geqq 0.$$

The three constraints have the same interpretation as in the economy $\mathscr{E}(p)$. The three terms on the left-hand side of (Pi) are the sources of net revenues to ν, from the activities of working his own shop at activity levels x^ν, hiring others to work his shop at levels y^ν, and selling his own labor power for the wage, in amount x_0^ν. Inequality (Pi) thus states that net revenue should not be exceeded by the cost of subsistence, which rephrases the requirement that ν not run down the value of his assets, which is the reproducibility requirement. Inequality (Pii) is the capital constraint: capital advanced is $pA(x^\nu + y^\nu)$, and so this inequality states that the activity levels chosen must be affordable. Inequality (Piii) is the quantity constraint on the labor supply of the individual.

Notice that wages are paid out of revenues, not in advance. If they were advanced, then (Pii) could appear as:

$$pA(x^\nu + y^\nu) + wLy^\nu \leqq p\omega^\nu + wx_0^\nu. \qquad \text{(Pii}')$$

The left-hand side of (Pii′) includes an additional term for the wages paid to hired workers which must be advanced out of capital, and the right-hand side includes a term of wages earned by ν from selling his labor power, which, since he would receive them at the period's beginning, become part of his financial assets. Absolutely nothing of consequence changes if we adopt the model (Pii′) with wages paid in advance; our convention is to keep wages paid out of revenues, as the algebra is slightly simpler, since there are two fewer terms in (Pii) than in (Pii′).

As before, we define, for each individual ν:

$$\mathscr{A}^{\nu}(p, w) \equiv \{(x^{\nu}, y^{\nu}, x_0^{\nu}) \text{ solving this program}\}.$$

We define next the equilibrium notion for the economy, which we call $\mathscr{E}(p, w)$, meant to conjure up the picture that this economy has a market for every produced good (at prices p), and labor power (at price w). (We could impose some normalization on the price vector (p, w), but do not choose to do so at this point.) The idea of a *reproducible solution* is the same as before: Facing prices (p, w) each producer chooses an optimal program $(x^{\nu}, y^{\nu}, x_0^{\nu})$. Prices (p, w) will be a reproducible solution if such optimal solutions can be chosen for all producers, with the consequences that total net output is sufficient to provide for aggregate consumption demand, total production inputs demanded can be supplied by aggregate initial endowment, and the supply and demand of labor power are equal. Formally:

Definition 2.1. A reproducible solution (RS) in the economy $\mathscr{E}(p, w|A, L, b, \omega^1, \ldots, \omega^N)$, or $\mathscr{E}(p, w)$, is a price vector (p, w) and associated set of actions such that:

(i) $\forall \nu, \quad (x^{\nu}, y^{\nu}, x_0^{\nu}) \in \mathscr{A}^{\nu}(p, w)$

(ii) $(x + y) \geqq A(x + y) + Nb,$
$x = \Sigma x^{\nu}, \quad y = \Sigma y^{\nu}$ (reproducibility)

(iii) $A(x + y) \leqq \omega \equiv \Sigma \omega^{\nu}$ (feasibility)

(iv) $Ly = x_0 \equiv \Sigma x_0^{n}$ (labor market equilibrium)

Notice that the gross activity level vector is $x + y$, where each non-superscripted variable is the total of all superscripted variables of the same letter, summed over all producers. Hence, (ii) states the reproducibility requirement that gross output be sufficient to replace inputs used plus supply all subsistence needs. The only new requirement for equilibrium in $\mathscr{E}(p, w)$ which did not appear in $\mathscr{E}(p)$ is the condition (iv) for the equilibration of the new market, for labor power. A requirement of equilibrium is that every labor-hiring plan and every labor-selling plan be realizable, which is assured by (iv). At an equilibrium of the type defined by Definition 2.1, every agent optimizes and the society reproduces, while the quantity constraints on labor and stocks are not violated.

2. Exploitation at reproducible solutions in $\mathscr{E}(p, w)$

Before analyzing reproducible solutions in $\mathscr{E}(p, w)$, a technicality must be dealt with. Note that if producer ν is sufficiently wealthy, then he may not work at all at an individually optimal (IO) solution. He may be able to reproduce himself by only hiring others. This possibility did not exist in $\mathscr{E}(p)$, and when it occurs there is some indeterminacy in ν's choice of action which it is convenient to eliminate. This is done by assuming:

Assumption 2 (NBC). Let (p, w) be prices such that $\exists(x^\nu, y^\nu, x_0^\nu) \in \mathscr{A}^\nu(p, w)$, for some ν, such that $x^\nu = x_0^\nu = 0$. Then among the optimal solutions to his program, ν chooses a solution y^ν which minimizes his capital outlay pAy^ν.

A producer who operates in this way is a *nonbenevolent capitalist* (NBC): a capitalist, since he only hires others; nonbenevolent, since he chooses to circulate the minimal amount of capital to achieve his zero work time, instead of circulating more and thus possibly creating additional employment. For some of the results below we need not assume NBC.

One might argue against the adoption of Assumption NBC on the grounds that if a producer could acquire his subsistence needs by not working at all himself, it is more appropriate to endow him with behavior which leads him to increase his consumption, rather than behavior which leads him to economize on capital. In Chapter 4 a full-fledged model of accumulation is studied which is essentially the polar opposite of the subsistence economy of Part I, and for that reason I choose here to maintain the subsistence character of agents. As well, since we are gradually building up to a model of capitalist economy, it will do no harm to endow our rich agents, who do not need to work, with embryonic capitalist behavior. But mostly, Assumption NBC imposes clarity and simplicity on a number of results, and hence it is a tool for simplifying the analysis at no great cost.

The task of the next several lemmas is to prove Theorem 2.1, which states that at a reproducible solution in $\mathscr{E}(p, w)$, total time worked is just socially necessary labor time. As the reader recalls, this permits us to classify producers as exploited or exploiting, according to whether they work longer or less long than time Λb, respectively.

We proceed to verify some simple facts.

Lemma 2.1. Let (p, w) be a RS for $\mathscr{E}(p, w)$. Assume NBC. Then $\forall \nu$, $p(I - A)x^\nu + (p - (pA + L))y^\nu + wx_0^\nu = pb$. (The reproducibility constraint holds with equality.)

Proof. Consider, first, ν who works. Either x_0^ν or x^ν is nonzero. If the producer's reproducibility constraint holds as a strict inequality, either x_0^ν or x^ν could be reduced without destroying the feasibility of the solution, thus reducing work time $Lx^\nu + x_0^\nu$, since $L > 0$ by Assumption 1.

Consider ν who does not work. If $(p - (pA + L))y^\nu > pb$, then y^ν could be reduced without destroying feasibility. This in turn reduces pAy^ν, a contradiction to Assumption NBC. QED

Lemma 2.2. Assume NBC. Let (p, w) be a RS for $\mathscr{E}(p, w)$ with $w > 0$. Then $p \geqq pA + wL$, and $p > 0$.

Proof. Suppose there is a sector j such that

$$p_j < pA_j + wL_j. \tag{1}$$

We show that no producer will operate sector j himself, nor will he hire others to operate that sector.

If he hires others to operate sector j at level y_j^ν, then his net revenue from that process is negative. By reducing y_j^ν to zero, his reproducibility constraint will become slack. This is still a feasible solution with ν working the same labor time as before, but by Lemma 2.1 it cannot be an individual optimum. Therefore $y_j^\nu = 0$ at an individual optimum, for all ν.

Suppose now that for some ν, $x_j^\nu > 0$. Then ν can reduce his operation of activity j by a small amount ϵ_j^ν, and by choice of j:

$$(p_j - pA_j)\epsilon_j^\nu < wL_j\epsilon_j^\nu. \tag{2}$$

The work time ν thereby saves is $L_j\epsilon_j^\nu$. Let ν sell labor time in amount $L_j\epsilon_j^\nu$. This new allocation, for ν, has the same total work time for him as before, but by (2) his revenue is greater than before. Hence, his reproducibility constraint is now slack, and by Lemma 2.1 this solution is not optimal; nor, therefore, was the original solution.

Hence, $x_j^\nu = y_j^\nu = 0$, for all ν. But since (x, y, x_0) is a RS, $x + y \geqq (I - A)^{-1}(Nb) > 0$, and so $x_j + y_j > 0$. This contradicts the existence of a sector j satisfying inequality (1). The first conclusion of the theorem follows, and the second thus follows, since $p \geqq wL(I - A)^{-1} > 0$. QED

As a consequence of Lemma 2.2, at a RS we have either $p = w\Lambda$ or $p \geq w\Lambda$. We shall say, in the second case, that at (p, w) there is a *possibility of positive profits* (PPP).

Theorem 2.1. Assume NBC. At a RS (p, w) of $\mathscr{E}(p, w)$:

$$x + y = (I - A)^{-1}(Nb) \tag{a}$$

$$Lx + x_0 = N\Lambda b \tag{b}$$

Proof. Summing the reproducibility constraint (Pi) over all producers, and using Lemma 2.1, and Definition 2.1, part (iv):

$$p(I - A)(x + y) = pNb. \tag{1}$$

By Definition 2.1, part (ii), it will follow that

$$(I - A)(x + y) = Nb \tag{2}$$

if $p > 0$.

Since (p, w) is a RS, $w > 0$, for if $w = 0$, the demand for labor will exceed the supply. Hence, by Lemma 2.2, $p > 0$.

Hence (2) holds. Premultiplying by $L(I - A)^{-1}$:

$$L(x + y) = Lx + x_0 = N\Lambda b. \quad \text{QED}$$

Hence total work time at a RS in $\mathscr{E}(p, w)$ is, as in $\mathscr{E}(p)$, precisely socially necessary labor time. As in $\mathscr{E}(p)$, we can, therefore, speak of a RS as being egalitarian if all producers work Λb, and inegalitarian and exploitative otherwise.

We prove next the analog of Theorem 1.5 of Chapter 1 for the economy with labor market.

Theorem 2.2. Assume NBC. Let $\omega \geq A(I - A)^{-1}(Nb)$, (p, w) an RS for $\mathscr{E}(p, w)$. The following are equivalent:

(A) Possibility of positive profits (PPP) (that is, $p \neq w\Lambda$).
(B) Existence of exploitation at (p, w).
(C) Some producer does not work.

Theorem 2.2 can be thought of as a Fundamental Marxian Theorem (FMT) for this economy, as it shows that exploitation is equivalent to the possibility of profits. (For other versions of the FMT in more classical Marxian economics, and a fuller discussion, see Morishima, 1973, and Roemer, 1980.) Moreover, Theorem 2.2 asserts the somewhat surprising fact that if there is any inegalitarianism in $\mathscr{E}(p, w)$, then there are some pure capitalists who do not work at all—subject to the caveat that the economy possess more than the bare minimum of resources necessary for reproduction, $\omega = A(I - A)^{-1}(Nb)$.

First , a lemma:

Lemma 2.3. Let (p, w) be prices at which PPP ($p \geq pA + wL$). If ν works at an IO, then $pA(x^\nu + y^\nu) = p\omega^\nu$.

Proof. If $pA(x^\nu + y^\nu) < p\omega^\nu$, then ν possesses some excess capital. He can choose a sector j in which $(p_j - (pA_j + L_j)) > 0$, and hire some workers to operate it, with his excess capital. This increases his net revenue, making his constraint (Pi) slack. Consequently, he was not at an IO, by Lemma 2.1. QED

Proof of Theorem 2.2.

(A) $\Rightarrow$ (C). At RS, $x + y = (I - A)^{-1}(Nb)$, and so $A(x + y) \leq \omega$. Since $p > 0$ (see Lemma 2.2), $pA(x + y) < p\omega$, and so $\exists \nu$, $pA(x^\nu + y^\nu) < p\omega^\nu$. By Lemma 2.3, ν does not work at his IO.

(C) $\Rightarrow$ *(B)*. Follows immediately from Theorem 2.1.

(B) $\Rightarrow$ *(A)*.

Suppose, on the contrary, $p = w\Lambda$. Every producer's program can then be written:

$$\min Lx^\nu + x_0^\nu$$

subject to

$$w(Lx^{\nu} + x_0^{\nu}) = w\Lambda b \quad \text{(Pi)}$$

$$\Lambda A(x^{\nu} + y^{\nu}) \leqq w\Lambda\omega^{\nu} \quad \text{(Pii)}$$

$$Lx^{\nu} + x_0^{\nu} \leqq 1 \quad \text{(Piii)}$$

By Lemma 2.1, and observing (Pi) above,

$$Lx^{\nu} + x_0^{\nu} = \Lambda b \; \forall \nu$$

and consequently there is no exploitation. QED

Theorem 2.2 is an analog, for $\mathscr{E}(p, w)$, to Theorem 1.5 of Chapter 1, since it states that when prices are not proportional to labor values there is exploitation.[1] That we get also the result that some producer does not work at equilibrium in $\mathscr{E}(p, w)$ is an artifact of the model, I think, of no particular significance. The genesis of the artifact is clear from the proof. If there is some excess aggregate stock, as postulated, then at equilibrium some producer has excess finance capital, in the sense that he can optimize without using his entire wealth. Such a producer will not be working, for every working producer has a binding wealth constraint.

3. The division of society into classes in $\mathscr{E}(p, w)$

In the economy $\mathscr{E}(p)$, there are, at an inegalitarian solution, two groups of producers: the exploiters and the exploited. (There may also be a marginal group who work precisely Λb.) These groups are not, however, classes in the Marxian sense, as all producers relate to the means of production in the same way: they all work their own means of production. In $\mathscr{E}(p, w)$, however, there are different classes. At a RS, different producers relate differently to the means of production. An optimal solution for an agent ν is a triple of vectors $(x^{\nu}; y^{\nu}; x_0^{\nu})$. Seven possible classes exist, according to whether these vectors are either zero or nonzero at the RS: that is, (0, +, 0),

1. If the organic compositions of capital are not all equal across sectors, then the converse of this statement holds also. This follows from Theorem 2.6 below. Only if the organic compositions are all equal is it possible to have reproducible solutions, with prices proportional to labor values (at a proportionality factor greater than the wage), which support profits and exploitation.

(+, +, 0), (+, +, +), (+, 0, 0), (0, +, +), (+, 0, +), and (0, 0, +) where "+" means a nonzero vector in the appropriate place. Producers who possess an RS of the form (0, +, 0) may be called *pure capitalists*, as they only hire others; the class of producers (0, 0, +) are *proletarians*, as they only sell labor power; the other classes shall be named later.

The use of the word *class* to describe these producers is a precise Marxian usage, for it characterizes the way in which an agent relates to the means of production—hiring labor power, selling labor power, working his own shop, or using some combination of these production relations.

The formal definition of class membership is:

Definition 2.2. Let (p, w) be any price vector. Agent ν is said to be a member of class (a_1, a_2, a_3) with respect to (p, w), where each a_i is the symbol + or 0, if ν possesses an individually optimal solution of the form (a_1, a_2, a_3) for the vector (x^ν, y^ν, x_0^ν).

The task of this section is to show that society decomposes into five classes, which always fall in a certain specified order, if we rank producers according to wealth. The class of pure capitalists will appear at the top of the hierarchy, and the proletarians will appear at the bottom. (See Theorem 2.5 below.) En route to this class decomposition theorem it is convenient to prove Theorem 2.3, which calculates precisely how long each producer works at a reproducible solution in $\mathscr{E}(p, w)$.

Let (p, w) be a RS for $\mathscr{E}(p, w)$. We define the maximal profit rate, across all sectors of the economy, as:

$$\pi_{\max} = \max_j \frac{(p - (pA + wL))_j}{pA_j} .$$

$\pi_{\max}$ is the maximal rate of profit on capital advanced, which does not include wages in our specification.

Theorem 2.3. Let (p, w) be a RS for $\mathscr{E}(p, w)$. Then the work time of ν at (p, w) is:

$$Lx^\nu + x_0^\nu = \max\left(0, \frac{pb - \pi_{\max} p\omega^\nu}{w}\right).$$

Proof. Rewrite the producer's program as:

$$\min Lx^\nu + x_0^\nu$$

subject to

$$p(I - A)(x^\nu + y^\nu) + w(x_0^\nu - Ly^\nu) \geqq pb \tag{Pi}$$

$$pA(x^\nu + y^\nu) \leqq p\omega^\nu \tag{Pii}$$

$$Lx^\nu + x_0^\nu \leqq 1 \tag{Piii}$$

$$x^\nu, y^\nu, x_0^\nu \geqq 0$$

If (x^ν, y^ν, x_0^ν) is a solution to the program, it therefore follows that $(\underline{x}^\nu, \underline{y}^\nu, \underline{x}_0^\nu)$ is also a solution, whenever:

$$\underline{x}^\nu + \underline{y}^\nu = x^\nu + y^\nu \tag{1}$$

and

$$\underline{x}_0^\nu - L\underline{y}^\nu = x_0^\nu - Ly^\nu \tag{2}$$

(Clearly $(\underline{x}^\nu, \underline{y}^\nu, \underline{x}_0^\nu)$ is feasible from (1) and (2); that it is optimal can be seen by premultiplying equation (1) by L and adding the result to equation (2).) Hence, if a solution (x^ν, y^ν, x_0^ν) to the program exists, then there is always a solution of the form $(0, \underline{y}^\nu, \underline{x}_0^\nu)$: simply set $\underline{x}^\nu = 0$, $\underline{y}^\nu = x^\nu + y^\nu$, $\underline{x}_0^\nu = Lx^\nu + x_0^\nu$, verifying that (1) and (2) hold.

That is, an agent can always optimize by not working in his own shop at all. It therefore follows that we may restrict our domain of feasible solutions to ones of the form $(0, y^\nu, x_0^\nu)$, without changing the optimal value of the program; and so the program may be rewritten:

$$\min x_0^\nu$$

subject to

$$(p(I - A) - wL)y^\nu + wx_0^\nu \geqq pb \tag{Pi'}$$

$$pAy^\nu \leqq p\omega^\nu \tag{Pii'}$$

$$x_0^\nu, y^\nu \geqq 0$$

But solving this program is equivalent to solving these two programs sequentially:

$$\max (p(I - A) - wL)y^\nu$$

subject to

$$pAy^\nu \leqq p\omega^\nu \qquad \text{(I)}$$
$$y^\nu \geqq 0$$

For given Π^ν,

$$\min x_0^\nu$$

subject to

$$\Pi^\nu + wx_0^\nu \geqq pb \qquad \text{(II)}$$
$$x_0^\nu \geqq 0$$

To prove Theorem 2.3, suppose $\pi_{\max} > 0$. Then the optimal value for program (I) is $\pi_{\max}p\omega^\nu$: agent ν simply hires labor in any $\pi_{\max}$ sector until his capital $p\omega^\nu$ is exhausted. (Notice that the objective function of (I) is just profits.) Setting $\Pi^\nu = \pi_{\max}p\omega^\nu$, program (II) is solved to yield $x_0^\nu = \max\left(0, \dfrac{pb - \Pi^\nu}{w}\right)$, as required.

If $\pi_{\max} = 0$, then $y^\nu = 0$ is an optimal solution of (I), and the optimal work time from (II) is $x_0^\nu = pb/w$, conforming to the required formula. QED

Theorem 2.4.

(A) At a RS (p, w) in $\mathscr{E}(p, w)$, the time ν works is strictly monotone decreasing in wealth $W^\nu \equiv p\omega^\nu$, as long as $W^\nu < pb/\pi_{\max}$.

(B) A RS in $\mathscr{E}(p, w)$ is egalitarian $\Leftrightarrow$ $\pi_{\max} = 0$ or all wealths are equal, $W^\nu = W^\mu \;\forall\, \nu, \mu$.

(C) The class of pure capitalists is $\{\nu | W^\nu \geqq pb/\pi_{\max}\}$.

Proof. From Theorem 2.3. QED

We may now discuss the class decomposition theorem. It is appropriate to give names to the five classes which exhaust society at a reproducible solution of $\mathscr{E}(p, w)$:

	(x^ν, y^ν, x_0^ν)	
1.	$(0, +, 0)$	big capitalists (landlords)
2.	$(+, +, 0)$	small capitalists (rich peasants)
3.	$(+, 0, 0)$	petty bourgeoisie (middle peasants)
4.	$(+, 0, +)$	semiproletarians (poor peasants)
5.	$(0, 0, +)$	proletarians (agricultural laborers)

The names in parentheses are added as a historical curiosus: they are the names Lenin and Mao Zedong gave to the five classes of peasantry. The identifications are not specious, as these writers defined the five classes the way they are defined here—for instance, a poor peasant was someone who worked his own land, but also hired himself out; a rich peasant worked his own land, but also hired others; a landlord only hired others, and so forth. For Lenin and Mao, the ordering of the five classes as listed also was the ordering according to the degree of wealth, and therefore the degree of exploitation of the various classes of peasantry. That result is a theorem in this model.[2]

2. In this passage, from "Analysis of the classes in Chinese Society," Mao characterizes the three bottom classes, which he calls the owner peasants, semi-owners, and poor peasants. It is interesting, as well, that he identifies labor selling with borrowing money on the credit market, an identification that is developed in Chapter 3. In this passage, Mao speaks of the landless as poor peasants; he elsewhere calls them rural proletarians. He also speaks of the landlords and rich peasants elsewhere in the article: "Although both the overwhelming majority of the semi-owner peasants and the poor peasants belong to the semi-proletariat, they may be further divided into three smaller categories, upper, middle and lower, according to their economic condition. The semi-owner peasants are worse off than the owner-peasants because every year they are short of about half the food they need, and have to make up this deficit by renting land from others, selling part of their labour power, or engaging in petty trading. In late spring and early summer when the crop is still in the blade and the old stock is consumed, they borrow at exorbitant rates of interest and buy grain at high prices; their plight is naturally harder than that of the owner-peasants who need no help from others, but they are better off than the poor peasants. For the poor peasants own no land, and receive only half the harvest or even less for their year's toil, while the semi-owner peasants, though receiving only half or less than half the harvest of land rented from others, can keep the entire crop from the land they own. The semi-owner peasants are therefore more revolutionary than the owner-peasants, but less revolutionary than the poor peasants" (Mao, 1926, pp. 16–17). A similar class characterization of the peasantry appears in Lenin's *Development of Capitalism in Russia:* "In the peasant mass of 97 million, however, one must distinguish three main groups: the bottom group–the proletarian and semi-proletarian strata of the population; the middle—the poor small peasant farmers; and the top group—the well-to-do small peasant farmers. We have analyzed above the main economic features of these groups as distinct *class* elements. The bottom group is the propertyless population, which earns its livelihood mainly, or half of it, by the *sale of labour-power*. The middle group comprises the poor small peasant farmers, for the middle peasant in the best of years just barely manages to make ends meet, but the *principal* means of livelihood of this group is "independent" (supposedly independent, of course) *small-scale farming*. Finally, the top group consists of the well-to-do small peasant farmers, who exploit more or less considerable numbers of allotment-holding farm labourers and day labourers and all sorts of wage-labourers in general" (Lenin, 1899, p. 508).

To make this precise, we must eliminate some duplication in the classes. Let Γ^ν be the set of optimal solutions (x^ν, y^ν, x_0^ν) of producer ν's optimization program P. We define disjoint classes as follows:

$$
\begin{aligned}
C^1 &= \{\nu | \Gamma^\nu \text{ contains a solution } (0, +, 0)\} \\
C^2 &= \{\nu | \Gamma^\nu \text{ contains a solution } (+, +, 0) \text{ but not one of form } (+, 0, 0)\} \\
C^3 &= \{\nu | \Gamma^\nu \text{ contains a solution } (+, 0, 0)\} \\
C^4 &= \{\nu | \Gamma^\nu \text{ contains a solution } (+, 0, +) \text{ but not } (+, 0, 0)\} \\
C^5 &= \{\nu | \Gamma^\nu \text{ contains a solution } (0, 0, +)\}
\end{aligned}
$$

That is, a given producer may have individually optimal solutions of different forms, thus placing him in several apparently different class positions. (In the proof of Theorem 2.3, it has already been shown that every producer has a solution of the form $(0, +, +)$; so that class description is useless for discriminating among agents.) We show that the above definition of classes is the appropriate one in the sense that it allows a disjoint and exhaustive class decomposition. A convenient shorthand is:

$$
\begin{aligned}
C^1 &= (0, +, 0) \\
C^2 &= (+, +, 0) \setminus (+, 0, 0) \\
C^3 &= (+, 0, 0) \\
C^4 &= (+, 0, +) \setminus (+, 0, 0) \\
C^5 &= (0, 0, +)
\end{aligned}
$$

Theorem 2.5. Let (p, w) be an inegalitarian RS for $\mathscr{E}(p, w)$. Let the producers be ordered by how long they work at (p, w). Then this ordering replicates the ordering of the five classes $C^1, \ldots, C^5$. That is: for $1 \leqq i < j \leqq 5$, any member of class C^j works longer than every member of class C^i. Furthermore, the five classes are exhaustive and pairwise disjoint.[3]

This theorem verifies that a producer's relation to the means of production corresponds to his wealth, or the degree to which he is exploited, in the economy with labor market $\mathscr{E}(p, w)$. It is apparent that the most fortunate production relations to enjoy in $\mathscr{E}(p, w)$ are those of labor hirers; the least fortunate relations are those of labor

3. If (p, w) is an egalitarian solution, then every producer is a member of class C^3.

sellers; and being self-employed is in between. This verifies traditional Marxian theory. There is thus an important asymmetry: the process of hiring is associated with being wealthier, and therefore doing better according to the exploitation-welfare criterion. Note that we have yet to verify where in the hierarchy of classes the cutoff point between exploited and exploiters occurs, the topic of the next section.

Proof of Theorem 2.5.

1. First, we easily observe that the class of agents C^1 comprises precisely the wealthiest agents, and therefore that class appears at the top of the hierarchy as claimed. This is obvious, since members of C^1 do not work at all, and are therefore the wealthiest group. Members of the other four classes all work. The wealth cutoff for membership in C^1 is given in Theorem 2.4, part (C). Next, it is obvious that the class $C^5 = (0, 0, +)$ consists precisely of those agents with zero wealth, the poorest agents. For if a producer possesses some positive wealth, he clearly optimizes by using his capital in some way: in particular, rather than only working himself for others, he could reduce his work time by hiring others to operate his capital. Thus, all members of the class C^5 fall at the bottom of the wealth ordering; they are the entirely dispossessed.[4]

2. There are, a priori, five possible class specifications left: $(+, +, 0)$, $(+, +, +)$, $(+, 0, 0)$, $(0, +, +)$, and $(+, 0, +)$. We show next that class membership in $(+, +, +)$ or $(0, +, +)$ is always redundant, in this sense:

Lemma 2.4. At a RS (p, w) in $\mathscr{E}(p, w)$, every member of $(+, +, +)$ or $(0, +, +)$ is also a member of $(+, 0, +)$ or $(+, 0, 0)$ or $(+, +, 0)$.

Proof. Let ν be a member of $(0, +, +)$ or $(+, +, +)$. Let his solution be (x^ν, y^ν, x_0^ν). We show:

Case 1. If $Ly^\nu < x_0^\nu$, then $\nu \in (+, 0, +)$.
Case 2. If $Ly^\nu = x_0^\nu$, then $\nu \in (+, 0, 0)$.
Case 3. If $Ly^\nu > x_0^\nu$, then $\nu \in (+, +, 0)$.

4. The proletariat and only the proletariat has *nothing* to lose but its chains.

This will suffice to prove the lemma. Suppose $Ly^\nu < x_0^\nu$. We assign ν a new action: he should fire all workers working for him, at activity levels y^ν, and augment his operation of his own means of production by y^ν. He should sell less of his own labor power in amount Ly^ν. Thus, his new action is

$$\xi^\nu = (x^\nu + y^\nu, 0, x_0^\nu - Ly^\nu).$$

It is easily checked that his net revenue is the same under ξ^ν as under (x^ν, y^ν, x_0^ν). Furthermore, ξ^ν is still individually feasible and his total work time is unchanged. Hence ξ^ν is individually optimal for ν, and $\xi^\nu \in (+, 0, +)$.

The other two cases are proved in like manner. QED to Lemma 2.4

3. Hence we can dispense with the class designations $(+, +, +)$ and $(0, +, +)$. To establish the stronger result of disjoint class membership in $\mathcal{C}^2$, $\mathcal{C}^3$, or $\mathcal{C}^4$ we use the same argument as is used in Lemma 2.4. Let Γ^ν be the set of individually optimal programs for producer ν, who is a member of $(+, 0, +)$, $(+, 0, 0)$, or $(+, +, 0)$. First notice that we can decompose producers into three disjoint groups as follows:

(a) If $Ly^\nu > x_0^\nu$ for all $\xi^\nu \in \Gamma^\nu$, then $\nu \in (+, +, 0)\setminus(+, 0, 0)$.
(b) If $\exists\xi^\nu \in \Gamma^\nu$ such that $Ly^\nu = x_0^\nu$, then $\nu \in (+, 0, 0)$.
(c) If $Ly^\nu < x_0^\nu$ for all $\xi^\nu \in \Gamma^\nu$, then $\nu \in (+, 0, +)\setminus(+, 0, 0)$.

Precisely one of these three statements holds for each ν under consideration.

4. Let us verify the first claim, labeled (a). Certainly, by Lemma 2.4, $\nu \in (+, +, 0)$. Suppose that ν possesses a solution in Γ^ν of the form $(+, 0, 0)$—call it $(x^\nu, 0, 0)$. Reverse the construction of Lemma 2.4, considering the solution defined by:

$$\xi^\nu = (0, x^\nu, Lx^\nu) \equiv (x'^\nu, y'^\nu, x_0'^\nu).$$

Calculate that $\xi^\nu \in \Gamma^\nu$ is optimal for ν; this contradicts the assumption in (a), since for ξ^ν, $Ly'^\nu = x_0'^\nu$. Hence claim (a) is proved. In like manner, (b) and (c) are true. Hence, C^1, C^2, C^3, C^4, and C^5 are disjoint and exhaustive.

5. We finally demonstrate that the wealth ordering of the three middle classes is: C^2, C^3, C^4. This consists of two statements:

(d) Every member of C^4 is poorer than any member of C^3.
(e) Every member of C^2 is richer than any member of C^3.

Consider (d). Let $\nu \in C^4$ and $\mu \in C^3$ be two producers. Suppose (d) is false, and ν and μ are chosen so that $W^\nu > W^\mu$. (Clearly we cannot have $W^\nu = W^\mu$, or the disjointness of C^3 and C^4 would be falsified.) Since $\mu \in C^3$, there is a solution $(0, y^\mu, x_0^\mu) \in \Gamma^\mu$ such that $Ly^\mu = x_0^\mu$, by the construction of paragraph 4 of this proof. Let $(0, y^\nu, x_0^\nu)$ be any solution in Γ^ν with its x^ν components equal to zero. (Γ^ν always possesses such solutions by the construction of Lemma 2.4, or of paragraph 4 above.) Since $W^\nu > W^\mu$, we must have $x_0^\nu < x_0^\mu$, and hence $Ly^\nu < x_0^\nu < x_0^\mu = Ly^\mu$. Thus, for any solution in Γ^ν of the form $(0, y^\nu, x_0^\nu)$, $Ly^\nu < Ly^\mu$. But this is impossible, since if ν is wealthier than μ, he can certainly optimize and hire more labor than μ, for an optimal solution consists of putting all one's capital into the π_{max} processes, in any arbitrary way. Thus, ν can replicate the investment choices made by μ, hiring the same number of workers as ν, and then hire some more workers with the capital he has left. This demonstrates claim (d). Claim (e) follows in like manner and the theorem is proved. QED

This verifies the classical Marxian tenet that class membership provides an accurate proxy of welfare or degree of exploitation. One can determine where in the wealth hierarchy a producer sits simply by observing how he relates to the means of production, without explicitly observing his wealth. Indeed, as will be shown below, one can also infer his exploitation status by observing his class position. In the class decomposition which exists when a labor market is present, labor selling is associated with poverty and labor hiring with being wealthy, with the class of agents who do not use the labor market at all located in the middle of the wealth spread. It is the case, moreover, that a producer's class position is endogenously determined: he chooses his class position as a consequence of optimizing against a capital constraint. Differential ownership of the means of production is responsible for differential class position.

4. The Class Exploitation Correspondence Principle (CECP)

In the last section I showed that at a reproducible solution, society is decomposed into five disjoint classes, which always fall in a certain specified order when producers are arranged according to wealth. This ordering of classes is endogenous, in the sense that class membership emerges from individual optimization facing the wealth constraint.

We know also that a producer's exploitation status emerges endogenously, and that the wealthy are exploiters and the poor are exploited. This follows immediately from the producers' optimization programs, for the wealthy are able to work less, and the length of time worked is the criterion for exploitation status. The question arises: Where in the hierarchy of classes is the wealth cutoff which separates the exploiters from the exploited, at a given reproducible solution? The answer to this question is the Class Exploitation Correspondence Principle (CECP).

The first step is to prove Theorem 2.6, of interest in its own right:

Theorem 2.6. Assume NBC. Let (p, w) be an inegalitarian RS for $\mathscr{E}(p, w)$. Then, for some positive number π, $p = (1 + \pi)(pA) + wL$. *Note:* As a consequence of Theorem 2.6, $\pi_{\max}$ of Theorem 2.3 can be replaced with π.

What this theorem tells us is that, once NBC is assumed, prices at a RS establish a well-defined exchange rate between "capital" and labor power. In particular, equilibrium prices are now the familiar Sraffian prices or Marxian prices of production (subject to a proviso on when wages are paid). It is noteworthy that equilibrium prices take this form in the subsistence economy under discussion, logically prior to the economy where capital accumulation is the objective. It is also noteworthy that a labor market (or, as we shall see, a credit market) is necessary to force equilibrium prices to be of this form. In the economy $\mathscr{E}(p)$ of Chapter 1, equilibrium prices do not equalize the profit rates among activities. Thus, a well-defined "return to capital" is only established with the advent of a labor market.

Proof of Theorem 2.6. Recall, from the proof of Theorem 2.3, that we can find the optimum of a producer's program by studying the optima of the two reduced programs, called (I) and (II). Suppose that the profit rate is not equalized across all sectors, and let $\pi_j < \pi_{\max}$. We show that no producer will operate sector j, and hence, by indecomposability of A, there can be no reproducible solution.

First, consider a producer who works at his optimum. Then, in solving program (I), he must make profits $\Pi^\nu \equiv [p - (pA + wL)]y^\nu$ as large as possible. Consequently, he can only hire workers to operate maximal-profit-rate sectors, and he will not operate sector j.

Second, consider a producer who does not work at the optimum. By Assumption NBC, he minimizes his capital outlay, which means he, too, will invest only in maximal-profit-rate sectors. The theorem follows. (This theorem can also be readily proved by examining the dual program to the producer's program (P).) QED

We next prove the Class Exploitation Correspondence Principle.

Theorem 2.7. Assume NBC. Let (p, w) be an inegalitarian RS in $\mathscr{E}(p, w)$. Then:

A. Every producer who must hire labor power to optimize (that is, a member of $C^1 \cup C^2$) is an exploiter; every producer who must sell labor power to optimize (that is, $C^4 \cup C^5$) is exploited.

B. If the organic compositions of capital among sectors are all identical, then a unique value of wealth is associated with the class (+, 0, 0), and a producer possessing that wealth is exploitation-neutral. If the organic compositions are unequal, then (+, 0, 0) corresponds to a nondegenerate interval of wealths and the class (+, 0, 0) may contain exploiting and/or exploited producers.

The key part of this theorem is part A, which asserts that selling of labor power is associated with being exploited and hiring of labor power is associated with exploiting. Part B asserts that this relationship is not an exact equivalence: except for a singular technology (equal organic compositions), there may be members of (+, 0, 0) who are not exploitation-neutral. This latter observation is the form the transformation problem takes in our model. For proof of part B and discussion, see the appendix to this chapter.

Proof of part A of Theorem 2.7.

1. According to Theorem 2.3, at an inegalitarian RS there is a unique value of wealth $\overline{W}$ associated with a working time of Λb, for

its possessor. It shall suffice to show that a producer with wealth $\overline{W}$ is in class $(+, 0, 0)$. For, by strict monotonicity of working time in wealth (Theorem 2.3), and the class hierarchy of Theorem 2.5, the theorem will then follow.

2. By the formula of Theorem 2.3 we solve for $\overline{W}$.

$$\overline{W} = \frac{pb - w\Lambda b}{\pi}$$

where $p = (1 + \pi)pA + wL$, by Theorem 2.6.

3. For abbreviation's sake, call the hypothetical producer with wealth $\overline{W}$ by the name $\overline{W}$. Showing that $\overline{W} \in (+, 0, 0)$ is equivalent to showing that $\overline{W}$ has an optimal solution of the form $(0, y^\nu, Ly^\nu)$. (See, for instance, the proof of Theorem 2.5, case 2.) Choose $y^\nu \equiv (I - A)^{-1}b$. Observe:

$$pAy^\nu = pA(I - A)^{-1}b = \frac{[p(I - A) - wL]}{\pi}(I - A)^{-1}b$$

$$= \frac{pb - w\Lambda b}{\pi} = \overline{W}.$$

Thus, producer $\overline{W}$ will precisely exhaust his capital if he hires workers to operate activities y^ν. Any way of exhausting his capital by hiring workers leads to an optimal solution for ν, since all sectors generate the maximal profit rate π. Notice, finally, that $Ly^\nu = \Lambda b$ by choice of y^ν, which by construction is $\overline{W}$'s optimal work time, and so $(0, y^\nu, Ly^\nu)$ is an optimal solution, as was to be demonstrated. QED

Together, Theorems 2.5 and 2.7 make up the Class Exploitation Correspondence Principle, as they verify the key Marxian insight that those who end up working for others are exploited and those who hire others are exploiters; furthermore, one's order in the exploitation and class hierarchy is a proxy for one's wealth and therefore one's welfare, measured by how long one works in this model. What is remarkable about the theorem is that producers' class status and exploitation status both arise endogenously as a consequence of optimizing behavior under institutions of competitive markets and differential ownership of the means of production. We do not postulate a priori that certain producers are "proletarians" and others are "pure capitalists" or "petty bourgeoisie"; rather, we let that emerge from the operation of the economy, as agents optimize given their constraints and the markets they can use.

In the models of this book, agents choose their class position by optimizing behavior. This appears to differ from the historical materialist description, where agents are viewed as being forced to occupy the class positions they do. In the latter description, optimization seems to be irrelevant. How might this be interpreted in the model $\mathscr{E}(p, w)$? If a producer has a feasible, though nonoptimal, solution placing him in a different class position from his class position determined by optimization, one might say he is not forced to occupy the latter position. Can a proletarian or semiproletarian find a feasible solution to his program in which he does not sell labor power, but only works in his own shop, or hires others? No. A proletarian has no produced assets, and hence must sell labor power at any feasible solution. For the semiproletarian, we know that even when he works all his own capital in the revenue-maximizing way, he does not produce enough revenue to reproduce; hence, he has no option but to sell labor power. Thus, any member of a labor-selling class is in fact *forced* to sell his labor power. The same does not hold for members of labor-hiring classes, who can feasibly reproduce by only working in their own shops.

To recapitulate, the task I am engaged in is to perturb the institutional characterization of an economy to see what are the institutional foundations of the phenomena of exploitation and class. In Chapter 1 it was shown that exploitation emerged in a subsistence economy without any institution for labor exchange. Now I show that if a labor market is introduced, then classes emerge, and class membership corresponds to exploitation status in a classical way. All this takes place still in the confines of a subsistence exchange economy, where producers do not accumulate. A further result is that equilibrium prices take the form of Marxian prices of production, equalizing the profit rate across all sectors, once the labor market is introduced. (This holds when the richest members of society act in a certain quasi-capitalist way, economizing on capital when they have a choice (Assumption NBC).)

Let us repeat the temporary resolution of the drama which has been unfolding. Although an institution for labor exchange is not necessary to produce exploitation, it appears from this chapter that some institution of labor exchange is, indeed, necessary to speak of

Marxian classes, if not exploitation. In the next chapter, the plot thickens: it is shown that classes and the CECP can be generated in a subsistence economy even when there is no institution for the exchange of labor. Both exploitation and class appear to be phenomena which can be conceived of even when there is no *direct* transfer of labor, either through a coercive or a noncoercive mechanism.

Appendix 2.1. The transformation problem and the CECP

To clarify the form the transformation problem takes in our discussion, we first prove part B of Theorem 2.7.

Theorem 2.7, part B. If the organic compositions of capital among sectors are all identical, then a unique value of wealth is associated with membership in class (+, 0, 0), and a producer possessing that wealth is exploitation-neutral. If the organic compositions are unequal, then the wealths associated with (+, 0, 0) comprise a nondegenerate interval and the class (+, 0, 0) contains exploited and exploiting producers. *Note:* The organic composition of capital in a sector is the ratio $\Lambda A_i/L_i$. For further reference, see Morishima (1973) or Roemer (1981).

Proof. Let (p, w) be the RS. Let $\nu \in (+, 0, 0)$. As was noticed in the proof of Theorem 2.7, part A, ν has an optimal solution of the form $(0, y^\nu, Ly^\nu)$. At this solution, his revenue is $p(I - A)y^\nu$, and so:

$$p(I - A)y^\nu = pb. \tag{1}$$

Furthermore, he is using all his wealth W^ν on hired labor, and so:

$$pAy^\nu = W^\nu. \tag{2}$$

From (1) and (2) it follows that:

$$\left[\frac{p(I - A)}{pA}\right]_{\min} \leqq \frac{pb}{W^{\nu}} \leqq \left[\frac{p(I - A)}{pA}\right]_{\max}, \tag{3}$$

where the bracketed expressions refer to the minimum and maximum of the component ratios of the vector ratio. Conversely, if (3) holds, then there is a nonnegative solution vector y^{ν} to (1) and (2). It will follow that $(0, y^{\nu}, Ly^{\nu})$ is an optimal solution for ν, and hence that $\nu \in (+, 0, 0)$, if it is true that $Ly^{\nu} \leqq 1$. If $Ly^{\nu} > 1$, then by consideration of (1) and Theorem 2.6:

$$\pi W^{\nu} + w < pb. \tag{4}$$

But $\pi W^{\nu} + w$ is the maximum revenue ν can achieve under any arrangement. Hence ν cannot possess a feasible solution to his program at prices (p, w), which is false. Hence $Ly^{\nu} \leqq 1$.

This shows that at a RS, $\nu \in (+, 0, 0)$ if and only if (3) holds. It is easily seen that the maximum and minimum of the vector ratio $p(I - A)/pA$ differ if and only if the organic compositions are not all identical. This proves the theorem, for if organic compositions are all equal, then the values of W satisfying (3) can only be a point, which, by part A of Theorem 2.7, must be that unique value of wealth which is exploitation-neutral; when there is a nondegenerate interval of wealths comprising $(+, 0, 0)$, then by the strict monotonicity of labor time in wealth there will be exploiters and/or exploited associated with the class $(+, 0, 0)$. QED

The classical transformation problem arises when the organic compositions of capital are not identical across sectors. Here we see the transformation problem takes the form of muddying the relationship between exploitation and class. Although it is always true that those who must sell labor power to optimize are exploited and those who must hire labor power to optimize are exploiters, the converse statement is true if and only if the organic compositions are equal in all sectors. The transformation problem makes ambiguous the exploitation status of producers in the class of petty bourgeoisie, $(+, 0, 0)$.

If the organic compositions of capital are all equal, then the class $(+, +, 0)$ is identical with the class C^2, and $(+, 0, +)$ is identical with C^4. The following theorems are easily proved.

Theorem A2.1. Let the organic compositions be unequal. Let $\nu \in (+, 0, 0)$ at a RS. Then ν has a solution of form $(+, +, 0)$ or $(+, 0, +)$, as well.

Corollary A2.2. If the organic compositions are unequal, there exists a (hypothetical) producer who is exploitation-neutral but who possesses an optimal solution where he hires or sells labor power.

That is, a consequence of the transformation problem, according to Corollary A2.2, is that we cannot unequivocally associate membership in a labor-hiring class with being an exploiter and membership in a labor-selling class with being exploited. Our way of dealing with this was to introduce the class specifications C^2, C^3, C^4 in which we considered the significant class relations to be those of *compulsory* labor hiring and *compulsory* labor selling (that is, ν belongs to C^2 only if he *must* hire labor power to optimize). In this way, we "solved" the transformation problem, by resolving the ambiguity in the relationship between class and exploitation which is evident in Corollary A2.2. The transformation problem arises again in Chapter 4.

Appendix 2.2.
The private ownership core of $\mathscr{E}(p, w)$

In Chapter 1 it was shown that the private ownership core of $\mathscr{E}(p)$ does not necessarily contain all the reproducible solutions. This was attributed to the lack of a sufficient number of markets in $\mathscr{E}(p)$. We verify that this was the correct explanation by showing that in $\mathscr{E}(p, w)$ reproducible solutions lie in the private ownership core. Thus the possibility of trading labor solves this unpleasant anomaly of $\mathscr{E}(p)$.

Theorem A2.3. The reproducible solutions of $\mathscr{E}(p, w)$ lie in its private ownership core.

Proof. It has been shown (in the proof of Theorem 2.3) that an agent always has a solution of the form $(0, y^\nu, x_0^\nu)$ to his program. Assign, then, each agent a solution of this form at the reproducible prices in question. It was observed, in Theorem 2.3, that the agent's program can be written, without loss of generality, as:

choose x_0^ν and y^ν to min x_0^ν

subject to

$$(p - (pA + wL))y^\nu + wx_0^\nu \geqq pb \tag{1}$$

$$pAy^\nu \leqq W^\nu. \tag{2}$$

Suppose the reproducible solution is not in the core, and let S be a blocking coalition. When S's members withdraw with their endowments $\omega^S = \Sigma_S\omega^\nu$, they can assign themselves activity vectors z^ν having these properties:

$$\begin{aligned} &\text{(i)} \quad Lz^\nu < x_0^\nu, \qquad \text{for all } \nu \in S \\ &\text{(ii)} \quad (I - A)z^S = |S|b, \qquad z^S = \Sigma_S z^\nu \\ &\text{(iii)} \quad Az^S \leqq \omega^S. \end{aligned}$$

Conditions (ii) and (iii) say that S can assign itself a reproducible allocation as a coalition, and (i) states that every member of S is faring better than he was at the RS in question, and so S is a blocking coalition. It follows from (i) that $x_0^\nu > 0$ for every $\nu \in S$; that is, blocking coalitions cannot include pure capitalists. Because of this, we can conclude that inequality (2) must hold with equality for all $\nu \in S$, since the only agents for whom $pAy^\nu < W^\nu$ at a reproducible solution are pure capitalists. But (1) holds with equality for all agents at an optimum. Thus:

$$\left.\begin{aligned} \pi pAy^\nu + wx_0^\nu &= pb \qquad (1') \\ pAy^\nu &= W^\nu \qquad (2') \end{aligned}\right\} \quad \text{for all } \nu \in S$$

where we use the equation $\pi pA = p - (pA + wL)$ in (1′). Substituting from (2′) into (1′) and solving for W^ν yields:

$$W^\nu = (pb - wx_0^\nu)/\pi \qquad \forall \nu \in S$$

and so

$$W^S = \Sigma_S W^\nu = (|S|pb - wx_0^S)/\pi. \tag{3}$$

Since, from (ii), $Lz^S = |S|\Lambda b$, it follows from (i) that $x_0^S > |S|\Lambda b$, and so from (3):

$$W^S < (|S|pb - |S|w\Lambda b)/\pi. \tag{4}$$

From (ii) and (iii) we have:

$$A(I - A)^{-1}|S|b \leqq \omega^S. \tag{5}$$

Premultiplying (5) by πp:

$$\pi pA(I - A)^{-1}|S|b \leqq \pi W^S. \tag{6}$$

Substituting $p(I - A) - wL$ for πpA in (6), and simplifying yields:

$$(|S|pb - |S|w\Lambda b)/\pi \leqq W^S, \tag{7}$$

which contradicts (4).

It follows that no coalition S can block the reproducible solution, and the theorem is proved. QED

In the next chapter, it is shown that appending a credit market to $\mathscr{E}(p)$ (instead of a labor market) produces an economy which is isomorphic to $\mathscr{E}(p, w)$. Thus we can assert that the reproducible solutions of the credit market economy lie in its core as well.

3

The Functional Equivalence of Labor and Credit Markets

1. A subsistence economy with credit market

This chapter develops one of the major points of Part I: the emergence of exploitation and of class has its genesis in the institutions of private ownership and competitive markets, not in the process of direct labor expropriation through an institution of labor exchange.

We begin again with the primitive economy $\mathscr{E}(p)$, without labor market. Instead of introducing a labor market, we may conceive of expanding the possibilities for trade by the opening of a credit market. The well endowed offer to lend capital at interest rate r. Producers can now engage in three types of activity: operating means of production on their own funds, operating means of production on borrowed funds, and lending out funds at interest.

For producer ν,

x^ν is the $\mathbb{R}^n_+$ vector of activities operated on own funds
y^ν is the $\mathbb{R}^n_+$ vector of activities operated on borrowed funds
z^ν is the scalar of funds lent out.

Producer ν's program, facing the price-interest rate pair (p, r), is:

$$\min Lx^\nu + Ly^\nu$$

subject to

$$\left.\begin{aligned} &(p - pA)x^\nu + (p - (1 + r)pA)y^\nu + rz^\nu \geqq pb && \text{(Qi)}\\ &pAx^\nu + z^\nu \leqq p\omega^\nu \equiv W^\nu && \text{(Qii)}\\ &Lx^\nu + Ly^\nu \leqq 1 && \text{(Qiii)}\end{aligned}\right\} \text{(Q)}$$

As before:

Definition 3.1. (p, r) is a RS for economy $\mathscr{E}(p, r) \Leftrightarrow$

1. $\exists(x^\nu, z^\nu, y^\nu) \in \mathscr{A}^\nu(p, r)$ (individual optimization)
2. $x = \Sigma x^\nu$, $y = \Sigma y^\nu$, $z = \Sigma z^\nu$ and $x + y \geqq A(x + y) + Nb$ (reproducibility)
3. $A(x + y) \leqq \omega$ (feasibility)
4. $pAy = z$ (clearing of credit market)

We shall truncate the analysis of $\mathscr{E}(p, r)$, as it is similar to the analysis of $\mathscr{E}(p, w)$. As before, we make a nonbenevolent capitalist assumption:

Assumption NBC. Let (p, r) be prices at which producer ν can solve program (Q) and not work at all. ν is a pure lender. Then ν lends out an amount z^ν minimal among all possible loans. (Precisely, $z^\nu = pb/r$.)

The analog of Theorem 2.5 is true in this model. At a RS there are five classes:

	(x, z, y)	
C^1 =	$(0, +, 0)$	pure lenders
C^2 =	$(+, +, 0)\setminus(+, 0, 0)$	mixed lenders
C^3 =	$(+, 0, 0)$	petty bourgeoisie
C^4 =	$(+, 0, +)\setminus(+, 0, 0)$	mixed borrowers
C^5 =	$(0, 0, +)$	pure borrowers

Theorem 3.1. Let (p, r) be an inegalitarian RS for $\mathscr{E}(p, r)$. Let the producers be ordered by how long they work at (p, r). Then this ordering is completely faithful to the ordering of the five classes: C^1, C^2, C^3, C^4, C^5. That is: for $1 \leqq i < j \leqq 5$, any member of class C^j works longer than every member of class C^i.

The analog of *Theorem 2.3* is also true:

Theorem 3.2. Let (p, r) be a RS for $\mathscr{E}(p, r)$. Then the time worked by producer ν is:

$$Lx^\nu + Ly^\nu = \max(0, \rho_{\min}(pb - rW^\nu))$$

where

$$\rho_{\min} = \min_j \left[\frac{L}{p - (1 + r)pA}\right]_j.$$

Also, the analog of Theorem 2.6 is true:

Theorem 3.3. Assume NBC. At a RS (p, r) there is a nonnegative number w such that $p = (1 + r)pA + wL$.

It should be mentioned that Theorem 3.3 is a consequence of the fact that the only sectors which will be operated in $\mathscr{E}(p, r)$ are those which minimize the ratio $L/[p - (1 + r)pA]$. Consequently, that vector ratio must in fact be a constant, for all sectors to operate, as they must.

The discussion in this section has been truncated because the proofs of theorems are identical to those for the economy $\mathscr{E}(p, w)$ studied in the previous chapter. The basic similarity in structure between the economies $\mathscr{E}(p, w)$ and $\mathscr{E}(p, r)$ is not a coincidence, for as we show next, the credit market and labor market are functionally equivalent: $\mathscr{E}(p, w)$ and $\mathscr{E}(p, r)$ are identical.

2. The isomorphism between $\mathscr{E}(p, w)$ and $\mathscr{E}(p, r)$

Suppose we are at a reproducible solution $(\bar{p}, \bar{r})$ in an economy $\mathscr{E}(p, r)$, operating on Credit Market Island. On a neighboring island, Labor Market Island, there is a subsistence economy with the same producers (same endowments) and the same technology as on CM Island, but the economy on LM Island appends a labor market to the produced commodity markets, instead of a credit market—that is, the economy of LM Island is of the type $\mathscr{E}(p, w)$. Is there a wage rate $\bar{w}$ with the property that $(\bar{p}, \bar{w})$ is a reproducible solution on LM Island, and such that each producer on LM Island works exactly as long as his twin on CM Island is working and is a member of the same class as his twin? And conversely, suppose $(\bar{\bar{p}}, \bar{\bar{w}})$ is a reproducible solution on LM Island. Can we calculate an interest rate $\bar{\bar{r}}$ with the property that $(\bar{\bar{p}}, \bar{\bar{r}})$ is a reproducible solution on CM Island, and such that each producer on CM Island works precisely as long, and is a member of the same class, as his twin on LM Island? The answer to these questions is yes.

Theorem 3.4. Let $(\bar{p}, \bar{r})$ be a RS of the economy with credit market $\mathscr{E}(p, r)$. Then there exists a wage $\bar{w}$ such that $(\bar{p}, \bar{w})$, is a RS of the economy with labor market $\mathscr{E}(\bar{p}, \bar{w})$. The mapping $\phi:(\bar{p}, \bar{r}) \to (\bar{p}, \bar{w})$ is an isomorphism with respect to exploitation and class properties. That is, each producer works the same amount of time at both RSs, and each producer remains a member of the "same" class. Conversely, every RS $(\bar{\bar{p}}, \bar{\bar{w}})$ of $\mathscr{E}(p, w)$ induces an isomorphic RS $(\bar{\bar{p}}, \bar{\bar{r}})$ of $\mathscr{E}(p, r)$.

Before proving Theorem 3.4 we discuss the method of the proof, for it is a constructive one which shows precisely why the labor and credit markets are functionally equivalent. Suppose we start with a reproducible solution $(\bar{p}, \bar{r})$ in $\mathscr{E}(p, r)$. According to Theorem 3.3, there is a natural wage generated, $\bar{w}$. To construct the isomorphic reproducible solution in $\mathscr{E}(p, w)$, we take a typical producer in $\mathscr{E}(p, r)$ and we reassign him activities in $\mathscr{E}(p, w)$ at prices $(\bar{p}, \bar{w})$ as follows: If he is working certain activities financed by his own funds in $\mathscr{E}(p, r)$, he is assigned those activities to operate on his own in $\mathscr{E}(p, w)$; if he is operating certain activities on borrowed funds in $\mathscr{E}(p, r)$, then in $\mathscr{E}(p, w)$ he is reassigned to sell his labor to those creditors, and operate those activities for them in their shops; if he is lending out capital in $\mathscr{E}(p, r)$, he is reassigned in $\mathscr{E}(p, w)$ to hire his debtors and have them operate in his shop the activities they were operating on his loans in their own shops, in $\mathscr{E}(p, r)$. The proof below simply checks that if these reassignments are carried out for all producers, then a reproducible solution in $\mathscr{E}(p, w)$ is constructed which preserves the exploitation and class status of each producer.

Proof.

1. Let $(\bar{p}, \bar{r})$ be a RS in $\mathscr{E}(p, r)$. We induce a RS in $\mathscr{E}(p, w)$ with the required properties.

$$\text{Choose } \bar{w} = \max_j \left(\frac{\bar{p} - (1 + \bar{r})\bar{p}A}{L}\right)_j .$$

(In fact, by Theorem 3.3, this choice is immediate.) It follows that the profit rate π generated by $(\bar{p}, \bar{w})$ is equal to $\bar{r}$.

2. We now assign an action to producer ν in $\mathscr{E}(\bar{p}, \bar{w})$. Let ν's action in $\mathscr{E}(\bar{p}, \bar{r})$ be (x^ν, z^ν, y^ν). We assign ν to sell his labor power in amount Ly^ν. That is, instead of borrowing funds and working time

Ly^ν on borrowed funds in $\mathscr{E}(\bar{p}, \bar{r})$, he works that same time on the labor market in $\mathscr{E}(\bar{p}, \bar{w})$. His net revenue from these two activities is the same:

$$\bar{w}Ly^\nu = \frac{\bar{p} - (1 + r)\bar{p}A}{L} Ly^\nu = (\bar{p} - (1 + \bar{r})\bar{p}A)y^\nu.$$

The producer(s) from whom ν borrowed funds pAy^ν in $\mathscr{E}(\bar{p}, \bar{r})$ is (are) hereby assigned to hire ν to operate those same activities (y^ν) in $\mathscr{E}(\bar{p}, \bar{w})$. In turn, it is easily checked that those producers get the same revenue from these two actions in the two economies. Finally, the x^ν vectors stay the same: ν continues to operate on his own account in $\mathscr{E}(\bar{p}, \bar{w})$ the activities he operated on his own account in $\mathscr{E}(\bar{p}, \bar{r})$.

According to this construction, the aggregate activity levels generated in $\mathscr{E}(\bar{p}, \bar{w})$ are identical to those operated in $\mathscr{E}(\bar{p}, \bar{r})$. Hence, the aggregate requirements for reproducibility hold in $\mathscr{E}(\bar{p}, \bar{w})$: that is, total net production is $(I - A)^{-1}(Nb)$ and $A(x + y) \leqq \omega$ in $\mathscr{E}(\bar{p}, \bar{w})$. Secondly, the labor market precisely clears, by the assignments made, since the credit market cleared in $\mathscr{E}(\bar{p}, \bar{r})$.

3. Finally, it must be verified that the actions constructed in $\mathscr{E}(\bar{p}, \bar{w})$ are individually optimal. This follows from Theorem 2.3 and Theorem 3.2. By construction of ν's action in $\mathscr{E}(\bar{p}, \bar{w})$, he works the same amount of time that he worked at $(\bar{p}, \bar{r})$ in $\mathscr{E}(\bar{p}, \bar{r})$. By Theorem 3.2, that work time is

$$\max\,(0, \rho_{\min}(\bar{p}b - \bar{r}W^\nu)).$$

Since $\rho_{\min} = 1/\bar{w}$ and $\pi = \bar{r}$, that work time equals

$$\max\,(0, \bar{p}b/\bar{w} - \pi W^\nu/\bar{w})$$

which, by Theorem 2.3, is optimal work time in $\mathscr{E}(\bar{p}, \bar{w})$ at prices $(\bar{p}, \bar{w})$. Hence the feasible action assigned to ν in $\mathscr{E}(\bar{p}, \bar{w})$ is in fact optimal.

4. That the mapping (induced by this construction) preserves classes as specified is seen immediately from the construction. Borrowing induces selling of labor power and lending induces hiring of labor power.

5. The converse construction, given a RS $(\bar{\bar{p}}, \bar{\bar{w}})$ in $\mathscr{E}(p, w)$, is induced by setting $\bar{\bar{r}} = \pi$ and proceeding in like manner. QED

Note: The importance of Assumption NBC to this proof should be mentioned. Consider how the solution in $\mathscr{E}(p, r)$ is induced by a solution $(\bar{\bar{p}}, \bar{\bar{w}})$ in $\mathscr{E}(p, w)$. Consider a producer ν who is selling his labor power at $(\bar{\bar{p}}, \bar{\bar{w}})$. The induced action in $\mathscr{E}(p, r)$, for him, is to borrow funds from his (former) employers in amount sufficient to operate the same activities, y^ν, himself, which he formerly operated for his employer(s). If the employer was a benevolent capitalist operating some activity which was not maximally profitable, then our producer ν, who must borrow funds, will not be optimizing in $\mathscr{E}(p, r)$. Assumption NBC entered the proof of Theorem 3.4 through Theorem 2.6 and Theorem 3.3.

A final issue remains. Suppose one creates an economy $\mathscr{E}(p, w, r)$ with both a labor market and a credit market. Are both markets necessary? Can anything be achieved which could not be achieved with only one of the markets? The following theorem shows that, not only are the separate economies with credit and labor markets isomorphic, but the two markets coexisting in the same economy are redundant.

We dispense with formal definitions of the producer's program and of the RS concept in the economy $\mathscr{E}(p, w, r)$, which can, by this time, be constructed by the reader.

Theorem 3.5. Let (p, w, r) be a RS in $\mathscr{E}(p, w, r)$. Then there is a set of optimal actions for all producers in which either the labor market or the credit market is used but not both, and reproducibility is preserved.

Proof. For prices (p, w, r) define the sectoral profit rates π_j in the usual way. It must be true that these are equal ($\pi_j = \pi$); for if not, then no one would operate the $\pi_{\min}$ sector either on his own account or with hired labor, by the usual revenue-maximizing argument. There are now several cases.

Case 1: $r < \pi$. Then every producer will have an individually optimal solution where he does not work at all. He borrows a large amount of capital at low interest r and hires workers to transform it into profits at the higher rate π, thus generating as much revenue as he pleases. This price vector cannot be reproducible.

Case 2: $r > \pi$. Then every producer with some capital will wish to lend it, as he gets a higher return than from hiring workers to operate it at rate of return π, or by operating it himself at the same implicit rate of return. No producer, however, will want to borrow capital, for the same reason. Hence no reproducible solution is possible.

Case 3: $r = \pi$. It follows by the construction made in the proof of *Theorem 3.4* that this RS can be converted into one which uses either of two markets above, without using the other. QED

The isomorphism Theorem 3.4 permits an interesting elaboration upon an old adage that it doesn't matter whether capital hires labor or labor hires capital in a competitive model. In the model of Chapter 2, capital hires labor; in the model of this chapter, labor hires capital. The isomorphism theorem states, truly, that it does not matter whether labor hires capital or capital hires labor: the poor are exploited and the rich exploit in either case. Thus, there is nothing in the institution of the labor market intrinsically necessary for bringing about the Marxian phenomena of exploitation and class. The same constellation of phenomena can be produced, in our subsistence economy, with a credit market instead. Again, competitive markets and private, differential ownerships of the means of production are the institutional culprits in producing exploitation and class, not the labor market.

Although I have insisted at various points that these models are not intended as historical descriptions, there are some historically relevant corollaries, of a negative sort, implied by the isomorphism theorem. In primitive societies the evidence points to the emergence of credit markets prior to labor markets (see, for instance, Pryor, 1977). There must be, therefore, important aspects of these markets which are not captured in models at the level of abstraction engaged in here, for in this discussion there is nothing to distinguish between the two markets. In fact, there are many differences between the two markets. Where credit markets operate, producers work for themselves, and where labor markets operate, some work for others. Hence, the relations between people are quite different in the two cases. The technology used in labor market economies may be quite different from that where producers work only for themselves; this, of course, is the claim of much of the recent literature on the labor process, of Braverman (1974) and others. The types of enforcement cost tend to differ between labor and credit market economies; in the former, supervision costs are incurred, and in the latter, collateral is necessary. Considerations of large-scale operation seem to favor the labor market. (These will come into play when the economy enjoys increasing returns to scale, unlike in the models here.) For on Credit Market Island, to operate on a large scale many producers must get together, either to borrow capital or to pool capital, for each is limited by his tight labor constraint. This may involve considerable organizational and informational problems, much more so than if one capitalist arranges to hire many workers on Labor Market Island. Indeed, credit markets are used along with labor markets as instruments of exploitation when economies of scale are not an issue, most typically in agricultural arrangements (sharecropping, for instance).

Given the asymmetries between the two types of market which exist at a finer level of detail than our model examines, what is the import of the isomorphism theorem? Recall that the motivation for constructing these models is to suggest to us what institutional specification is necessary to generate a more general theory of exploitation. What the isomorphism theorem tells us is *not* that the adoption of labor markets, instead of credit markets, in real economies has been essentially fortuitous, but rather than we should not think of a labor market as a logically necessary institution in our general conception of exploitation and class, at a certain level of abstraction.

If Marxists wish to claim that there is something in the social relations surrounding the labor process which is intrinsically necessary to generate exploitation and class, that claim cannot be made at the level of the "pure" Marxian theory of value. (Of course, the models of Part I are not models of capitalist economy, but it should be clear that the functional equivalence of labor and credit markets would hold there, as well.) A resurrection of a Marxian theory of class with an important position for the labor market must depend on the imperfections mentioned—transaction costs, economies of scale, information, risk.

Although labor markets have been historically relevant in bringing about Marxian exploitation, I think it is methodologically useful to acknowledge the logical expendability of the labor market, at the appropriate level of abstraction, for we are thereby liberated to think more easily about exploitation when the labor market no longer exists. The fundamental feature of capitalist exploitation is not what happens in the labor process, but the differential ownership of productive assets.[1]

3. The existence of reproducible solutions in $\mathscr{E}(p, w)$ and $\mathscr{E}(p, r)$

Up to this point we have studied the properties of reproducible solutions, assuming they exist. In this section, existence theorems are proved for reproducible solutions in the economy with credit market $\mathscr{E}(p, r)$.[2] By the preceding section, this is equivalent to solving the existence problem for the economy with labor market.

According to Theorem 3.3, any RS in $\mathscr{E}(p, r)$ must have the form $p = (1 + r)pA + wL$. Since only relative prices matter, we may normalize this system of prices by choosing $w = 1$ as numeraire, and conclude:

Lemma 3.1. All reproducible solutions belong to the one-parameter family $(p(r), r)$ where $p(r) = L(I - (1 + r)A)^{-1}$. *Note:* It is due to this severe restriction on the domain of admissible price vectors that the existence problem is tractable for $\mathscr{E}(p, r)$. For $\mathscr{E}(p)$, this is not the case. The existence problem for $\mathscr{E}(p)$ is considerably more delicate.

---

1. Erik Wright argues (in personal correspondence) that the social relations must be quite different on the two islands. For if agents are labor minimizers, then some enforcement mechanism is needed on LM Island to guarantee that hired workers do not shirk, whereas, he claims, on CM Island such enforcement is not needed—borrowers will work without external discipline. (Even if wages are paid at the end of the work period, some procedure is needed on LM Island to verify that work was performed.) This, however, is not strictly true. If a borrower has no collateral, some enforcement mechanism is needed on CM Island to guarantee that he works, for if he simply consumes the loan, the creditor loses. Historically, it is the case that creditors (in the rural U.S. South after the Civil War, for instance) supervised their debtors closely. I am not, therefore, convinced that the social relations on the two islands are necessarily that different. But if labor enforcement is necessary on both islands, then my claim that the locus of exploitation lies in differential ownership of the means of production, and not in labor process/enforcement considerations, is weakened. If, to make sense of the optimization in these models, we admit that labor enforcement is a necessary assumption, then it is difficult to claim that such an assumption is at a lower level of abstraction than the current specification of the model.

2. This section verifies the existence of reproducible solutions in $\mathscr{E}(p, r)$ and $\mathscr{E}(p, w)$. Without loss of continuity in the main story it may be skipped by the reader who is unenthusiastic about technicalities.

For our present purposes, it is convenient to characterize the program of producer ν in a slightly different way than it was characterized in section 2. In the credit market economy $\mathscr{E}(p, r)$, producer ν shall:

$$\text{choose } z^\nu \in \mathbb{R}^n_+, \quad Q^\nu \in \mathbb{R} \text{ to min } Lz^\nu$$

subject to

$$p(I - A)z^\nu + rQ^\nu \geqq pb \tag{Pi}$$

$$pAz^\nu + Q^\nu \leqq p\omega^\nu \tag{Pii}$$

$$Lx^\nu \leqq 1 \tag{Piii}$$

$$z^\nu \geqq 0$$

Q^ν is the amount of *net loans* producer ν makes. z^ν is the vector of activity levels ν operates, on all funds, his own or borrowed. Clearly this program is equivalent to the previous characterization of ν's problem in $\mathscr{E}(p, r)$. In this notation, a RS is:

Definition 3.2. (p, r) is a RS for $\mathscr{E}(p, r) \Leftrightarrow$

1. $\exists(z^\nu, Q^\nu) \in \mathscr{A}^\nu(p, r)$ (individual optimization)
2. $z = \Sigma z^\nu$, $(I - A)z \geqq Nb$ (reproducibility)
3. $Az \leqq \omega$ (aggregate feasibility)
4. $Q = \Sigma Q^\nu = 0$ (clearing of credit market)

Assumption NBC in this economy takes this form: among his individually optimal solutions $(z^\nu, Q^\nu) \in \mathscr{A}^\nu(p, r)$, a producer chooses one which minimizes Q^ν. (That is, no producer lends out more capital than he has to.)

A. Existence of reproducible solutions when $\omega = \Sigma\omega^\nu = A(I - A)^{-1}(Nb) \equiv \bar{\omega}$

It is convenient to study this case separately, when total endowments are the absolute minimum necessary for a reproducible allocation to exist. As we shall see, this singular case gives rise to a continuum of reproducible solutions, whereas the nonsingular case has isolated solutions. For specificity, call this economy $\mathscr{E}(p, r; \bar{\omega})$.

By Lemma 3.1, we may refer to a candidate for a RS simply by its parameter r. We do this for the remainder of the section. By Lemma

3.1, r may range over the domain $D = [0, r^*)$ where $1/(1 + r^*)$ is the Frobenius eigenvalue of A. r^* is positive since A is a productive matrix.

Lemma 3.2. Let $r \in D$, $r > 0$. Let $(z^\nu, Q^\nu) \in \mathscr{A}^\nu(p, r)$ for $\mathscr{E}(p, r; \bar{\omega})$ be such that $z = \Sigma z^\nu = (I - A)^{-1}(Nb)$. Then r is a RS.

Note: Lemma 3.2 informs us that conditions 3 and 4 of Definition 3.2 may be dispensed with in the definition of RS.

Proof. Since $(I - A)z = Nb$, $p(I - A)z = pNb$. By summing inequalities (Pi) for all producers, we conclude that $rQ \geqq 0$. Since $r > 0$, $Q \geqq 0$.

Since $pAz \equiv pA(I - A)^{-1}(Nb) = p\bar{\omega}$, we conclude by summing inequalities (Pii) that $Q \leqq 0$. Hence, $Q = 0$. Since $z = (I - A)^{-1}(Nb)$, part 2 of definition 3.2 follows immediately. QED

Note: The assumption $r > 0$ above is vital. Suppose $r = 0$. Then, by NBC, no producer will lend. Hence, a RS will exist only if there are no borrowers. When $r = 0$, $p = \Lambda$, and when $p = \Lambda$ the best a producer can do is work time Λb. Hence $r = 0$ will generate a RS in $\mathscr{E}(p, r)$ if and only if the distribution of ω^ν is such that each producer can optimize without the credit (or labor) market. We have proved:

Theorem 3.6. There is a RS at $r = 0$ for $\mathscr{E}(p, r)$ if and only if the prices $p = \Lambda$ are a RS in the economy $\mathscr{E}(p)$ without credit/labor market. *Note:* Theorem 3.6 is valid for any $\omega \geqq \bar{\omega}$.

Lemma 3.3. In $\mathscr{E}(p, r; \bar{\omega})$, let $\bar{r} > 0$ be an interest rate for which $0 \leqq p(\bar{r})b - \bar{r}p(r)\omega^\nu \leqq 1$, for producer ν. Then ν possesses feasible solutions at $\bar{r}$, and his set of optimal solutions is:

$$\mathscr{A}^\nu(\bar{r}) = \{z^\nu \geqq 0 | Lz^\nu = \bar{p}b - \bar{r}\bar{p}\omega^\nu\}.$$

(There is a notational abuse here: actually $\mathscr{A}^\nu(\bar{r})$ is defined as a set of pairs (z^ν, Q^ν). We are only concerned about the projection of this pair onto its first component.)

Proof. We assume first that producer ν has an optimal solution at $\bar{r}$, and show it has the required form.

Case 1: Producer ν works at his optimum. In this case, it is easily verified that inequalities (Pi) and (Pii) both hold as equalities. Since an optimum exists, ν's program becomes:

$$\min Lz^\nu$$

subject to

$$\bar{p}(I - A)z^\nu + \bar{r}Q^\nu = \bar{p}b \qquad \text{(P'i)}$$

$$\bar{p}Az^\nu + Q^\nu = \bar{p}\omega^\nu \qquad \text{(P'ii)}$$

$$z^\nu \geqq 0,\ Q^\nu \in \mathbb{R}$$

Since Q^ν is unrestricted in sign, we may set $Q^\nu = \bar{p}\omega^\nu - \bar{p}Az^\nu$ by (P'ii), and, substituting into (P'i) and using the fact that $\bar{p}(I - A) = \bar{r}\bar{p}A + L$, conclude that the program is

$$\min Lz^\nu$$

subject to

$$Lz^\nu = \bar{p}b - \bar{r}\bar{p}\omega^\nu.$$

$$z^\nu \geqq 0.$$

This shows that any optimal solution for ν is of the prescribed form. Conversely, if z^ν satisfies $0 < Lz^\nu = \bar{p}b - \bar{r}\bar{p}\omega^\nu \leqq 1$, then reading the argument in reverse shows that z^ν is feasible and optimal.

Case 2: $\bar{p}b - \bar{r}\bar{p}\omega^\nu = 0$. In this case, producer ν possesses an optimal solution $(z^\nu, Q^\nu) = (0, \bar{p}b/\bar{r})$. That is, he lends out his entire capital. Thus $\mathcal{A}^\nu(\bar{r}) = \{0\} = \{z^\nu \geqq 0 | Lz^\nu = \bar{p}b - \bar{r}\bar{p}\omega^\nu\}$, as required. QED

We verify next a lemma which states that, for *any* $\bar{r} \in D$, the optimal work times at prices $(\bar{p}, \bar{r})$ add up to what aggregate work time has to be at any RS:

Lemma 3.4. Let $\omega = \bar{\omega}$. Let $r \in D$. Then

$$\sum_{\nu=1}^{N} (pb - rp\omega^\nu) = N\Lambda b.$$

Proof. We must show:

$$pNb - rp\bar{\omega} = N\Lambda b. \tag{1}$$

Substituting $p = L(I - (1 + r)A)^{-1}$ and $\bar{\omega} = A(I - A)^{-1}(Nb)$ and dividing by N, (1) becomes:

$$L(I - (1 + r)A)^{-1}b - rL(I - (1 + r)A)^{-1}A(I - A)^{-1}b = \Lambda b. \tag{2}$$

It is therefore sufficient to verify:

$$L(I - (1 + r)A)^{-1} - rL(1 - (1 + r)A)^{-1}A(1 - A)^{-1} = \Lambda. \tag{3}$$

We proceed to reduce (3) to an identity.

Expanding the inverted matrices in (3) by geometric expansion gives for the left-hand side of (3):

$$L\sum_{i=0}^{\infty}(1 + r)^i A^i - rL\left(\sum_{i=0}^{\infty}(1 + r)^i A^i\right) A \left(\sum_{j=0}^{\infty} A^j\right),$$

which can be written:

$$L\sum_{i=0}^{\infty}(1 + r)^i A^i - rL\sum_{i=0}^{\infty}\sum_{j=0}^{\infty}(1 + r)^i A^{i+j+1}.$$

Grouping terms of the double sum differently gives:

$$L\sum_{i=0}^{\infty}(1 + r)^i A^i - rL\sum_{\substack{k=0\\(k=i+j)}}^{\infty}\left(\sum_{i=0}^{\infty}(1 + r)^i\right) A^{k+1}$$

or

$$L\sum_{i=0}^{\infty}(1 + r)^i A^i - rL\sum_{k=0}^{\infty}\left(\frac{(1 + r)^{k+1} - 1}{r}\right) A^{k+1}$$

or

$$L\sum_{i=0}^{\infty}(1 + r)^i A^i - L\sum_{i=1}^{\infty}[(1 + r)^i - 1]A^i$$

or

$$L + L\sum_{i=1}^{\infty} A^i$$

or

$$L \sum_{i=0}^{\infty} A^i,$$

which is equal to Λ as required. QED

Theorem 3.7. Let $\bar{r}$ be any positive number in D such that:

$$\forall \nu,\ 0 \leqq \bar{p}b - \bar{r}\bar{p}\omega^\nu \leqq 1. \tag{*}$$

Then $\bar{r}$ is a RS for $\mathscr{E}(p, r; \bar{\omega})$.

Proof. As long as (*) holds, every producer has an individually optimal solution $\bar{z}^\nu$ for prices $(\bar{p}, \bar{r})$, by Lemma 3.3. By Lemma 3.3 and Lemma 3.4,

$$\Sigma L\bar{z}^\nu = N\Lambda b = L(I - A)^{-1}(Nb). \tag{1}$$

Now partition $(I - A)^{-1}(Nb)$ into $\Sigma\bar{z}'^\nu$ such that:

$$\Sigma\bar{z}'^\nu = (I - A)^{-1}(Nb),\ z'^\nu \geqq 0,\ L\bar{z}'^\nu = \bar{p}b - \bar{r}\bar{p}\omega^\nu.$$

This can be done by (1). By Lemma 3.3 $\bar{z}'^\nu$ is also individually optimal for ν. But the existence of the partition $\{\bar{z}'^\nu\}$ shows, by Lemma 3.2, that $\bar{r}$ is in fact a RS associated with actions $\bar{z}'^\nu$. QED

Corollary 3.8. Let $\Lambda b < 1$. Then there is a half-open interval $(0, \hat{r}] \subseteq D$ such that $\forall r \in (0, \hat{r}]$, r is a RS for $\mathscr{E}(p, r; \bar{\omega})$.

Proof. Let $\Psi^\nu(r) \equiv p(r)b - rp(r)\omega^\nu$. $\Psi^\nu(r)$ is a continuous function of r. Furthermore $\Psi^\nu(0) = \Lambda b$ for all ν. Since $0 < \Lambda b < 1$, there is a largest interval $(0, \hat{r}]$ with the property that:

$$\forall \nu,\ r \in (0, \hat{r}],\quad 0 \leqq \Psi^\nu(r) \leqq 1.$$

By Theorem 3.7, QED

Note: Corollary 3.8 almost characterizes reproducible solutions in $\mathscr{E}(p, r; \bar{\omega})$. What is not assured is this: perhaps, for some $r' > \hat{r}$, the functions $\Psi^\nu(r')$ could all return to the [0, 1] interval, in which case r' would also be a *RS*. There seems no obvious guarantee that this cannot happen, although its occurrence is most likely a singular one.

B. Existence of reproducible solutions when $\omega \geq \bar{\omega}$

We fix $\omega \geq \bar{\omega}$ and refer to the economy as $\mathscr{E}(p, r; \omega)$. Observe, first, that Lemma 3.3 continues to hold for $\mathscr{E}(p, r; \omega)$. Second, observe that Lemma 3.4 becomes:

Lemma 3.5. Let $\omega \geq \bar{\omega}$. Let $r \in D$. Then

$$\sum_{j=1}^{N} (pb - rp\omega^\nu) < N\Lambda b.$$

This follows since $p\omega > p\,\bar{\omega}$.

Third, observe that Lemma 3.2 continues to hold for $\mathscr{E}(p, r; \omega)$. The analog of Theorem 3.7 is:

Theorem 3.9. Let $r > 0$, $r \in D$. r is a RS for $\mathscr{E}(p, r; \omega) \Leftrightarrow$

$$\sum_{\nu=1}^{N} \max\,(0, pb - rp\omega^\nu) = \Lambda Nb$$

and

$$pb - rp\omega^\nu \leqq 1 \quad \text{for all } \nu.$$

Proof.

$\Rightarrow$ Follows from Theorem 2.3 and the fact that at a RS total net output is $z = (I - A)^{-1}(Nb)$.

$\Leftarrow$ The proof follows that of Theorem 3.7. To all ν for whom $pb - rp\omega^\nu > 0$, assign an action z'^ν such that $Lz'^\nu = pb - rp\omega^\nu$, and $\Sigma z'^\nu = (I - A)^{-1}(Nb)$. To all ν for whom $pb - rp\omega^\nu \leqq 0$, assign the action $z'^\nu = 0$.

By Lemma 3.3, these actions are individually optimal; by Lemma 3.2, the global solution is a RS. QED

Note that in this case where $\omega \geq \bar{\omega}$, there will not be an interval of solutions $(0, \bar{r})$ as in the case $\omega = \bar{\omega}$. In fact, there will usually be at most one solution. To see this, define the function:

$$\hat{\Psi}(r) \equiv \sum_{1}^{N} \max\,(0,\, pb - rp\omega^{\nu})$$

and

$$\hat{\Psi}^{\nu}(r) \equiv \max\,(0,\, pb - rp\omega^{\nu}).$$

Note that $\hat{\Psi}^{\nu}(0) = \Lambda b$ for all ν. $\hat{\Psi}^{\nu}(r)$ and $\hat{\Psi}(r)$ are continuous. If $\Lambda b < 1$, then for all sufficiently small positive r, $0 < \hat{\Psi}^{\nu}(r) < 1$, and so by Lemma 3.5, for all such r, $\hat{\Psi}(r) < N\Lambda b$. Thus, no such r can be a RS. The usual case will be that there is a unique $\bar{r}$ such that $\hat{\Psi}(r) = N\Lambda b$. Clearly this can only occur when some ν has excess capital, that is, when $pb - rp\omega^{\nu} < 0$.

It is possible, however, that a type of reswitching occurs, which would generate several values of r for which $\hat{\Psi}(r) = \Lambda Nb$, and hence several reproducible solutions. This can happen as follows. When r is very small, we think of there being an excess supply of labor power for sale, since the wage is high. When r becomes large, there should be an excess demand for labor power. One might think, therefore, that a unique value of r exists at which the supply and demand for labor power are equal. This, however, may not be the case: for as r increases, relative prices may change in such a way that one producer's endowment is increasing in value relative to the subsistence bundle and another's is decreasing in relative value. The labor power offered for sale by the first producer will decrease, while the second producer will increase his offering of labor power, due to his impoverishment. Thus, no simple rule exists which permits the statement that an increase in r will increase the excess demand for labor power.

More interesting is the possibility that there may be *no* reproducible solution. Suppose Λb is very close to unity, and there are some very poor producers (small ω^{ν}). By the time r increases to the value $\bar{r}$ where $\hat{\Psi}(\bar{r}) = N\Lambda b$, the poor producers' work time will have increased more than is feasible; that is, $\bar{p}b - \bar{r}\bar{p}\omega^{\nu} > 1$ for them. In particular, if $\omega^{\nu} = 0$, then $\hat{\Psi}(r) = p(r)b$ is strictly increasing toward infinity in r. If Λb is close to 1 then $p(r)b \geqq 1$ will be achieved for a small value of r. If there is no terribly wealthy producer it will still be the case that $\hat{\Psi}(r) > 0$ for all agents at that r, and hence no RS exists.

Clearly there will never exist a solution with $r = 0$ in the presence of such extreme poverty. Hence, if Λb is close to 1 and there exist producers who are sufficiently poor, then there will be no reproducible solutions for the economy $\mathscr{E}(p, r; \omega)$, where $\omega \geq \bar{\omega}$.

We have a rather surprising result: if there is no excess capital in the economy ($\omega = \bar{\omega}$), then there is always a continuum of equilibria for the economy with credit/labor market. However, if there is excess capital, there may be no equilibrium! Consequently, there are economies which can reproduce themselves in the communal fashion of Chapter 1 (Theorem 1.2), but in which the market cannot find a way.

Finally, it must be pointed out that this type of market failure is due to the assumption of NBC. If we drop Assumption NBC, then the following holds:

Theorem 3.10. Without Assumption NBC, every economy $\mathscr{E}(p, r)$ for which $\omega \geqq A(I - A)^{-1}(Nb)$ possesses a RS at $r = 0$ and $p = \Lambda$.

Proof. At prices Λ, and interest rate 0, the best a producer can do is work Λb. Redistribute stocks among the agents so that each possesses identical wealth. At this wealth distribution, all agents in fact have an optimal solution at which they work Λb, and which aggregates to a globally reproducible solution—namely, $x^\nu = (I - A)^{-1}b$. Furthermore, the redistribution which was enacted was costless to borrowers, since $r = 0$, and was costless to lenders, since they could not have done better for themselves with more capital. This redistribution does, however, defy NBC, since we have required the rich to lend their excess capital to the poor at zero interest. QED

Hence, the introduction of the extra market (labor or credit) solves the problem of reproducibility, if we do not insist upon NBC, in the rather trivial fashion of Theorem 3.10. (The construction of Theorem 3.10 is, of course, a surrogate communal economy.) If our producers are sufficiently self-interested to abide by NBC, there will, however, be in general one market-clearing interest rate, if the economy is sufficiently productive ($\Lambda b \ll 1$); there may be *no* market solution if the economy is marginally productive ($\Lambda b \approx 1$); or there may be a perverse reswitching in which several isolated RSs exist.

4. Exploitation versus alienation

The models in Part I show that if producers have differential ownership of the means of production then a regime of competitive markets is sufficient to produce the exploitation and class characterization of capitalism predicted by classical Marxism. It is more enlightening, perhaps, to emphasize what is not necessary to produce this result: there need not be an institution for the exchange of labor. Exploitation can be mediated entirely through the exchange of produced commodities, and classes can exist with respect to a credit market instead of a labor market—at least at this classical level of abstraction.

This is not to say that coercion is not necessary to produce Marxian exploitation and class; rather, it suffices for the coercion to be at the point of maintaining property relations, and not at the locus of extracting surplus labor directly from the worker. Surely the latter struggle in the workplace exists also in capitalism. But the argumentation here implies that such coercion is of secondary importance in understanding exploitation and class. It is a mistake to elevate the struggle in the process of production between worker and capitalist to a more privileged position in the theory than the fact of differential ownership of productive assets. I must emphasize that I do not mean that study of the process of labor exchange and extraction does not have an important place in the theory, because at a more concrete specification of the economy than the models here allow, other factors enter (such as enforcement of property relations and costs of supervision) which make the labor market an important locus.

Nevertheless, a misplaced emphasis on the labor process can lead to faulty, or at least nonmaterialist, analysis. If, for instance, one observes that the labor process appears much the same in existing socialism as it does in capitalism, then one might conclude that existing socialist countries are not essentially different from capitalist countries, insofar as the exploitation of workers is concerned. This is, indeed, the inference of many Marxists who emphasize the labor process and industrial democracy as the defining characteristic of the mode of production, rather than property relations. There is, I think, a distinction between *alienation* and *exploitation.* Workers may always feel alienated, to some extent, in a labor process which employs the detailed division of labor, one-man management, and so on, but whether exploitation exists (or, more precisely, whether it is capitalist exploitation) is another matter. There is not a one-to-one correspondence between regimes of property relations and organizational forms of work, and when two different regimes give rise to similar organizational work forms, it is the former which defines the nature of exploitation and surplus extraction, and the latter which defines the nature of alienation. That is a conclusion implied by the analysis here. The labor process approach, on the other hand, takes the organization of work as the touchstone for passing judgment on a form of economic organization, and alienation in work is thus elevated to a higher analytical plane than the relations of exploitation.

Capitalist exploitation is the appropriation of the labor of one class by another class, realized because of their differential ownership or access to the nonhuman means of production. This can be accomplished, in principle, with or without any direct relationship between the exploiters and the exploited in the process of work. One might argue that there is exploitation without alienation in $\mathscr{E}(p)$, since each producer is in control of the labor process in $\mathscr{E}(p)$, that is, works for himself in his own shop. Conversely, as will be seen in Part III, capitalist exploitation can be eliminated, with or without eliminating relations of authority (and thereby alienation?), in the process of work. Given this muddy relationship between the organization of work (alienation) and property relations (exploitation), what is the proper mixture of the two criteria for understanding the laws of motion of society? Historical materialism directs us to emphasize property relations (exploitation) as key; it may be incorrect in so doing, but one must at least understand the implications of taking the other approach.

Part II

Exploitation and Class in an Accumulating Economy

In Part I the origins of exploitation and class were studied in a precapitalist, subsistence economy, where all producers have access to the same technology and have the same subsistence needs but differ according to their endowments of produced goods. The distribution of endowments gives rise to a class structure and a hierarchy of exploitation. A producer was said to be exploited if he has to work more time than is "socially necessary" in order to produce a bundle of goods which can be traded for his subsistence needs. The central theorem of Part I is the Class Exploitation Correspondence Principle. Agents in the economy, facing a set of prices and a wage rate, decide whether to sell labor power, hire labor power, work for themselves, or do some combination of these three activities. Thus, individual optimization determines a *class structure,* a class being a particular way of relating to the means of production, in the Marxian sense. (For instance, all agents who optimize by selling some labor power and working part-time for themselves constitute one class, which might be called the class of semiproletarians.) The Class Exploitation Correspondence Principle (CECP) states that all producers who optimize by selling labor power are exploited at the economy's equilibrium, and all agents who optimize by hiring labor power are exploiters; furthermore, the five classes which exist in this economy always appear in a certain classical order with respect to the welfare ordering of society's members in terms of the exploitation criterion.

In Part II a model which schematically represents capitalist economy, as opposed to subsistence economy, will be studied. I wish to define a notion of exploitation which is faithful to the classical Marxian idea that agents are exploited when they have to work more time than is socially necessary to acquire what they get. I shall construct the model so that, as before, classes are endogenously determined by individual optimization, and then prove that the CECP is valid for capitalist economy. The validation of the CECP in the model of capitalist economy—or, more precisely, the model with accumulation—will show that the association between class and exploitation is robust, even when several simple features of the subsistence model no longer obtain. Alternatively, if one wishes heuristically to accept the correspondence of classes and exploitation as a Marxian premise, then the theorem indicates that the definition of exploitation which is offered in this chapter is an appropriate one from the Marxian point of view, as it preserves this fundamental principle. This is a nontrivial point, since the definition of exploitation we offer is considerably more general than the classical Marxian one: in particular, we define exploitation below without reference to any subsistence concept.[1]

In passing from a subsistence economy to a model of an economy in which agents are accumulators, it becomes necessary to define a (Marxian) concept of exploitation which is independent of any notion of subsistence. This, incidentally, is a worthwhile task in itself for Marxian economics, since most workers in advanced capitalist economies today do not receive a wage which can be called a subsistence wage under any interpretation except a tautological one (that is, whatever workers receive is subsistence). In addition, it might be argued that a Marxian notion of exploitation should be independent of the subjective preferences of agents, as whether an agent is exploited should be an objective fact over which he has no control. Hence, the first task of Chapter 4 is to propose a definition of exploitation which generalizes the Marxian idea of surplus value, but is independent of any concept of subsistence, and of the agents' sets of preferences over goods.

In Chapter 4 I develop the idea of exploitation and the CECP for the accumulation economy with the Leontief technology. This is the simplest case. In an appendix the problem of exploiting and exploited coalitions of producers is studied. This somewhat technical diversion is necessary, because a problematic phenomenon arises in

1. Actually, two definitions of exploitation are proposed here, and this statement applies to both.

the model of capitalist economy: it is possible for there to be exploiting producers but no exploited producers, and conversely. This apparent anomaly of the theory is resolved by introducing the concepts of minimal exploited coalitions and minimal exploiting coalitions, the topic of the appendix. (The theory of the appendix emerges as central, later on, in the discussion of exploitation in economies with increasing returns. See Chapter 7.) In Chapter 5 I generalize the discussion of exploitation and class to an economy whose technology is specified as a convex cone (that is, production is only required to exhibit constant returns to scale). This will be the first time in this book in which the concepts under study are dealt with in a more general technology than the Leontief technology. In particular, a special case of a conical technology is the von Neumann technology, which suffices to model fixed capital and joint products, and another special case is the Cobb-Douglas neoclassical technology. It will be shown that the CECP holds for the conical technology, thus verifying the robustness of that principle. But the purpose of Chapter 5 is not simply generalization for its own sake, for a fascinating corollary concerning a classical issue of Marxian value theory follows from the proof of the CECP in the general case. When faced with the conical technology, we require a generalization of the definition of labor value embodied in a bundle of commodities. In general, the vector of labor values, Λ, does not exist. There are several candidates for a suitable generalized definition. The definition which must be adopted in order for the CECP to hold is one in which labor value embodied depends on the market. One cannot define the labor content of commodities until one knows equilibrium prices. This fact provides new and important evidence on the classical question of whether labor value can be conceived of independently of market phenomena.

In Chapter 6 we perturb the basic model of Chapter 4 in a different way: we allow producers to be endowed with different amounts of labor. This is a rudimentary way of approaching the problem of differential skill. Another interpretation is that agents have different preferences for leisure, and some choose to work longer than others. In the model with differential labor endowments (or supplies), there is a well-defined notion of Marxian exploitation, and the CECP continues to hold; but it is no longer true that exploitation or class position is a proxy for wealth. There may be some very wealthy producers who are exploited, and some poor producers who are exploiters. This example makes more compelling the search for a general theory of exploitation, as the labor theory seems to provide curious prescriptions, from a Marxist viewpoint, in some cases.

Part II, then, serves two purposes. From the point of view of a study in the classical Marxian theory of value, it (a) provides a definition of exploitation in terms of surplus labor which depends neither on an assumption of subsistence consumption, nor on the subjective preferences or actual consumption of workers; (b) develops the theory of exploitation and class for an accumulating economy; (c) shows the dependence of labor value on the market, when the technology is more general than a Leontief matrix. From the point of view of our search for a general concept of exploitation, it appears to push the labor theory of exploitation to the limits of credibility, forcing us to inquire into what ethical conception we are trying to capture with the notion of the transfer of surplus labor.

4

The Class Exploitation Correspondence Principle

1. A model of accumulation

Our schematic model of capitalist economy is that all agents are accumulators, seeking to expand the value of their endowments (capital) as rapidly as possible. All agents have access to the same technology, but they differ (as in Part I) in their bundles of endowments. A common Leontief technology is available to all agents. An agent can engage in three types of economic activity: he can sell his labor power, he can hire the labor power of others, or he can work for himself. His constraint is that he must be able to afford to lay out the operating costs, in advance, for the activities he chooses to operate, either with his own labor or hired labor, funded by the value of his endowment.

Explicitly:

A is an $n \times n$ productive, indecomposable input matrix
L is a strictly positive $1 \times n$ vector of direct labor inputs
(p, w) is a $1 \times (n + 1)$ price and wage vector
x^ν is an $n \times 1$ vector of activity levels
y^ν is an $n \times 1$ vector of activity levels
z^ν is a scalar
ω^ν is an $n \times 1$ vector of endowments

Facing prices (p, w) the νth producer chooses a $(2n + 1) \times 1$ activity vector (x^ν, y^ν, z^ν) to

$$\left.\begin{aligned} &\max\,(p - pA)x^\nu + (p - (pA + wL))y^\nu + wz^\nu \equiv \Pi^\nu(p, w) \\ &\text{subject to} \\ &pA(x^\nu + y^\nu) \leqq p\omega^\nu \qquad (1.1a) \\ &Lx^\nu + z^\nu \leqq 1 \qquad (1.1b) \\ &x^\nu, y^\nu, z^\nu \geqq 0 \end{aligned}\right\} (1.1)$$

x^ν is the vector of activity levels agent ν chooses to operate himself with technology (A, L); y^ν is the vector of activity levels he hires others to operate for him; z^ν is the amount of his labor time he sells. The objective function maximizes net revenues; (1.1a) is the agent's capital constraint and (1.1b) is his labor constraint. Let $\mathscr{A}^\nu(p, w)$ be the set of actions (x^ν, y^ν, z^ν) which solve ν's program at prices (p, w).

The equilibrium concept is:

Definition 4.1. A price vector (p, w) is a *reproducible solution* for the economy $(A, L, \omega^1, \ldots, \omega^N)$ with N producers if:

(R1) $(\forall \nu)(\exists (x^\nu, y^\nu, z^\nu) \in \mathscr{A}^\nu(p, w))$ (profit maximization)
(R2) $A(x + y) \leqq \omega$, where $x = \Sigma x^\nu$, $y = \Sigma y^\nu$ (feasibility of production)
(R3) $Ly = z \equiv \Sigma z^\nu$ (labor market equilibrium)
(R4) $(I - A)(x + y) \geqq 0$ (reproducibility)

The concept of a reproducible solution is the same as for the subsistence economies of Part I. A price vector reproduces the economy if every producer can choose an individually optimal point (R1) which is globally feasible given society's total endowment of produced goods (R2) and which allows trades in labor power to equilibrate (R3); moreover, we demand that society should not run down any physical stock of a produced good, which is accomplished by insisting that net output be a nonnegative vector (R4).

Note the absence of any subsistence concept in this economy, or indeed any consumption demand by agents. Agents are pure-and-simple accumulators; we wish to model, in as simple and stark a way as possible, an economy whose agents are motivated by the desire to accumulate, just as the economies of the previous part modeled stark subsistence economies. We could make this model somewhat less stark by insisting that each agent, although an accumulator, has to consume at least some minimal vector b. This would add one more constraint to the individual's program (1.1), and would change the reproducibility constraint (R4) to $(I - A)(x + y) \geqq Nb$. Such a change adds nothing to the model, however, and so we choose to keep things clean by positing, as it were, that $b = 0$.[1]

Notice that time is of the essence in the model, as what constrains production decisions is the fact that inputs must be paid for today, and revenues from output accrue tomorrow. Nevertheless, we have assumed the same price vector (p, w) is used to price goods in the two periods. In the previous models of subsistence economy this was also done; there it was shown that this was legitimate because an equilibrium in the subsistence economy is in fact a stationary state. However, an equilibrium in the accumulation economy is not a stationary state, because endowments grow. The expectations of agents that prices will remain the same may be unfulfilled. Consequently, we must observe that the equilibrium of Definition 4.1 is in fact descriptive of the steady state. We shall not investigate the existence question of a steady state here. A steady state in the sense of Definition 4.1, which makes the equilibrium concept consistent with a conventional temporary equilibrium price expectation structure of the agents, exists when initial aggregate endowments $\omega = \Sigma\omega^{\nu}$ lie on the von Neumann ray of the economy. (For a detailed discussion of a related model which verifies this, see the appendix of Roemer, 1980a.)

We proceed to characterize the equilibrium solutions of the model, by showing first that reproducible solutions (p, w) must equalize profit rates across sectors. The intuition behind the equalization of profit rates across all sectors at a reproducible solution is this. At a reproducible solution, a nonnegative vector of net outputs must be produced (statement (R4) of Definition 4.1). Since the matrix A is indecomposable, this requires that every sector be operated at a positive level. But revenue maximizers will operate only those sectors which enjoy the maximal profit rate over all sectors. Hence, for every sector to operate, all sectors must enjoy the maximal profit rate, which is to say the profit rate must be equal across sectors. This intuition is formalized by the following proof.

1. This is, of course, just like the familiar assumption in certain growth models that the savings rate of capitalists is unity. In this model, every agent is a potential capitalist.

Consider the dual program to (1.1):

$$\left.\begin{aligned} &\text{choose } \alpha,\ \beta \text{ to min } \alpha W^\nu + \beta \\ &\text{subject to} \\ &\alpha pA + \beta L \geqq p(I - A) \qquad x^\nu \qquad (1.2a) \\ &\alpha pA \geqq p - (pA + wL) \qquad y^\nu \qquad (1.2b) \\ &\beta \geqq w \qquad z^\nu \qquad (1.2c) \end{aligned}\right\} \quad (1.2)$$

where $W^\nu \equiv p\omega^\nu$, and the complementary primal variables are listed next to the appropriate dual constraint. Let $(\hat{\alpha}, \hat{\beta})$ be an optimal solution to (1.2).

Case 1: $w > 0$. Suppose $\hat{\beta} > w$. Then a comparison of (1.2a) and (1.2b) shows that (1.2a) is a strict vector inequality. (This uses the assumption postulated that $L > 0$.) Hence, by duality, $x^\nu = 0$. Also $z^\nu = 0$ since $\hat{\beta} > w$. Hence ν does not work at all at his optimum. But this is impossible, since $w > 0$. (ν can increase his revenues if he has some spare time by selling labor power.) Therefore $\hat{\beta} = w$. Now constraints (1.2a) and (1.2b) are identical and the program (1.2) can be simplified:

$$\begin{aligned} &\text{choose } \alpha \text{ to min } \alpha W^\nu + w \\ &\text{subject to} \\ &\alpha pA \geqq p - (pA + wL). \end{aligned} \qquad (1.3)$$

Define $\pi_i = ([p - (pA + wL)]/pA)_i$ as the profit rate in sector i, and $\pi_{\max} \equiv \max_i \pi_i$. Then the solution of (1.3) is

$$\hat{\alpha} = \max\,(0, \pi_{\max}).$$

By complementary slackness, from (1.2a) and (1.2b), we conclude:

$$x_i^\nu = 0 = y_i^\nu \quad \text{unless } \pi_i = \pi_{\max} \text{ and } \pi_{\max} \geq 0.$$

Only sectors generating the maximum profit rate are operated, either by hired labor or on one's own. No sector is operated if $\pi_{\max} < 0$. Notice that this argument is independent of ν. Hence, since reproducibility (R4) requires all sectors to operate, a necessary condition for

(p, w) to be a reproducible solution is:

$$\forall i, \quad \pi_i = \pi_{\max} \quad \text{and} \quad \pi_{\max} \geq 0$$

or

$$p = (1 + \pi)pA + wL \tag{1.4}$$

for some number $\pi \geq 0$.

Case 2: $w = 0$. In this case, program (1.2) immediately becomes:

$$\text{choose } \alpha, \beta \text{ to min } \alpha W^{\nu}$$

subject to

$$\left.\begin{aligned} &\alpha pA + \beta L \geqq p(I - A) && (1.4a) \\ &\alpha pA \geqq p(I - A) && (1.4b) \end{aligned}\right\} (1.4)$$

$$\alpha, \beta \geqq 0.$$

If $\hat{\beta} > 0$, then constraints (1.4a) are all slack at the optimum, and as before we see from (1.4b):

$$\hat{\alpha} = \begin{cases} \max\limits_i \left[\dfrac{p(I - A)}{pA}\right]_i = \pi_{\max}, & \text{if } \pi_{\max} \geq 0, \\ 0, & \text{if } \pi_{\max} < 0. \end{cases}$$

The only activities which operate are those for which $\pi_i = \pi_{\max}$, when $\pi_{\max} \geq 0$, and no activities operate if $\pi_{\max} < 0$. Again, reproducibility requires $\pi_i = \pi_{\max} \geq 0$ for all i. If $\hat{\beta} = 0$, then (1.4a) becomes identical to (1.4b) and the same situation prevails. Summarizing:

Theorem 4.1. Let (p, w) be a nontrivial reproducible solution.[2]

(A) Then prices must equalize profit rates in all sectors: that is, there is a nonnegative number π such that

$$p = (1 + \pi)pA + wL. \tag{1.5}$$

2. A nontrivial reproducible solution is one where some activity is operated.

(B) At an optimum, ν's revenues are $\pi W^\nu + w$.

Notice that part (B) follows immediately from the duality theorem of linear programming, since the value of ν's dual program is always $\pi W^\nu + w$.

An important observation follows from the fact that ν's revenues are $\pi W^\nu + w$. Notice that ν can always achieve precisely that revenue by hiring himself out for the entire day (and receiving wage w for his efforts), plus hiring others to "operate" his capital W^ν, bringing in revenues πW^ν. That is:

Lemma 4.1. At a RS, ν always possesses an individually optimal solution (x^ν, y^ν, z^ν) with $x^\nu = 0$.

We next use Theorem 4.1 to characterize solutions of the model. The model in fact has a knife-edge property. According to Theorem 4.1, there can only be three types of reproducible solutions:

$$\begin{array}{llll} \text{(i)} \ (p, w) & \text{where } p = (1 + \pi)pA + wL, & \pi > 0, & w > 0 \\ \text{(ii)} \ (\bar{p}, 0) & \text{where } \bar{p} = (1 + \bar{\pi})\bar{p}A, & \bar{\pi} > 0, & w = 0 \\ \text{(iii)} \ (p, w) & \text{where } p = pA + wL, & \pi = 0, & w > 0. \end{array}$$

In all cases, $p > 0$.

Theorem 4.2.

(A) Let (p, w) be a nontrivial reproducible solution where $\pi > 0$ and $w > 0$. Then the knife-edge relationship $N = LA^{-1}\omega$ between the labor supply (N) and aggregate capital (ω) must hold. Conversely, if $N = LA^{-1}\omega$ then: (1) if $A^{-1}\omega \geqq \omega$, *any* price vector (p, w) of type (i) supports a reproducible solution; (2) if $A^{-1}\omega \ngeqq \omega$, there is no RS.

(B) If $N > LA^{-1}\omega$, then the only reproducible solution is $(\bar{p}, 0)$ where $\bar{p} = (1 + \bar{\pi})\bar{p}A$.

(C) If $N < LA^{-1}\omega$, then the only reproducible solution is (p, w) where $p = pA + wL$ (and $\pi = 0$).

Proof. Consider a nontrivial reproducible solution (p, w), where $x + y = \Sigma(x^\nu + y^\nu) \neq 0$. Since $(I - A)^{-1}$ exists, in fact $(I - A)(x + y) \geq 0$, and since $(I - A)^{-1} > 0$ by indecomposability of A, in fact $x + y > 0$. That is, all activities must operate at a (nontrivial) reproducible solution. By considering the objective function of program (1.1), it is seen that this can only occur if $p \geqq pA$. (If $p_i < pA_i$, no producer will operate sector i.) By productiveness of A, this implies $p \geq pA$ (since A's eigenvalue cannot be unity), and hence $p > 0$ (since $(I - A)^{-1} > 0$).

Suppose, now, that (p, w) is of the form $\pi > 0$. Then every agent at his optimum must have a binding capital constraint (from (1.1a)):

$$pA(x^\nu + y^\nu) = p\omega^\nu, \tag{1.6}$$

for if not, he could increase his revenues by offering to hire more workers and putting them to work on his slack capital, since $\pi > 0$. Adding (1.6) over all ν gives:

$$pA(x + y) = p\omega. \tag{1.7}$$

In the light of (R2) and our observation that $p > 0$, (1.7) implies

$$A(x + y) = \omega. \tag{1.8}$$

Hence $(x + y) = A^{-1}\omega$ (assuming A^{-1} exists) and

$$L(x + y) = Lx + z = LA^{-1}\omega = N, \tag{1.9}$$

since $Ly = z$ (R3) at a reproducible solution. Hence the demand for labor is N. If $w > 0$, the supply of labor offered is also N, since any agent with slack labor could increase his revenues by selling the extra labor power. Hence (p, w) with $\pi > 0$ and $w > 0$ can only be a reproducible solution if $N = LA^{-1}\omega$.

To prove the converse statement in part (A), we need only show that the aggregate activity levels $x + y = A^{-1}\omega$ can (a) arise from individual optimization, and (b) reproduce the system. Given $N = LA^{-1}\omega$, it is easily seen that $x + y = A^{-1}\omega$ can be the outcome of individual optimization by Lemma 4.1: let $x = 0$ and $y = A^{-1}\omega$. Each agent is indifferent to which sectors he operates with hired labor, since they all enjoy the same profit rate. By Lemma 4.1 and $N = LA^{-1}\omega$, agents can be assigned vectors $(0, y^\nu, 1) \equiv (x^\nu, y^\nu, z^\nu)$ which are individually optimal and and which aggregate to the required activity levels. Does $x + y = A^{-1}\omega$ reproduce the system, satisfy (R4)? Only if $(I - A)(A^{-1}\omega) \geqq 0$, or if $A^{-1}\omega \geqq \omega$. Thus, if $A^{-1}\omega \geqq \omega$, then all price vectors of type (i) are reproducible solutions; if $A^{-1}\omega \ngeqq \omega$, then there are no reproducible solutions.

In part (B), where $N > LA^{-1}\omega$, we have a capital-limited economy, with excess labor. As long as $w > 0$, all labor will wish to be employed since slack labor can always increase its revenues by hiring out. Thus the only reproducible solution is $w = 0$, and $\bar{p} = (1 + \bar{\pi})\bar{p}A$, where $\bar{p}$ is the Frobenius eigenvector of A. This in fact supports a reproducible solution, since agents are indifferent to offering their extra labor power for sale at $w = 0$, according to (1.1). This may be thought of as the subsistence wage case. When there is not sufficient capital in the economy to employ all labor, wages are driven down to subsistence level.

In part (C), where $N < LA^{-1}\omega$, there is a labor-limited economy. As long as $\pi > 0$, all agents with capital wish to gainfully employ it, which is impossible. Hence $\pi = 0$ is the only possible reproducible solution. Conversely, a reproducible solution of type (iii) can be arranged in this case. This concludes the proof of Theorem 4.2. QED

In summary, at the knife edge the profit rate is indeterminate. In the capital-limited economy, the profit rate is maximal and the wage is driven to zero; in the labor-limited economy, the opposite occurs. This appears to be a rather uninteresting set of equilibria, and it derives from the stark specification of the model. Recall that in the subsistence economies of Chapters 2 and 3 there was a more pleasant situation: an essentially unique profit rate π prevailed which equilibrated the demand and supply for labor, in nonpathological cases. The essential difference between the two models appears to be the satiability of agents in the subsistence economy. Once an agent's labor time was reduced to zero, he was willing to allow capital to lie unused which, for other agents, has a positive shadow price. In the present model, agents are insatiable and are driven to use all their capital as long as positive profits can be made. The fixed proportions technology generates the knife-edge problem, since changes in relative prices are incapable of stimulating substitution of factors in production. We could change the equilibrium possibilities for the economy with utility functions including an accumulation-leisure tradeoff. We have, however, avoided specifying such utility functions, wishing to portray only the starkest kernel of the accumulation issue, so that we can examine the issues of exploitation and class in the most unfettered way. And this simple model suffices for that task.

2. A definition of exploitation

Consider a reproducible solution (p, w) for the economy $(A, L, \omega^1, \ldots, \omega^N)$ involving the total activity vector $x + y$. In classical Marxian economics, a worker is considered exploited because the bundle of goods he purchases with his wage, the subsistence bundle, embodies less labor time than he worked. In our model, agents do not purchase goods, they accumulate; nor is the subsistence notion important. We propose a generalization of the Marxian notion of exploitation. Consider all bundles of goods an agent could feasibly purchase with his revenues. An agent is exploited if there is no such bundle which embodies as much labor as the time he worked. More precisely:

Definition 4.2. Let (p, w) support a reproducible solution $x + y$. A *feasible assignment* for this reproducible solution is any distribution of net output $\{f^\nu\}$, $\nu = 1, N$ such that:

$$(1)\quad \Sigma f^\nu = (I - A)(x + y)$$
$$(2)\quad pf^\nu = \Pi^\nu(p, w).$$

The class of all feasible assignments is called $\mathcal{F}$.

(Recall that $\Pi^\nu(p, w)$ is the optimal value for ν's program (1.1).) Let $\mathcal{F}^\nu$ be the set of bundles f^ν which ν receives under the various feasible assignments.

A feasible assignment is any distribution of society's net output to its members, distributed so each agent receives an affordable bundle. Recall that the labor value of a bundle of goods v is $L(I - A)^{-1}v \equiv \Lambda v$.

Definition 4.3. An agent ν is *exploited* at the reproducible solution if and only if

$$\max_{f^\nu \in \mathcal{F}^\nu} \Lambda f^\nu < Lx^\nu + z^\nu.$$

Agent ν is an exploiter if and only if

$$\min_{f^\nu \in \mathcal{F}^\nu} \Lambda f^\nu > Lx^\nu + z^\nu.$$

An agent is exploited when the amount of labor embodied in *any* bundle of goods he could receive, in a feasible distribution of society's net product, is less than the labor he expended. Similarly, an exploiter is one whose revenues unambiguously command goods embodying more labor time than he worked.

Notice that this definition is independent of subjective preferences, if we endow the agents with utility functions for produced commodities. Clearly any feasible assignment can be thought of as arising from some set of preferences. (The converse, however, is not true, because an arbitrary set of utility functions will not give rise to demands which necessarily aggregate to $(I - A)(x + y)$.) The intent of the definition is to capture the notion that an agent is exploited when the goods he can command through the market embody less social labor time than he expended.

This definition is not precisely a generalization of the usual definition of exploitation of workers who are said to be exploited if the labor embodied in their subsistence bundle is less than the time they worked: $\Lambda b < 1$. In that model, it is conceivable that another bundle, b', exists which a worker could afford to buy with his wage and for which $\Lambda b' > 1$. Consequently, he would not be exploited according to Definition 4.3, although perhaps consumption of b' would not permit the worker to survive.[3] Despite this anomaly, I think Definition 4.3 captures accurately the intention of the Marxian concept of the expropriation of surplus labor: producers or agents are exploited when their income does not permit them to command as much labor through the goods they can buy as the labor they provided in production.

Several comments are in order. First, in general, there may be agents who are neither exploiters nor exploited. Under some feasible assignments a producer may receive a bundle f^ν where $\Lambda f^\nu < Lx^\nu + z^\nu$, and under another assignment he may receive a bundle f^ν where $\Lambda f^\nu > Lx^\nu + z^\nu$. We shall be interested in analyzing this gray area of agents. The existence of the gray area is intimately related to the classical "transformation problem" of the nonproportionality of prices and labor values. Second, there may exist reproducible solutions with exploiters but no exploited agents, or vice versa. This may ap-

3. For the consequences of letting workers choose their consumption bundles in classical Marxian economics, see Roemer (1981), chaps. 7–8.

pear to be a defect of the model, but it is actually a nice point. The resolution of this issue is discussed in the appendix.

More important is the philosophical question of why one might choose to call this phenomenon exploitation. In the subsistence economies of Part I, there was some prima facie rationale for calling agents who worked long hours, exploited, since every agent's objective was to minimize labor performed. In the accumulation model, however, this is not the case. Why should it be relevant to classify an agent as exploited by comparing his labor supplied to labor commanded? For the moment, this will not be defended; the justification of the normative term exploitation must await Part III. We are, after all, attempting to construct a generalized Marxian theory of exploitation. All that is asked at this point is that the definitions be evaluated in the light of the classical Marxian one in terms of surplus value, rather than against some other conception of justice or exploitation.

3. The characterization of producers' exploitation status and class position

We wish to characterize, at a reproducible solution (p, w), the wealths $W^{\nu} = p\omega^{\nu}$ which will be associated with exploited agents, and with exploiting agents. It is obvious from the Definition 4.3 that there are two cutoff points: if ν's wealth is greater than a certain amount, ν is an exploiter; if ν's wealth is less than a certain amount, ν is exploited. To characterize simply these two cutoff points, we require:

Assumption of a Large Economy (ALE). Every agent can spend all his revenue on the purchase of any one good.

In other words, ALE guarantees that, given any agent ν and any good i, there is a feasible assignment in which ν receives a bundle consisting of only good i. This means each agent's revenue is small compared to the entire economy's net product.

Theorem 4.3. Let (p, w) be a RS with $w > 0$, and $p = (1 + \pi)pA + wL$. Let ALE hold. If $\pi > 0$, then:

$$\nu \text{ is exploited} \Leftrightarrow W^\nu < \frac{1 - \rho_{\max} w}{\pi \rho_{\max}}$$

$$\nu \text{ is an exploiter} \Leftrightarrow W^\nu > \frac{1 - \rho_{\min} w}{\pi \rho_{\min}}$$

where $\rho_i = \Lambda_i/p_i$ and $\rho_{\max} = \max_i \rho_i$, $\rho_{\min} = \min_i \rho_i$. If $\pi = 0$, there are no exploiters and no exploited agents.

Proof. From Theorem 4.1, the revenues of agent ν are $\Pi^\nu(p, w) = \pi W^\nu + w$. How can ν receive goods embodying maximal labor value for his money? By spending his entire revenue on the good with the maximal labor value-price ratio,[4] $(\Lambda/p)_{\max}$. By ALE, there is, in fact, a feasible assignment which assigns this particular bundle to agent ν. ν is exploited if the labor value he thus commands through goods is less than the time he worked—that is, if:

$$\left[\frac{\Lambda}{p}\right]_{\max} (\pi W^\nu + w) < 1. \tag{3.1}$$

(3.1) is equivalent to $W^\nu < (1 - \rho_{\max} w)/\pi \rho_{\max}$.

In like manner, ν is an exploiter if, when he spends his entire revenues on the good with the minimal labor value-price ratio, $\rho_{\min}$, he nevertheless commands more labor time in his goods than he worked:

$$\left[\frac{\Lambda}{p}\right]_{\min} (\pi W^\nu + w) > 1, \tag{3.2}$$

or

$$W^\nu > (1 - \rho_{\min} w)/\pi \rho_{\min}. \qquad \text{QED}$$

(*Note:* When $\pi = 0$, it follows from (3.1) and (3.2) that there are no exploiters or exploited, since $p = w\Lambda$.)

Hence the gray area of agents who are neither exploited nor exploiters consists of all agents possessing wealth W such that $(1 -$

4. The maximal ratio of two vectors is signified:

$$\left[\frac{\Lambda}{p}\right]_{\max} \equiv \max_i \left[\frac{\Lambda_i}{p_i}\right].$$

$\rho_{\max}w)/\pi\rho_{\max} \leqq W \leqq (1 - \rho_{\min}w)/\pi\rho_{\min}$. Notice that this interval of wealths is a single point if and only if $\rho_{\min} = \rho_{\max}$, which occurs if and only if prices are proportional to labor values. If $\pi > 0$, this arises if and only if organic compositions of capital are equal in all sectors. Thus, when $\pi > 0$, the existence of a nontrivial gray area is equivalent to the transformation problem.

Theorem 4.3 characterizes a producer's exploitation status in terms of his wealth $W^{\nu} \equiv p\omega^{\nu}$ at a particular reproducible solution (p, w). Next, we characterize a producer's class position in terms of his wealth. We will then be prepared to explore the relationship between exploitation status and class position, by comparing the characterizations of the two phenomena in terms of their common index, wealth.

An agent's class membership is determined by whether he hires labor power, sells labor power, or works for himself when he optimizes. An agent, for instance, is said to belong to the class $(+, 0, +)$ if he possesses an individually optimal solution of the form $(x^{\nu}, y^{\nu}, z^{\nu})$ with $x^{\nu} \neq 0 \neq z^{\nu}$ and $y^{\nu} = 0$. As in Part I, there are eight possible classes, depending on how we arrange the + and 0 symbols in the three cells. In Lemma 4.1 we have shown that every agent is a member of class $(0, +, +)$. We use as before the set-theoretic notation $\nu \in C^1 \setminus C^2$ to mean that ν is a member of class C^1 but not of class C^2. We can now easily characterize class membership in the model.

Theorem 4.4. At the RS (p, w):

(A) $\nu \in (+, +, 0)\setminus(+, 0, 0) \Leftrightarrow \forall$ individually optimal solutions of form $(0, y^{\nu}, z^{\nu})$, $Ly^{\nu} > 1$

(B) $\nu \in (+, 0, 0) \Leftrightarrow \exists$ an individually optimal solution of form $(0, y^{\nu}, z^{\nu})$, $Ly^{\nu} = 1$

(C) $\nu \in (+, 0, +)\setminus(+, 0, 0) \Leftrightarrow \forall$ individually optimal solutions of form $(0, y^{\nu}, z^{\nu})$, $Ly^{\nu} < 1$, and $W^{\nu} \neq 0$

(D) $\nu \in (0, 0, +) \Leftrightarrow W^{\nu} = 0$.

Let us denote these four classes as:

$$C^H = (+, +, 0)\setminus(+, 0, 0)$$
$$C^{PB} = (+, 0, 0)$$
$$C^S = (+, 0, +)\setminus(+, 0, 0)$$
$$C^P = (0, 0, +).$$

C^H is the class of agents who must hire labor power to optimize; C^S consists of those who must sell labor power to optimize, but have some capital; C^{PB} is the "petty bourgeois" class of agents who can optimize without either hiring or selling labor power; C^P is the class of pure proletarians who have no capital.

Note that Theorem 4.4 is the analog of Theorem 2.5.

Proof of Theorem 4.4.

Part (C). Recall that by Lemma 4.1 ν always has a solution with $x^\nu = 0$. Consider any solution for ν of form $\xi^\nu = (0, y^\nu, z^\nu)$. Note that $z^\nu = 1$ if $w > 0$, and $y^\nu \neq 0$ since $W^\nu \neq 0$. (In the case $w = 0$, $z^\nu = 1$ is still an optimal solution for ν, since there is no preference for leisure.) Define a new solution:

$$\bar{\xi}^\nu = (\bar{x}^\nu, \bar{y}^\nu, \bar{z}^\nu) \quad \text{where } \bar{x}^\nu = y^\nu$$
$$\bar{y}^\nu = 0$$
$$\bar{z}^\nu = 1 - Ly^\nu.$$

Check that $\bar{\xi}^\nu$ is a feasible solution for ν (program (1.1)). (Notice that ν uses the same amount of capital in both solutions, and the same amount of labor.) Check also that the solution $\bar{\xi}^\nu$ generates the same revenue as ξ^ν, so that $\bar{\xi}^\nu$ is individually optimal. Hence, $\nu \in (+, 0, +)$, since $Ly^\nu < 1$ and $y^\nu \neq 0$.

Suppose $\nu \in (+, 0, 0)$; let $(x^\nu, 0, 0)$ be optimal. Then $Lx^\nu = 1$, or else ν was not optimizing: since $w > 0$, he could have sold slack labor power for increased revenue. Form the solution $\bar{\xi}^\nu = (\bar{x}^\nu, \bar{y}^\nu, \bar{z}^\nu)$ defined by:

$$\bar{x}^\nu = 0$$
$$\bar{y}^\nu = x^\nu$$
$$\bar{z}^\nu = 1.$$

Check that $\bar{\xi}^\nu$ is individually optimal for ν; this contradicts the assumption that $Ly^\nu < 1$ for all individually optimal solutions. Hence $\nu \in (+, 0, +)\setminus(+, 0, 0)$.

The converse direction follows by making these same constructions.

Parts (A), (B), and (D) have proofs with the same format. QED

Corollary 4.5. At a RS (p, w), society is exhaustively partitioned into the four pairwise disjoint classes C^H, C^{PB}, C^S, and C^P.

Proof. Both exhaustiveness and pairwise disjointedness follow immediately from Theorem 4.4. QED

A quick review is useful. Since every agent belongs to the class (0, +, +), that class description is not interesting. The class partition C^H, C^{PB}, C^S, C^P is much more interesting because of Corollary 4.5, and because it distinguishes unambiguously between labor hiring and labor selling. The possibility of a Class Exploitation Correspondence Principle for this economy now materializes: to wit, is it true that every member of C^H is an exploiter and every member of C^S and C^P is exploited?

To approach this question, we require a characterization of the class memberships C^H, C^{PB}, C^S, and C^P according to wealths, for we have already in Theorem 4.3 a characterization of the exploitation status of an agent according to his wealth.

Theorem 4.6. Let (p, w) be a RS with $\pi > 0$. Then:

$$\nu \in C^H \Leftrightarrow W^\nu > \left[\frac{pA}{L}\right]_{\max}$$

$$\nu \in C^{PB} \Leftrightarrow \left[\frac{pA}{L}\right]_{\min} \leqq W^\nu \leqq \left[\frac{pA}{L}\right]_{\max}$$

$$\nu \in C^S \Leftrightarrow 0 < W^\nu < \left[\frac{pA}{L}\right]_{\min}$$

$$\nu \in C^P \Leftrightarrow W^\nu = 0.$$

To prove Theorem 4.6, first notice—from Theorem 4.4 and the canonical optimal solutions of the form $(0, y^\nu, z^\nu)$ of Lemma 4.1—that the four classes must fall in the order C^H, C^{PB}, C^S, C^P as wealth decreases. Recall how the solution $(0, y^\nu, z^\nu)$ was constructed. Agent ν hires himself out all day ($z^\nu = 1$), and then hires others to work his entire capital stock. If, in so doing, the amount of labor ν employs, Ly^ν, is always greater than the amount of labor μ employs, Ly^μ, then ν must have more capital than μ—for one of ν's options is to invest in precisely the same sectors as μ, and by hypothesis, he can hire more labor than μ by so doing. (Since all sectors achieve the same profit rate π, it is immaterial in which sectors a capitalist invests. The reason there is indeterminacy as to the amount of labor ν employs, Ly^ν, is because organic compositions of capital may differ across sectors and so ν can exhaust his capital according to $pAy^\nu = W^\nu$ using different activity vectors y^ν, and hence different labors Ly^ν—all generating the same amount of profit, πW^ν.) Hence, from Theorem 4.4, the ordering of the four classes by wealths follows.

Second, it is obvious that $\nu \in C^P$ if and only if $W^\nu = 0$; for if $W^\nu > 0$, then $(0, 0, +)$ cannot be optimal for ν, as his revenue is only w and not $\pi W + w$. (We use $\pi > 0$ here.)

From these two remarks, to complete the proof of the theorem we need only show that:

$$\nu \in C^{PB} \Leftrightarrow \left[\frac{pA}{L}\right]_{\min} \leqq W^\nu \leqq \left[\frac{pA}{L}\right]_{\max}.$$

This constitutes the heart of the argument; its proof is essentially the same as that of Theorem 2.7, part (B). For variety's sake, we present an alternative proof using duality.

An agent ν who possesses an optimal solution to (1.1) of the form $(+, 0, 0)$ possesses the same optimal solution to the following restricted program:

$$\left.\begin{aligned} &\max\ p(I - A)x^\nu \\ &\text{subject to} \\ &pAx^\nu \leqq W^\nu && (3.3a) \\ &Lx^\nu \leqq 1. && (3.3b) \end{aligned}\right\} \quad (3.3)$$

In the program (3.3), agent ν has no option to sell or hire labor power: he optimizes solely with respect to the activities he can operate himself, using his own resources.

The dual to the restricted program is:

$$\left.\begin{aligned} &\min\ \alpha W^\nu + \beta \\ &\text{subject to} \\ &\alpha pA + \beta L \geqq p(I-A). && (3.4a) \end{aligned}\right\} \quad (3.4)$$

Note that $(\pi, w) = (\alpha, \beta)$ is an optimal solution to (3.4). Feasibility of

(π, w) for (3.4) follows, since $p = (1 + \pi)pA + wL$. Optimality follows since by hypothesis the solution of (3.3) for ν is the same as the solution of (1.1) for ν, and the solution of (1.1) is $\pi W^\nu + w$ by Theorem 4.1. Finally the solution of (3.3) has the same value as the solution of (3.4) by duality.

For the solution (π, w), (3.4a) becomes a vector *equation*. That is, the point (π, w) lies on every constraint line of the constraint set for program (3.4). In Figure 6 we make a picture of program (3.4) in $\mathbb{R}^2$. (π, w) lies on every constraint line as required. For the objective function $\alpha W^\nu + \beta$ to achieve its optimum at (π, w), it is clearly necessary and sufficient that the slope of the contour lines $\alpha W^\nu + \beta = k$ lie between the maximal and minimal slopes of the various constraints; that is:

$$\left[\frac{pA}{L}\right]_{\min} \leqq W^\nu \leqq \left[\frac{pA}{L}\right]_{\max}.$$

(The slope of the ith constraint is $-(pA_i/L_i)$, and the slope of the contour lines is $-W^\nu$.) This completes the proof. QED

Note: The restriction $\pi > 0$ of Theorem 4.6 is important. If $\pi = 0$, the value of every agent's objective function becomes $\pi W^\nu + w = w$, and so it is clear that every agent has an optimal solution of form (0, 0, +). This situation is one of no interest, as agents become identical, since capital ceases to matter. When $\pi = 0$, there will be no exploitation. This is, in fact, a variant of the so-called Fundamental Marxian Theorem (FMT) of Morishima (1973), Roemer (1980a) and others. The variant of the FMT for the subsistence economy was proved in Chapter 2. In this model it is an immediate fact, since the revenues of all agents are identical when $\pi = 0$.

4. The Class Exploitation Correspondence Principle (CECP)

We now have two independent characterizations of class membership and exploitation according to wealth, according to Theorems 4.6 and 4.3. We proceed to compare the two characterizations to conclude a relationship between exploitation and class.

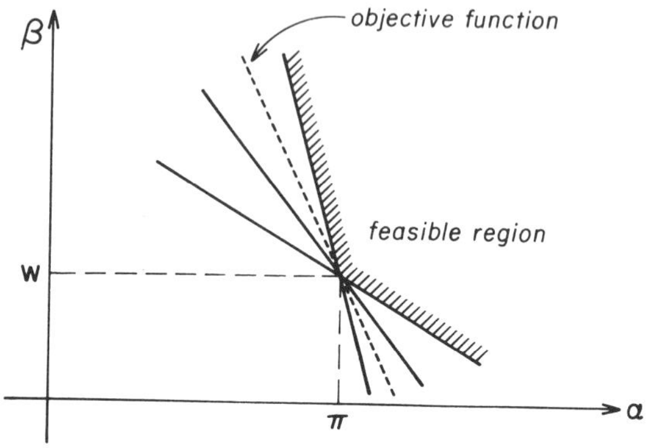

Figure 6 The linear program (3.4)

Theorem 4.7. Let (p, w) be a RS with $\pi > 0$. Let the Assumption of Large Economy (ALE) hold. Then:

(A) Every member of C^H is an exploiter;
(B) Every member of $C^S \cup C^P$ is exploited.

Figure 7—a picture of the two real lines, along which are arranged the four crucial numbers of Theorem 4.3 and Theorem 4.6—shows the relationship we wish to prove. Thus, Theorem 4.7 is proved if we verify these two inequalities:

$$\left[\frac{pA}{L}\right]_{\max} \geqq \frac{1 - w\rho_{\min}}{\pi\rho_{\min}} \tag{4.1}$$

$$\left[\frac{pA}{L}\right]_{\min} \leqq \frac{1 - w\rho_{\max}}{\pi\rho_{\max}}. \tag{4.2}$$

We verify (4.1). Suppose it were false. Then:

$$\left[\frac{pA}{L}\right]_j < \frac{1 - w\rho_{\min}}{\pi\rho_{\min}}, \quad \text{for all } j. \tag{4.3}$$

Consequently this vector inequality holds:

$$\pi pA\rho_{\min} < L - w\rho_{\min}L \tag{4.4}$$

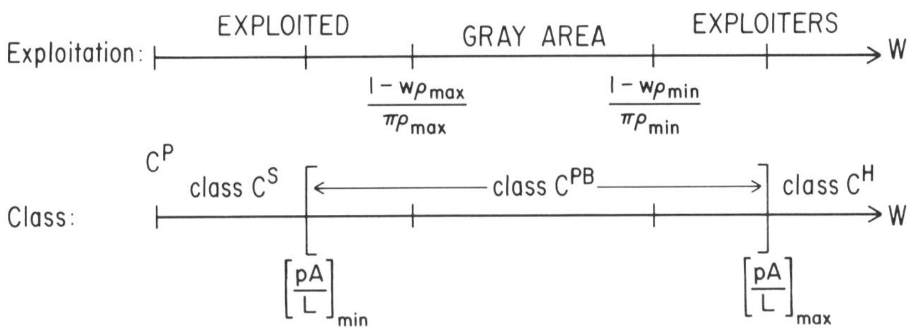

Figure 7 Relationship of exploitation to class

and by definition of π and p the left-hand side can be written to yield:

$$[p(I - A) - wL]\rho_{\min} < L - wL\rho_{\min} \tag{4.5}$$

which implies:

$$p(I - A) < \frac{1}{\rho_{\min}} L \tag{4.6}$$

and since $(I - A)^{-1} > 0$:

$$p < \frac{1}{\rho_{\min}} L(I - A)^{-1} \equiv \frac{1}{\rho_{\min}} \Lambda. \tag{4.7}$$

But (4.7) is impossible by the definition of $\rho_{\min}$, since $\rho_{\min} p_i = \Lambda_i$ for some i. By contradiction, (4.1) is verified. A symmetrical argument verifies (4.2). QED

Hence the CECP is verified for our model of an accumulation economy, even given our quite restrictive criterion for deciding on the exploitation status of agents. Exploitation status depends neither on any subsistence concept nor on subjective preferences; nevertheless, the association between labor selling and labor hiring with being exploited and exploiting continues to hold. Although there is a nontrivial gray area of agents, who are neutral from the exploitation point of view, this gray area of agents lies always entirely in the class of petty bourgeoisie.

We may now discuss the precise form the transformation problem takes in this model. Suppose the organic compositions of capital are equal in the economy (A, L). (That is, $\Lambda A_i/L_i$ is the same for all sectors i.) Then $\rho_{\min} = \rho_{\max}$ and $(pA/L)_{\max} = (pA/L)_{\min}$. It follows from (4.1) and (4.2) that $(pA/L) = (1 - w\rho)/\pi\rho$ in this case. Hence, the wealths associated with class C^{PB} constitute a single point, and the gray area of agents, who are neither exploited nor exploiting, reduces to that same point. The class C^H is *precisely* the set of agents who exploit, and the class union $C^S \cup C^P$ is *precisely* the set of agents who are exploited.

When, however, the organic compositions of capital are unequal, then in general (4.1) and (4.2) are strict inequalities. Thus, there are in general agents in the class C^{PB} who are exploiters or exploited. Although the gray area is always contained in the class C^{PB}, the converse is not true. Hence class membership does not provide a completely unambiguous proxy for an agent's exploitation status.

The transformation problem renders ambiguous the exploitation status of agents in the class (+, 0, 0). But Theorem 4.7 can be viewed as providing a resolution to the transformation problem, if one believes such questions require resolution. For it says that although the nonproportionality of labor values and prices produces a gray area of agents whose exploitation status is ambiguous, in fact that gray area is always contained in the class (+, 0, 0).

5. A preference-dependent definition of exploitation

Some pains have been taken thus far to define exploitation status independently of agents' preferences. We offer now an alternative definition of exploitation which is preference-dependent, and observe that the CECP continues to hold for it. Suppose the net product is actually distributed to agents (as investment and consumption goods), and that agent ν receives a bundle $\bar{f}^\nu$. Define an agent as exploited when $\Lambda\bar{f}^\nu < Lx^\nu + z^\nu$ and as an exploiter when $\Lambda\bar{f}^\nu > Lx^\nu + z^\nu$. Accordingly, only the singular agent will be exploitation-neutral; in general, the gray area disappears.

It is an easy observation that the CECP continues to hold under the preference-dependent specification of exploitation. For if $\nu \in$

C^H, then we know the labor value of *any* bundle of goods that ν purchases with his revenues contains more labor than he expended; in particular, this holds for the bundle $\bar{f}^\nu$, and thus all members of C^H continue to be exploiters under the second definition. Similarly for members of $C^S \cup C^P$—they continue to be exploited. The new definition of exploitation simply shrinks the gray area of agents, and so, a fortiori, the CECP holds. As with the first definition of exploitation, the exploitation status of agents in the class C^{PB} is ambiguous because of the transformation problem.

If one wishes to adopt the convention that an agent is exploited if the bundle of goods he actually purchases with his revenues embodies less labor than he expended in production, then we have shown that the relationship between class and exploitation (the CECP) is independent of subjective preferences. This is so even though a person's exploitation status may not be independent of his preferences, if he is in the gray area.

So far as the formalism is concerned, either definition passes the test of maintaining the CECP. The preference-independent definition provides the more startling result, because of the large gray area of agents it introduces. However, the analysis of Chapter 6 will indicate another argument for possibly preferring the preference-dependent definition of exploitation. Suppose agents do not maximize revenues, but rather utility, which is a function of revenues and leisure. Then agents will, in general, offer different amounts of labor ℓ^ν at the optimum, which they expend either in their own shops or working for others. We may continue to define an agent as exploited if the labor he commands through goods purchased is less than the labor he expends:

$$\Lambda f^\nu < \ell^\nu = Lx^\nu + z^\nu.$$

But if so, exploitation status already depends on preferences (for leisure), and so there is nothing gained by examining labor commanded over all feasible assignments of goods, in terms of preserving some objectivity in the definition. If we wish to define exploitation with reference to the labor an agent actually expends, rather than the labor he *could* expend in some counterfactual, then we must admit the preference-relatedness of exploitation in any case. This argument holds only when different labor-leisure choices are an important feature of the economy we wish to capture.

6. Summary

To review, we have introduced a definition of exploitation for the accumulation economy which captures the notion that a producer is exploited if he cannot buy goods embodying as much labor as he contributed in the production process. An exploiter is one who commands more labor through the goods he can purchase than he expended, regardless of how he dispenses his money. This leaves room for a large gray area of agents who are neither exploited nor exploiters, as they are able to dispense their income in purchasing some bundle embodying precisely the labor they worked. We showed that society is decomposed into four classes according to whether producers choose to hire others, sell their labor power, operate their own shop, or do some combination of these activities. If a utility function with a preference for leisure is allowed, the five-class decomposition of Part I results.

Note that the definition of exploitation is independent of any subsistence concept: we do not define the "value of labor power" with reference to any particular bundle of commodities the worker consumes, as in the previous chapters. Nor need exploitation status depend on what bundle an agent chooses to consume, although it may (section 5). Our characterization can thus be independent of subjective preferences and of any subsistence notion. We have generalized the traditional Marxian notion of exploitation and now evaluate exploitation status by comparing labor expended with the potential to command labor, embodied in goods.

Given this very general definition of Marxian exploitation, it is remarkable that the CECP continues to hold. Even though the gray area of agents who are neither exploited nor exploiters may be large, it is always contained in the class of petty bourgeoisie, (+, 0, 0). That is, those who must hire labor power to optimize are always exploiters, and those who must sell labor power are exploited. The fact that the CECP is preserved in turn indicates that the definition of exploitation we have proposed here is an appropriate generalization of the traditional Marxian concept of exploitation.

There is, however, an anomaly which arises from this definition of exploitation: there may be exploited coalitions of agents, but no exploited individual producers.[5] This phenomenon is studied in the

5. In particular, the existence of an exploiter implies the existence of an exploited coalition, but not necessarily of an individual who is exploited.

appendix. We then proceed to Chapter 5, where we inquire into the robustness of the CECP by investigating a model of production more general than the Leontief model studied thus far. The final resolution will be that the CECP continues to hold for the more general constant returns technologies, but there are some surprises before reaching that conclusion.

Appendix 4.1. Exploited and exploiting coalitions of producers

The definition of exploitation which has been studied proposes, in a sense, the strongest possible criterion for an agent to be exploited or exploiting.[6] In the definition of Chapter 4, section 2, we do not consider an agent to be exploited if he *happens* to purchase a bundle of goods which embodies less labor time than he worked; he is only exploited if he could not feasibly have purchased a bundle of goods embodying as much labor time as he worked. Because of the severity of the exploitation criterion there is a *large* gray area of agents who are neither exploited nor exploiting. It is therefore a theorem of some power that this gray area is always contained entirely in the class of agents $(+, 0, 0)$. In this way, the ambiguity in the classification of agents by their exploitation status seems well resolved.

There is, however, another way of examining the agents' exploitation status which gives rise to further questions. It is possible that there can be economies where exploiters exist but where there are no exploited individuals (or vice versa). If an agent j is an exploiter, then the complementary coalition to him, $N - \{j\}$, is certainly an *exploited coalition*, in the sense that in toto that coalition never receives goods under feasible assignments embodying as much labor as they collectively worked; but no *individual* in the complementary coalition need be exploited. The agent(s) who receive(s) the bundle embodying less labor than he worked can change as we range over feasible assignments. In general, $N - \{j\}$ will contain some individual exploiters.

6. A more general treatment of the material in this appendix is developed in Chapter 7, sections 7 and 8.

From a philosophical point of view, this phenomenon need not be troublesome. We view exploitation as a social phenomenon, and the existence of exploitation need not imply, in principle, the existence of individual exploiters or exploited. Nevertheless, the ambiguity requires us to analyze more carefully the set-theoretic nature of exploitation in the economy. In particular, the study can be guided by this question: Despite the nonexistence, in general, of individual members of society who are exploited or exploiters, can we identify two coalitions of agents which we consider to be the "canonical exploited coalition" and the "canonical exploiting coalition"?

For preciseness we repeat:

Definition A4.1. Let S be a set of agents at a RS. Then S is an *exploited coalition* if, under all feasible assignments $\{f^\nu\}$ in the economy, $\Sigma_S \Lambda f^\nu < \Sigma_S(Lx^\nu + z^\nu)$; S is an *exploiting coalition* if, under all feasible assignments, $\Sigma_S \Lambda f^\nu > \Sigma_S (Lx^\nu + z^\nu)$.

Note that Lemma A4.1 follows immediately from the aggregate employment identity, that the labor embodied in total net output equals total labor employed. (That is, $\Lambda(I - A)(x + y) = Lx + z$.)

Lemma A4.1. S is an exploited coalition if and only if S', its complement, is an exploiting coalition.

In general, there are many exploited and exploiting coalitions at a RS. It would not be correct to think of an agent as in some sense unlucky if he is a member of an arbitrary exploited coalition. For instance, the wealthiest member of society will be a member of some exploited coalition if there is an exploiting agent other than him. (Let the other exploiting agent be j; then the wealthiest agent is a member of the exploited coalition $N - \{j\}$.) This motivates us to examine *minimal* exploited coalitions: for their status as exploited coalitions depends on the presence of every member.

Definition A4.2. An agent is *vulnerable* if he is a member of some minimal exploited coalition, $\mathcal{V}^t$. An agent is *culpable* if he is a member of some minimal exploiting coalition, $\mathcal{C}^t$. $\mathcal{V} = \cup\mathcal{V}^t$ is the coalition of vulnerable agents and $\mathcal{C} = \cup\mathcal{C}^t$ is the coalition of culpable agents.

We propose to consider $\mathcal{V}$ as the "canonical exploited coalition" in the economy, and $\mathcal{C}$ as the "canonical exploiting coalition." $\mathcal{V}$ contains, of course, all the exploited individuals, but in general it contains much more. ($\mathcal{C}$ also contains all individual exploiters.) Moreover, as long as there is some exploiting coalition in society, both $\mathcal{V}$ and $\mathcal{C}$ are nonempty, even if there are no individual exploiters or exploited.

For the rest of the analysis we fix a reproducible solution; let W_N be the total wealth of the N agents in society at the RS. Let $W \leqq W_N$ be any wealth level; we define the function $\phi(W)$ as the maximal amount of labor value that can be embodied in goods at the RS, purchasable with wealth W. That is:

$$\phi(W) = \max\{\Lambda f | f \leqq (I - A)(x + y) \text{ and } pf = W\}.$$

For specificity, the function $\phi(W)$ is graphed in Figure 8 for an economy with seven agents. Various crucial levels of wealth have been named in the figure. W_n is defined as that wealth which would just allow its possessor to purchase goods from society's net output embodying n units of labor: that is $\phi(W_n) = n$. The property of ϕ crucial for the analysis is its concavity, which is obvious. For if W is small, then it can all be spent on goods which maximize the value-price ratio, Λ/p; as W grows, goods with smaller Λ/p-ratios must be purchased, and hence dollars become less efficient in purchasing labor value. Hence the concavity of ϕ. Actually, ϕ is piece-wise linear, with as many linear segments on its graph as there are goods in the economy. It is drawn smoothly since the piece-wise linearity plays no role in the analysis.

From the concavity of $\phi(W)$, it immediately follows that:

Lemma A4.2. $(W_n - W_{n-k})$ is increasing in n, for $k \leqq n$.

(This is evident from Figure 8, and its proof is immediate.)

Note the relevance of the function $\phi(W)$ for our analysis. A set S with s members is exploited if and only if the wealth of S, $W(S)$, satisfies $\phi(W(S)) < s$. Exploited individual agents are precisely those for whom $\phi(W^\nu) < 1$.

We now prove a fact which helps put together the story for the canonicality of the sets $\mathcal{C}$ and $\mathcal{V}$:

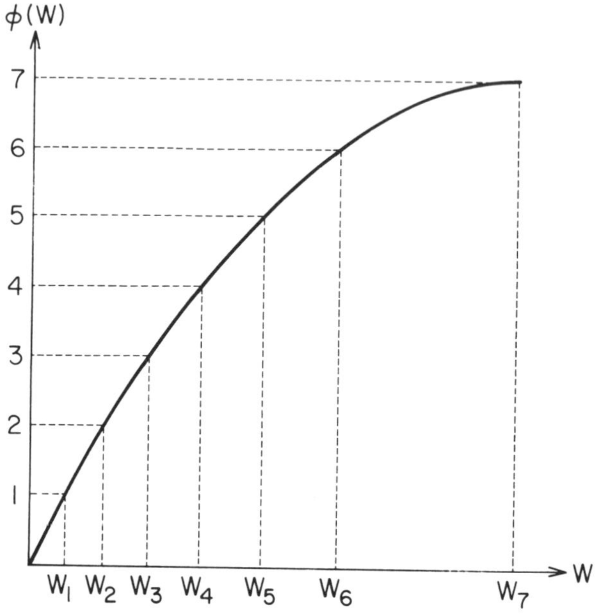

Figure 8 The function $\phi(W)$

Theorem A4.1. $\mathscr{V}$ is an exploited coalition and $\mathscr{C}$ is an exploiting coalition.

This follows from:

Lemma A4.3. Let R and S be two exploited coalitions whose intersection $R \cap S$ is not an exploited coalition. Then $R \cup S$ is an exploited coalition.

Proof. Label the sets so that $\#R \leqq \#S$. If $R \subseteq S$, we are done. If $R \cap S = \phi$ we are done since the union of disjoint exploited coalitions is exploited (this follows from Definition A4.1). Hence we may assume $R \not\subseteq S$ and $R \cap S \neq \phi$. Let $T = R \setminus S$. We have assumed $T \neq \phi$ and $T \not\subseteq R$. Let $t = \#T$, $r = \#R$, $s = \#S$.

We must show $S \cup R = S \cup T$ is an exploited set. Suppose this is false. Then:

$$W(S \cup T) \geqq W_{s+t} \tag{1}$$

where $W(S \cup T)$ means the total wealth of the coalition $S \cup T$. By definition, since S is exploited:

$$W(S) < W_s. \tag{2}$$

Now:

$$W(T) = W(S \cup T) - W(S) \tag{3}$$

since $S \cap T = \phi$ by definition of T. It follows from (1)–(3) that:

$$W(T) > W_{s+t} - W_s. \tag{4}$$

By choice, $s \geqq r$, so $s + t > r$. Hence, from Lemma A4.2:

$$W_{s+t} - W_s \geqq W_r - W_{r-t}. \tag{5}$$

From (4) and (5):

$$W(T) > W_r - W_{r-t}. \tag{6}$$

Now:

$$W(R) = W(R \setminus T) + W(T) > W(R \setminus T) + W_r - W_{r-t}. \tag{7}$$

Notice that $R \setminus T = R \setminus (R \setminus S) \equiv R \cap S$. Thus $R \setminus T$ is not an exploited coalition by hypothesis and so:

$$W(R \setminus T) \geqq W_{r-t}. \tag{8}$$

Combining (8) with (7) yields:

$$W(R) > W_r \tag{9}$$

which says that R is not an exploited coalition, which contradicts the original supposition that $S \cup R$ is not exploited. QED

Proof of Theorem A4.1. Inductive application of Lemma A4.3 to the class of minimal exploited coalitions shows that $\mathcal{V}$ is an exploited coalition. (That is, $\mathcal{V}^1 \cup \mathcal{V}^2$ is exploited; $(\mathcal{V}^1 \cup \mathcal{V}^2) \cup \mathcal{V}^3$ is exploited; and so on. This follows since a proper subset of a minimal exploited set cannot be an exploited set.) QED

The proof that $\mathcal{C}$ is an exploiting coalition is exactly the same. We must introduce the relevant dual function to $\phi(W)$, which we call $\psi(W)$. $\psi(W)$ is the minimal amount of labor power embodied in goods which can be purchased using wealth W:

$$\psi(W) = \min\{\Lambda f | f \leqq (I - A)(x + y),\ pf = W\}.$$

$\psi(W)$ is drawn in Figure 9. $\psi(W)$ is in fact a reflected image of $\phi(W)$, in this sense:

$$\phi(W_N - W) = N - \psi(W).$$

That is, if a coalition with wealth W can minimally purchase n units of embodied labor time, then its complement, with wealth $W_N - W$, can maximally purchase $N - n$ units of embodied labor time.

Application of the argument given above to the function ψ proves, in like manner, that $\mathcal{C}$ is an exploiting coalition.

We now complicate the argument by introducing another important set. Let $\{\mathcal{W}^\tau\}$ be the *maximal* exploited coalitions. We shall propose another candidate for the canonical exploited coalition: $\mathcal{W} = \bigcap \mathcal{W}^\tau$. First notice:

Lemma A4.4. The sets $\mathcal{W}^\tau$ are precisely the complements of the sets $\mathcal{C}^t$.

Proof. Let $\mathcal{W}^\tau$ be a maximal exploited coalition. Its complement $(\mathcal{W}^\tau)'$ is exploiting, by Lemma A4.1. If $(\mathcal{W}^\tau)'$ is not a minimal exploiting set, there is an agent $j \in (\mathcal{W}^\tau)'$ who can be removed, and $(\mathcal{W}^\tau)' - \{j\}$ is still exploiting. Thus by Lemma A4.1, $\mathcal{W}^\tau \cup \{j\}$ is exploited, which means that $\mathcal{W}^\tau$ is not a maximal exploited coalition. QED

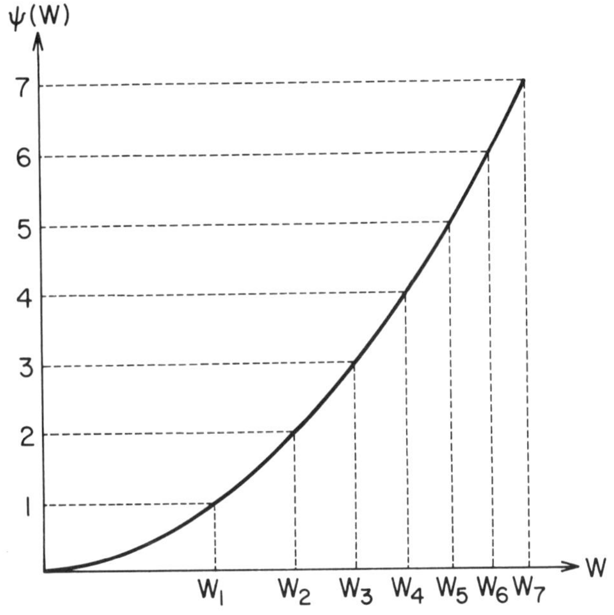

Figure 9 The function $\psi(W)$

Corollary A4.2. $\mathcal{W}$ is an exploited coalition.

Proof. $\mathcal{W} = \cap\mathcal{W}^\tau$ and so $\mathcal{W}' = \cup(\mathcal{W}^\tau)' = \cup\mathcal{C}^t = \mathcal{C}$ by Lemma A4.4. By Theorem A4.1, $\mathcal{C}$ is exploiting, and so $\mathcal{W}$ is exploited by Lemma A4.1. QED

Despite a plethora of sets, we must introduce the one missing notion. Let $\{\mathcal{D}^\tau\}$ be the maximal exploiting coalitions and $\mathcal{D} = \cap\mathcal{D}^\tau$. $\mathcal{D}$ is another candidate for a canonical exploiting set. The reasoning of Corollary 4.2 has also proved that $\mathcal{D}$ is an exploiting set, since $\mathcal{D}' = \cup\mathcal{V}^t = \mathcal{V}$.

We study next the relationship between $\mathcal{V}$ and $\mathcal{W}$. Notice that $\mathcal{V}$, as the union of minimal exploited sets, is like a "max min" and $\mathcal{W}$ is like a "min max." This motivates us to carry through this analogy, and ask whether we always have max min $\leqq$ min max, as is true of very general functions.

Theorem A4.3. $\mathcal{V} \subseteq \mathcal{W}$ and $\mathcal{C} \subseteq \mathcal{D}$ (that is, max min $\leqq$ min max).

Proof. (We need only prove that $\mathcal{V} \subseteq \mathcal{W}$. Then the second statement follows by De Morgan's laws.) We need show:

$$\cup \mathcal{V}^t \subseteq \cap \mathcal{W}^\tau$$

for which it is necessary and sufficient to show:

$$\forall t, \tau \; \mathcal{V}^t \subseteq \mathcal{W}^\tau.$$

Suppose for some t and τ, $\mathcal{V}^t \not\subseteq \mathcal{W}^\tau$. If $\mathcal{V}^t$ and $\mathcal{W}^\tau$ were disjoint, then $\mathcal{W}^\tau \cup \mathcal{V}^t$ would be an exploited set, which contradicts the maximality of $\mathcal{W}^\tau$. Hence

$$\mathcal{V}^t \cap \mathcal{W}^\tau = Q \neq \phi.$$

Since Q is a proper subset of $\mathcal{V}^t$ it is not an exploited set by the minimality of $\mathcal{V}^t$. But now Lemma A4.3 applies, and asserts that $\mathcal{V}^t \cup \mathcal{W}^\tau$ is an exploited set, which contradicts the maximality of $\mathcal{W}^\tau$. QED

Corollary A4.4. $\mathcal{V} \cap \mathcal{C} = \phi$.

Proof. Since $\mathcal{V} \subseteq \mathcal{W}$, $\mathcal{V} \cap \mathcal{W}' = \phi$. But $\mathcal{W}' = \mathcal{C}$. QED

This corollary contributes more to our story that $\mathcal{V}$ and $\mathcal{C}$ are canonical exploited and exploiting sets. No agent can be both vulnerable and culpable.

Definition A4.3. An agent j is *strongly neutral* if he is neither vulnerable nor culpable. The coalition of strongly neutral agents is called $\mathcal{S}$: $\mathcal{S} = N \setminus (\mathcal{V} \cup \mathcal{C})$.

We now ask under what conditions we have a duality theorem, that is, when is "min max $\leqq$ max min" as well?

Theorem A4.5 (duality theorem).

(a) $\mathcal{W} \setminus \mathcal{V} = \mathcal{S}$ and $\mathcal{D} \setminus \mathcal{C} = \mathcal{S}$
(b) $\mathcal{W} = \mathcal{V}$ and $\mathcal{D} = \mathcal{C}$ if and only if $\mathcal{S} = \phi$.

Proof. From Corollary A4.4, we can write the set of all agents as a pairwise disjoint union of three sets:

$$N = \mathcal{C} \cup \mathcal{V} \cup \mathcal{S}.$$

By De Morgan's laws, $\mathcal{C}' = \mathcal{W}$, and hence $\mathcal{W} = \mathcal{V} \cup \mathcal{S}$. Likewise $\mathcal{V}' = \mathcal{D}$, and so $\mathcal{D} = \mathcal{C} \cup \mathcal{S}$. This proves part (a). Part (b) follows. QED

Hence the duality theorem, "max min = min max," holds precisely when all agents are either vulnerable or culpable. In this case there is no ambiguity as to which of the sets $\mathcal{V}$ or $\mathcal{W}$ should be considered the canonical exploited set, as the two sets are identical, and the same for $\mathcal{C}$ and $\mathcal{D}$. If, however, there are some strongly neutral agents at the reproducible solution, then we may wish to identify the canonical exploited set as $\mathcal{V}$ and the canonical exploiting set as $\mathcal{C}$.

We summarize this classification of society by:

Theorem A5.6.

(A) If there is any exploited set or exploiting set of agents, then $\mathcal{V} \neq \phi \neq \mathcal{C}$.

(B) $\mathcal{V} \cup \mathcal{C} \cup \mathcal{S} = N$ is a partition of society.

(C) $\mathcal{V}$ is an exploited coalition and $\mathcal{C}$ is an exploiting coalition.

(D) $\mathcal{V}$ consists of all agents poorer than some wealth $\underline{W}$; $\mathcal{C}$ consists of all agents wealthier than $\overline{W}$; $\mathcal{S}$ consists of all agents with wealth in the interval $(\underline{W}, \overline{W})$.

Proof. (A) is a simple derivation: if there is an exploited set, then there is an exploiting set, its complement. Some subset of the first set is a minimal exploited set and some subset of the complement is a minimal exploiting set.

(B) and (C) have been proved above.

Proof of (D): Let $\underline{W}$ be the wealth of the wealthiest agent, μ, in $\mathcal{V}$ and suppose the claim is false; there is an agent $\nu \notin \mathcal{V}$ such that $W^\nu < \underline{W}$. μ is a member of some minimal exploited set $\mathcal{V}^t$. Form the set

$$Q = \mathcal{V}^t \setminus \{\mu\} \cup \{\nu\}.$$

A fortiori, Q is an exploited set, since

$$W(\mathcal{V}^t) < W_q, \text{ where } q = \#Q = \#\mathcal{V}^t,$$

and

$$W(Q) < W(\mathcal{V}^t).$$

Either Q is a minimal exploited set or it contains one. If the former, then $\nu \in \mathcal{V}$. If not, Q contains a proper minimal exploited set $\bar{Q}$; but $\bar{Q}$ must contain ν, since all other proper subsets of Q are proper subsets of $\mathcal{V}^t$, and hence are not exploited sets. Hence in any case ν is vulnerable. QED

We have shown there is some inherent ambiguity in the exploitation status of members of society in the sense that there may be strongly neutral agents. It is natural to ask if there is any sense in which the set $\mathcal{S}$ can be ignored. For instance, we might be justified in ignoring the set $\mathcal{S}$ if we could show that as economies become large, the set of strongly neutral agents becomes small. Unfortunately (or not), this is not so. The following example shows that we can construct an economy with N members, $N - 2$ of whom are strongly neutral.[7]

An *economy* for these purposes is specified by the function $\phi(W)$. (Any increasing, concave, piece-wise linear function with $\phi(0) = 0$ and $\phi(W_N) = N$ can be the ϕ-function associated with some reproducible solution of some economy). The example is best comprehended by referring to Figure 8. We have an economy with seven agents. We given them wealths:

$$W^1 = W_1$$
$$W^2 = W_2 - W_1$$
$$W^3 = W_3 - W_2$$
$$\vdots$$
$$W^7 = W_7 - W_6.$$

7. The example is due to R. E. Howe.

Now make the first agent a little poorer, and the last a little richer:

$$W^1 = W_1 - \epsilon$$
$$W^\nu = W_\nu - W_{\nu-1} \quad \text{for } \nu = 2, \ldots, 6$$
$$W^7 = W_7 - W_6 + \epsilon.$$

Observe that all exploited coalitions contain agent 1. In fact, the exploited sets are simply: {1}, {1, 2}, {1, 2, 3}, . . . , {1, 2, 3, 4, 5, 6}, since the wealth of the jth set in that sequence is $W_j - \epsilon$. It is easily verified that any other set is too rich to be exploited. Consequently there is only one minimal exploited set: {1}. Then 1 is the only vulnerable agent. A similar argument shows that 7 is the only culpable agent. Thus 2, . . . , 6 are strongly neutral. Clearly this construction works for an economy with N agents. Furthermore, there is an open neighborhood of this distribution in wealth space which preserves the result of $N - 2$ strongly neutral agents, so this is not a singular example.

There is a second way in which one might hope strongly neutral could be ignored. If the addition (or subtraction) of strongly neutral agents to (or from) a set of agents never changed the exploitation status of that set, then we would be justified in treating the strongly neutral agents as irrelevant from the point of view of exploitation. In fact, such is the case for the example just given. Nevertheless, the contention is false, in general. To see this, consider an economy with four agents, where wealths are assigned thus:

$$W^1 = W_1 - \epsilon$$
$$W^2 = (W_2 - W_1) + \epsilon$$
$$W^3 = (W_3 - W_2) - \epsilon$$
$$W^4 = (W_4 - W_3) + \epsilon.$$

The exploited coalitions are {1} and {1, 2, 3}. Hence $\mathscr{V} = \{1\}$. The exploiting sets are {2, 3, 4} and {4}. Hence $\mathscr{C} = \{4\}$. Thus $\mathscr{S} = \{2, 3\}$. But {1, 2} is a neutral set. Thus the augmentation of the exploited set {1} with the strongly neutral agent 2 changes the exploitation status of that set. Consequently, it does not appear there is any sense in which the strongly neutral agents can be ignored.

What the analysis of the section has shown is that in general the gray area can be whittled down a good deal. We can first of all discard those exploiting and exploited agents who are in the gray area because of the transformation problem; we can then distinguish vulnerable agents and culpable agents in the gray area—agents who are individually neutral, but belong to minimal exploited or exploiting sets. After taking them out, the grayest of the gray area remains, the strongly neutral agents.

Note that the key result in developing the theory of vulnerable sets is Lemma A4.3, which depended on the concavity of the function $\phi(W)$.

In summary, Theorem A4.6 allows us to maintain that the correct general criterion is not whether an individual is exploited or exploiting, but whether he is vulnerable or culpable. According to that theorem, as long as exploitation exists at a RS (which is to say, as long as there is at least one exploited coalition), then there are vulnerable and culpable agents (although not necessarily exploited and exploiting ones). Furthermore, no agent is both vulnerable and culpable, a result which depends on the concavity of $\phi(W)$.

The analysis of this appendix is not simply a curiosus; it has a broader application in allowing us to capture, in Chapter 7, a game-theoretic characterization of exploitation in economies with increasing returns.

5

The Dependence of Labor Value on the Market

1. A summary of the idea

Up to this point we have assumed that producers have access to a special technology, a Leontief point-input point-output matrix, in which each good is produced by precisely one process. There are no joint products; there is no substitution between factors. One might naturally inquire whether our basic result, the Class Exploitation Correspondence Principle, is true under the assumption of a more general technology. Can we even define class and exploitation in the presence of a more general production set? In this chapter we assume only that the production set is a convex cone; this models the assumption of constant returns to scale, and permits us to incorporate assumptions of joint production, fixed capital, differential turnover times of processes, substitution between factors, and so on. In Marxian work, it has become not unusual to generalize theorems which are true in the Leontief context to the general activity analysis model. One should note that our assumption in this chapter of a production set which is a convex cone includes the activity analysis model as a special case.

Once we properly set up the model, we will prove the Class Exploitation Correspondence Principle for the general conical technology. This verifies that the correspondence is robust, and not an artifact of the special Leontief assumptions. If that were the only purpose of the argument following, however, I think it would deserve only appendix status. The elevation of this material to chapter status derives from a surprise, and remarkable resolution of that surprise, which we encounter in trying to prove the CECP for the conical technology.

The surprise is this. The first chore facing us under the assumption of a general conical production set is to define the concept of labor value embodied in a commodity bundle, so that we can define exploited and exploiting producers. (Recall how exploitation was defined in the previous chapter.) There is an accepted way of doing this for the von Neumann activity analysis model, introduced by Morishima (1973, 1974), and extended to a general convex production set in Roemer (1980a, 1981). Up to this point, this generalization of the definition of labor value has been accepted as the appropriate definition for activity analysis or convex production sets, as it appears reasonable, and preserves the main analytic result of the received theory, the so-called Fundamental Marxian Theorem, that exploitation is equivalent to profit-making (for discussion, see Morishima, 1973, Roemer, 1981, or Steedman, 1977). The rub, however, is that if we use the received definition of labor value embodied, the CECP is false for the cone (or even the activity analysis) technology!

Are we to conclude that the CECP is a fragile idea which fails as soon as we introduce, for instance, fixed capital? An alternative to this resolution is to ask whether, perhaps, our *model* of exploitation is incorrect for the cone technology. As will be shown below, if we adopt another definition of labor value embodied for the general cone technology, which is also a generalization of the definition of labor values $\Lambda = L(I - A)^{-1}$ of the Leontief model, then the CECP is true.

This resolution is not simply a mechanical one; something important is learned about the logical status of the labor value concept from the choice of definition we must make to preserve the theorem. Here is a summary. To calculate the former, received definition of labor value embodied, consider a bundle of commodities c, a vector. Scan the entire production set for ways of producing c as a *net* output. Among all such ways of producing c, there is one which minimizes *direct* labor input. Define the labor value embodied in c as that amount of labor. (Notice that although we have defined the labor value embodied in c as a certain amount of direct labor, it is direct labor used to produce c as a *net* output, and so it captures the *embodied* labor, direct and indirect, in producing c from scratch, as it were.) Consider now the alternative definition of labor value embodied which must be adopted to prove the CECP. Instead of scanning the production set for *all* processes which can produce c as net output, limit the scan to those processes which are in fact maximally profitable *at the going equilibrium prices.* The only candidates for feasible ways of producing c, in our attempt to determine its labor content, are those processes which capitalists would be willing to operate, at the equilibrium prices.

Perhaps it is clarifying to present these two definitions in the context of the activity analysis model with which readers are familiar. Let the technology be specified $(B, A; L)$ where B is an $n \times m$ commodity output matrix, A is an $n \times m$ commodity input matrix, and L is a $1 \times m$ vector of direct labor inputs. (There are n goods and m processes.) Let c be an $n \times 1$ vector of commodities. Then the received (Morishima) definition of the labor value embodied in c is given by the solution to this program:

$$\left.\begin{array}{ll} \quad \text{choose } x^* \text{ to min } Lx & \\ \text{such that} & \\ \quad (B - A)\, x \geqq c & (1.1) \\ \quad x \geqq 0 & \\ \quad \text{Define l.v.}(c) \equiv Lx^* & \end{array}\right\} \text{Definition 1}$$

In Definition 1, x can be any activity vector which permits c to be produced as a net output, as we see from (1.1).

For the alternative definition, let (p, w) be the equilibrium prices. Define labor value of c by the solution to this program:

$$\left.\begin{array}{ll} \quad \text{choose } x' \text{ to min } Lx & \\ \text{such that} & \\ \quad (B - A)\, x \geqq c & (2.1) \\ \quad pBx = (1 + \pi)pAx + wLx & (2.2) \\ \quad x \geqq 0 & \\ \quad \text{Define l.v.}(c) = Lx' & \end{array}\right\} \text{Definition 2}$$

Definition 2 directs us to consider only activity vectors x which operate the processes achieving the maximal profit rate π. The price vector satisfies, by definition of π:

$$pB \leqq (1 + \pi)pA + wL;$$

together with (2.2), this implies that a component x_i' of x' can be positive only if process i achieves the maximal profit rate π; that is, only if

$$pB_i = (1 + \pi)pA_i + wL_i.$$

Notice that both Definitions 1 and 2 are generalizations of the standard definition of labor value in the Leontief environment; for equilibrium prices in the Leontief case equalize the rate of profit across all sectors so that restriction (2.2) of Definition 2 is no restriction at all. Thus both definitions are identical for Leontief technology, and both define l.v.(c) as Λc where $\Lambda = L(I - A)^{-1}$.

What is the significance of the fact that the CECP is true if Definition 2 is adopted, but false if Definition 1 is taken as the definition of labor value in the case of the activity analysis, or conical, technology? Notice that in Definition 1 the labor value of a commodity bundle is independent of prices; it is solely a function of the technology. In Definition 2, however, labor value depends on equilibrium prices. One cannot define the labor embodied in commodities until one knows what the market equilibrium is. In general, there may be several equilibria, or reproducible price vectors, for our accumulation economy. The amount of labor embodied in c depends on which one we are in. This is not determined by the data of the economy, in particular, by the technology. Equilibrium prices must be known before labor value can be said to exist.

One can now see the importance of this result for a classical debate in Marxian value theory concerning the relative priority of prices versus labor values. It has been an aspect of what some call the orthodox or fundamentalist position in Marxian economics to claim that labor values exist "logically prior" to equilibrium prices in the hierarchy of concepts in economic theory. Labor values are the phenomenon and prices the epiphenomenon. In an attack on the fundamentalist position, Steedman (1977) argued that labor values do not precede prices, but prices and values have a common ancestor—the technology and real wage. What the present argument implies is that one must take a position even more heretical from the point of view of fundamentalist orthodoxy: labor values and prices do not have a common ancestor; rather, prices precede values. One cannot define labor value until one knows equilibrium prices.[1]

In fact—and this is a secondary point for our purposes—even more general definitions than Definition 2 for labor value will suffice to prove the CECP. We need not insist on labor minimization.[2] Let $X(c)$ be the set of activity levels which produce c efficiently as a net output using only profitable processes:

$$X(c) = \{x \geqq 0 \mid \quad \text{(i)} \quad (B - A)x \geqq c$$
$$\text{(ii)} \quad pBx = (1 + \pi)pAx + wLx$$
$$\text{(iii)} \quad \nexists x' \text{ satisfying (i) and (ii) for which } (B - A)x \geq (B - A)x'\}$$

Any systematic way for choosing a vector $x^* \in X(c)$, and defining l.v.(c) as Lx^*, will maintain the CECP. The labor-minimizing way is only one convenient, systematic procedure for choosing a labor-evaluating activity vector from $X(c)$ to define l.v.(c).

With ex post wit, it is possible to see why Definition 2 provides a philosophically more satisfactory generalization of the "socially necessary labor" concept than Definition 1. Marx makes the point that labor value is a concept which arises with capitalist production—commodity production more generally, perhaps—but not with production in general. Value is a concept which adheres to goods produced in capitalist production, not simply goods as such. This distinction is nicely captured by the distinction between Definitions 1 and 2. In Definition 1, value is a completely technological concept; in Definition 2, we take account of the specifically capitalist imperative that the only socially feasible processes are ones which bring the going rate of profit. Thus, labor value as defined by Definition 2 is socially necessary labor, given capitalist relations of production; Definition 1 provides us with a technological definition of labor value

1. It should be pointed out that Steedman had a glimmer of this idea in his book (1977, p. 65) but did not see its full implications, as he did not revise Morishima's Definition 1 of labor value embodied in the von Neumann technology; nor did I. It only became possible to see the full implications of this idea with the development of the analysis of the correspondence between exploitation and class.

2. I am indebted to Birgit Grodal for raising an astute question which gave rise to this observation.

which is independent of the social relations of production. In this sense, Definition 2 seems superior from the classical point of view that value is a concept which specifically adheres to commodities produced under capitalist relations of production. This classical point is reinforced, since the present theory of class and exploitation directs us to choose Definition 2 as the appropriate one.

It is worthwhile summarizing the epistemological nature of this argument, for it is an example of how formal model building can convey genuinely new information about our conceptualization of reality. (Often, model building allows us to verify intuitions in a formal manner, but does not convey new information.) We begin with a certain intuitive theory of an aspect of social life, namely, that class corresponds to exploitation status in the manner we have described: compulsory labor hirers are exploiters and compulsory labor sellers are exploited. We verify this intuition by constructing models of the theory developed in Chapters 2 through 4. (For my usage of the terms *theory* and *model,* see the introduction to Roemer, 1981). In trying to verify the theory in a more general model, we run into a roadblock; the formal verification of the theory fails. A first response might be to decide that the theory has only a limited validity, that an intuition about the world is simplistic and, at its heart, incorrect. But such a response presupposes that our model of the theory is correct; perhaps our formal model can be changed. Our intuitive faith in the theory directs us to explore ways of modifying the model which will allow us to preserve the theory. In so exploring, we discover a new construction of the model which does, indeed, make the theory formally true. This in turn directs us to new insights concerning the correct relationships among the conceptual terms of our model—in this case, labor value and price. Thus, we learn that labor value cannot be conceived of as existing logically prior to prices, but rather it must be the other way around, if we wish to verify our intuition of the relationship between exploitation and class.

Although the formal version of the Class Exploitation Correspondence Principle emerges as a *theorem* of the model, in fact its epistemological role in our understanding is as a *postulate*. We seek a model which will make our postulated belief true. Guided by this postulate, we learn something about what the formal model must look like, and hence something about the logical relationship of our primitive terms. While we used Marxian value theory to conceive of and prove the CECP, now the CECP directs us to an extension of our understanding of Marxian value theory. An astute observer faced with the a priori choice between Definitions 1 and 2 for the definition of labor values might intuitively prefer Definition 2; but only with an analytical result like the CECP would he be compelled to choose that definition as the correct one.[3] And this choice, of course, is one which cannot possibly be made at the level of resolution of the theory represented by the Leontief model.[4]

In the next section the CECP is proved for a general cone technology. In section 3 I reconstruct the proof of the theorem for the special case of the von Neumann technology. Readers who are comfortable with the model of a production set as a convex cone may skip section 3, and readers who are more comfortable with the von Neumann model may get their mathematics from section 3, although the model is more fully developed in section 2. Finally, section 4 presents more evidence that Definition 2 provides the "correct" notion of embodied labor time in the von Neumann model, by examining the concept of compounded dated labor that is implied by it.

2. The model of production and accumulation for a cone technology

A. Reproducible solutions

Let P be the production set, which is assumed to be a convex cone.[5] P has elements of the form $\alpha = (-\alpha_0;\ -\underline{\alpha};\ \overline{\alpha})$ where $\alpha_0 \in \mathbb{R}_+$, $\underline{\alpha} \in \mathbb{R}^n_+$, $\overline{\alpha} \in \mathbb{R}^n_+$. Thus, elements of P are vectors in $\mathbb{R}^{2n+1}$. The first compo-

3. Thus, we are effectively proving a definition. For a beautiful discussion of proof-generated definitions, and the Platonic pedagogy which obscures how this strategy is central to the development of mathematical ideas, see Lakatos (1976).

4. More generally, however, we may think of the particular Leontief technology (A, L) which is operated as being chosen from a book of blueprints consisting of many techniques. (A, L) is the technique which maximizes profits at going prices. Hence, even in the Leontief model, the evaluation of labor value must be restricted to profit-maximizing processes, for in general some nonprofitable technique might assign a lower labor content to some commodity bundle. If we admit, then, of the existence of other unused techniques, then the price-dependent definition of labor value must be adopted even when the only observable technique is Leontief. I thank Paul Rhode for this observation.

5. Marxian value theory, where the production set is assumed to be only convex, is developed in Roemer (1980a). The material presented there is not necessary for this section, although it might aid in comprehension.

nent, $-\alpha_0$, is the direct labor input of the process α; the next n components, $-\underline{\alpha}$, are the inputs of goods used in the process; and the last n components, $\overline{\alpha}$, are the outputs of the n goods from the process. We denote the net output vector arising from α as $\hat{\alpha} \equiv \overline{\alpha} - \underline{\alpha}$. We assume that P is a closed convex cone containing the origin in $\mathbb{R}^{2n+1}$. Another assumption is needed later.

We specify the program for the individual accumulator, which is the generalization of program (1.1) of Chapter 4. The price vector is $(p, 1)$. (We may avoid the case where the wage is zero without problem, so we normalize setting the wage equal to unity.) The producer ν chooses a vector $\alpha = (-\alpha_0, -\underline{\alpha}, \overline{\alpha})$ which he operates himself, a vector $\beta = (-\beta_0, -\underline{\beta}, \beta)$ which he hires others to operate using his capital, and a scalar of labor time sold, γ_0. (We omit the superscripts ν from these three vectors for clarity.) His program is:

$$\left.\begin{aligned}&\max\ [p(\overline{\alpha} - \underline{\alpha})] + [p(\overline{\beta} - \underline{\beta}) - \beta_0] + [\gamma_0]\\ &\text{such that}\\ &p\underline{\alpha} + p\underline{\beta} \leqq p\omega^\nu \equiv W^\nu\\ &\gamma_0 + \alpha_0 \leqq 1\\ &\alpha, \beta \in P; \quad \gamma_0 \geqq 0\end{aligned}\right\} \qquad \text{(P5)}$$

That is, ν maximizes revenues subject to his capital constraint and labor constraint. The three bracketed terms in the maximand are the revenues from operating his own shop, hiring others, and selling labor power, respectively.

The definition of a reproducible solution is simply a translation of Definition 4.1 of Chapter 4 into the new notation, that is:

Definition 5.1. A price vector $(p, 1)$ is a *reproducible solution* for the economy $(P; \omega^1, \omega^2, \ldots, \omega^N)$ with N producers if:

(R1) $(\forall\nu)(\exists(\alpha^\nu; \beta^\nu; \gamma_0^\nu) \in \mathscr{A}^\nu(p, 1))$ (profit maximization) where $\mathscr{A}^\nu(p, 1)$ is the set of optimal solutions to ν's program (P5)

(R2) $\underline{\alpha} + \underline{\beta} \leqq \omega$ (feasibility of production) where $\underline{\alpha} = \Sigma_\nu\, \underline{\alpha}^\nu$, $\underline{\beta} = \Sigma_\nu\, \underline{\beta}^\nu$

(R3) $\gamma_0 = \beta_0$ (labor market equilibrium) where $\gamma_0 = \Sigma_\nu\, \gamma_0^\nu$ and $\beta_0 = \Sigma_\nu\, \beta_0^\nu$

(R4) $\hat{\alpha} + \hat{\beta} \geqq 0$ (reproducibility) where $\hat{\alpha} = \Sigma_\nu\, (\overline{\alpha}^\nu - \underline{\alpha}^\nu)$, $\hat{\beta} = \Sigma_\nu\, (\overline{\beta}^\nu - \underline{\beta}^\nu)$

B. Class division of society

At a given price vector $(p, 1)$, an agent optimizes by choosing an action $(\alpha, \beta; \gamma_0)$, which can be displayed as a vector in $\mathbb{R}^{4n+3}$. As before, we consider an agent as enjoying a certain *class position*, according to whether he possesses an optimal solution with α, β, or γ_0 zero or nonzero vectors. For example, if he possesses a solution of the form $(\alpha; 0; \gamma_0)$ with $\alpha \neq 0 \neq \gamma_0$, then we say he belongs to the class $(+; 0; +)$.

The class characterization of society is developed in the same manner as in Lemma 4.1 and section 1 of Chapter 4.

Lemma 5.1. Every agent has an optimal solution to his program (P5) of form $(0; \beta; \gamma_0)$, if he has any optimal solution at prices $(p, 1)$. (Note: This is the analog of Lemma 4.1.)

Proof. Let $(\alpha, \beta, \gamma_0)$ be a solution to (P5) for our agent. Define a new solution by:

$$\alpha' = 0$$
$$\beta' = \beta + \alpha$$
$$\gamma' = \gamma_0 + \alpha_0 .$$

It is easily checked that $(\alpha'; \beta'; \gamma')$ is a feasible solution to (P5), generating the same revenue as $(\alpha, \beta, \gamma_0)$, and so it is optimal. QED

Definition 5.2. Let $\alpha = (-\alpha_0, -\underline{\alpha}, \overline{\alpha}) \in P$, and let prices $(p, 1)$ rule. Then the *profit rate* at α is defined as $\pi(\alpha, p) = (p\hat{\alpha} - \alpha_0)/p\underline{\alpha}$.

It is clear that if $(p, 1)$ supports a reproducible solution, the profit rates of points in P must be bounded—or else producers would not be able to choose optimal solutions. By closedness of P, a *maximal profit rate* is attained in P, which we call $\pi^{\max}$.

Corrollary 5.2. At an optimal solution to (P5), agent ν's revenue is $\pi^{\max}W^{\nu} + 1$.

Proof. By Lemma 5.1, ν has an optimal solution of the form $(0, \beta, \gamma_0)$. Since the wage is positive, $\gamma_0 = 1$. (The agent must work all day to maximize revenue.) The revenues from hiring others, received by ν, are maximally $\pi^{\max}W^{\nu}$, by definition of $\pi(\alpha, p)$. Hence his revenue at $(0, \beta, \gamma_0)$ must be $\pi^{\max}W^{\nu} + 1$. QED

Theorem 5.1. At a RS with $\pi^{\max} > 0$, the class division of society is precisely as in Theorem 4.4; that is:

(A) $\nu \in (+, +, 0)\setminus(+, 0, 0) \Leftrightarrow \forall$ individually optimal solutions of form $(0, \beta^\nu, \gamma_0)$, $\beta_0^\nu > 1$

(B) $\nu \in (+, 0, 0) \Leftrightarrow \exists$ an individually optimal solution of form $(0, \beta^\nu, \gamma_0^\nu)$, $\beta_0^\nu = 1$

(C) $\nu \in (+, 0, +)\setminus(+, 0, 0) \Leftrightarrow \forall$ individually optimal solutions of form $(0, \beta^\nu, \gamma_0^\nu)$, $\beta_0^\nu < 1$ and $W^\nu > 0$

(D) $\nu \in (0, 0, +) \Leftrightarrow W^\nu \equiv p\omega^\nu = 0$

Proof. Same as Theorem 4.4; employ Lemma 5.1. QED

We proceed to characterize class membership in terms of agents' wealth. Recall the definitions:

C^H = the class of producers $(+, +, 0)\setminus(+, 0, 0)$
C^{PB} = the class of producers $(+, 0, 0)$
C^S = the class of producers $(+, 0, +)\setminus(+, 0, 0)$
C^P = the class of producers $(0, 0, +)$

Theorem 5.2. In this model, Theorem 4.6 holds. When $\pi^{\max} > 0$:

$$\nu \in C^H \Leftrightarrow W^\nu > \max_{\beta \in \bar{P}} \left[\frac{p\beta}{\beta_0}\right]$$

$$\nu \in C^{PB} \Leftrightarrow \min_{\beta \in \bar{P}} \left[\frac{p\beta}{\beta_0}\right] \leqq W^\nu \leqq \max_{\beta \in \bar{P}} \left[\frac{p\beta}{\beta_0}\right]$$

$$\nu \in C^S \Leftrightarrow 0 < W^\nu < \min_{\beta \in \bar{P}} \left[\frac{p\beta}{\beta_0}\right]$$

$$\nu \in C^P \Leftrightarrow W^\nu = 0$$

where $\bar{P} = \{\beta \in P | \pi(\beta, p) = \pi^{\max}\}$ is the set of profit-maximizing processes. Note the qualification of Theorem 4.6. Here, the minimization and maximization of the "capital-wages ratio" is taken over only those activities in P which achieve the maximal profit rate. In the Leontief model, *all* activities achieve the maximal profit rate at a reproducible solution, and so this distinction was not evident.

Proof of Theorem 5.2. We wish to characterize the wealths associated with class membership (+; 0; 0). Note, according to the construction of Lemma 5.1, that ν possesses an optimal solution of form (+; 0; 0) if and only if he has a solution of form (0; β; 1) with $\beta_0 = 1$. Compute $(p\underline{\beta}/\beta_0)_{\min}$ and $(p\underline{\beta}/\beta_0)_{\max}$ where β ranges over $\overline{P}$. (It does no harm if the max is infinite.) If

$$\min_{\beta\in\overline{P}}\left[\frac{p\underline{\beta}}{\beta_0}\right] \leqq W^{\nu} \leqq \max_{\beta\in\overline{P}}\left[\frac{p\underline{\beta}}{\beta_0}\right], \tag{1}$$

then by convexity of $\overline{P}$, there is a process in $\overline{P}$, call it β, such that $p\underline{\beta}/\beta_0 = W^{\nu}$. The ray through β belongs to $\overline{P}$, since P and $\overline{P}$ are cones. Hence ν can invest all his wealth in some process along the β ray, and he will thereby hire one unit of labor. That is, ν chooses a multiple of β, call it $t\beta$, in which he invests all his wealth:

$$tp\underline{\beta} = W^{\nu}.$$

It follows that $t\beta_0 = 1$.

But with choice of activity $t\beta$, ν will make revenues $\pi^{\max}W^{\nu} + 1$ at action (0; $t\beta$; 1), since $t\beta \in \overline{P}$. It follows by the second sentence of this proof that $\nu \in$ (+; 0; 0). The converse—that $\nu \in$ (+; 0; 0) implies W^{ν} lies in the appropriate interval—follows in like manner by consideration of Lemma 5.1.

The proof of the other parts of the theorem follow quickly, as in Theorem 4.6. QED

C. Exploitation

To define exploitation in terms of surplus value, we must first define the *labor value* of a vector of commodities. Our definition of labor value shall depend, in part, on the particular equilibrium the economy is in. Let $c \in \mathbb{R}^n_+$ be a vector of produced commodities. Let

$$\phi(c; p) = \{\alpha \in \overline{P} \mid \hat{\alpha} \geqq c\}.$$

$\phi(c; p)$ is the set of those profit-rate-maximizing actions which produce, as net output vectors, at least c. The dependence of ϕ on p is through the profit-maximizing set $\overline{P}$.

Definition 5.3. The labor value of c is:

$$\text{l.v.}(c) \equiv \min\{\alpha_0 | (-\alpha_0, -\underline{\alpha}, \overline{\alpha}) \in \phi(c; p)\}.$$

The labor value of c, or "socially necessary labor time to produce c," is the smallest amount of direct labor which must be employed to produce at least c as net output, *using only profit-maximizing activities.* Definition 5.3 is the version of Definition 2, section 1 of this chapter, for the cone technology. By convexity and closedness of $\overline{P}$, and the assumption that $0 \in P$, it can be shown that l.v.(c) is well defined if $\phi(c; p)$ is not empty (see Roemer, 1980a, for the argument).

What is special about this definition is that in computing socially necessary labor time we restrict our search for labor-cheap ways of producing c to processes which are earning the maximal profit rate—that is, to processes which capitalists would *in fact* operate at the equilibrium prices $(p, 1)$. It is a consequence of Lemma 5.1 that no point in P achieving a profit rate less than $\pi^{\max}$ will be chosen by any agent, either to operate on his own or to operate with hired labor. Thus, in fact, the only processes we will observe at the reproducible solution are processes in $\overline{P}$, and we define these observable processes as the universe for the computation of socially necessary labor time. In the definition of labor value in Morishima (1974) and Roemer (1980a), no such restriction was put on the universe: rather, labor minimizing was done over the larger set $\phi(c)$:

$$\phi(c) = \{\alpha \in P | \hat{\alpha} \geqq c\}.$$

This distinction involves the conception of what constitutes socially necessary labor. The labor value of a bundle will in general be greater defined over the restricted set $\phi(c; p)$ than over $\phi(c)$. Moreover, in general labor value will change with different reproducible price vectors. There are two formal justifications for choosing the restricted set $\phi(c; p)$ as an appropriate universe for defining labor value. First, both the definition using $\phi(c; p)$ and the one using $\phi(c)$ are generalizations of labor value in the Leontief model, because *all* processes enjoy the maximal profit rate at a reproducible solution in the indecomposable Leontief model. Secondly, the Fundamental Marxian Theorem continues to hold using the $\phi(c; p)$ definition.[6]

6. This can be checked by reading through the proof of Theorem 3.1 in Roemer (1980a), substituting the new definition. An assumption of independence of production, like Assumption 7 of that paper, must be made concerning the restricted production set $\overline{P}$.

There appears therefore to be no formal reason to prefer the $\phi(c)$ generalization of labor value for the cone model to the $\phi(c; p)$ generalization.

In fact, as has been argued, the $\phi(c; p)$ definition seems a priori preferable. For socially necessary labor time embodied in a bundle c, under Definition 5.3, is the amount of labor time *actually* embodied in c, if c were to be produced by capitalists choosing processes guided by today's prices. The socially necessary labor time of the $\phi(c)$ definition cannot be realized at today's prices, for in general, capitalists would have to operate some inferior processes to achieve it. In addition, under the $\phi(c; p)$ definition, *labor values are themselves a function of prices,* as the set $\bar{P}$ is a function of prices.

The reader should perhaps be reminded that the CECP shall be true under the definition of labor values via $\phi(c; p)$ but false under the $\phi(c)$ definition. Thus, if we take the CECP as a basic Marxian principle, then we are directed to adopt the $\phi(c; p)$ definition as the preferred or "correct" one. This is perhaps the strongest argument that has been made for the dependence of labor value phenomena on the market.

It must be remarked that under Definition 5.3, l.v.(c) is not in general defined for all bundles c; it is defined only for those bundles which are producible at prices $(p, 1)$, that is, for which $\phi(c; p)$ is nonempty. Conceptually, this is appropriate: goods which are not *commodities,* that is, which capitalists will not produce, have no labor value. Labor value is not the labor time embodied in the production of goods in general, but in the production of goods for the market. This also fits nicely with classical Marxian ideas, that value is a phenomenon associated with commodity production specifically, not a technological phenomenon.[7]

The definition of exploitation is the same as in Chapter 4. We define a *feasible assignment* as any distribution of aggregate net output, $\hat{\alpha} + \hat{\beta}$ at the reproducible solution, to producers so that each producer is assigned a bundle of goods he can just afford. A producer is exploited if the maximum labor value embodied in his assigned

7. Another price-dependent definition of labor value in the context of the von Neumann model has been independently developed by Flaschel (1980). He examines the *square* matrices of input and output coefficients defined by the processes in the von Neumann technology which are maximally profitable at a particular equilibrium, and defines additive labor values with reference to this system. I believe my general proof of the CECP in this chapter will apply with Flaschel's definition, as well.

bundle, maximized over all feasible assignments, is less than the time he worked, which is unity; he is an exploiter if the minimal labor value embodied in his assigned bundles is greater than one. Otherwise, he is a neutral agent in the gray area. Summarizing:

Definition 5.4. Let $(p, 1)$ support a reproducible solution with net output $\hat{\alpha} + \hat{\beta}$. A *feasible assignment* is any collection of nonnegative vectors $\{f^\nu\}$ such that:

(i) $\Sigma f^\nu = \hat{\alpha} + \hat{\beta}$
(ii) $pf^\nu = \Pi^\nu (p, 1)$ for all ν.

The class of feasible assignments is $\mathcal{F}$, and the set of bundles assigned to ν in $\mathcal{F}$ is $\mathcal{F}^\nu$. A producer ν is exploited if and only if:

$$\max_{f^\nu \in \mathcal{F}^\nu} \text{l.v.}(f^\nu) < 1$$

and ν is an exploiter if and only if:

$$\min_{f^\nu \in \mathcal{F}^\nu} \text{l.v.}(f^\nu) > 1.$$

We next assume, as in Chapter 4:

Assumption of a Large Economy (ALE). For any agent ν and any good i, there exists a feasible assignment in which ν receives a bundle consisting of only good i. That is, net output of every good is sufficiently large that every agent can spend his entire revenue on any good.

We now characterize the wealth levels of exploiters and exploited. Agent ν has revenue $\pi^{\max}W^\nu + 1$. To ascertain whether he is an exploiter, we shall assign him a bundle of goods, under a feasible assignment, which minimizes the labor value he can buy with his revenue. If that labor value exceeds one, then he is an exploiter. Consider the set of all commodity bundles of labor value unity:

$$\theta = \{c \in \mathbb{R}^n_+ | \text{l.v.}(c) = 1\}.$$

Let

$$\theta^* = \{\alpha \in \bar{P} | (\exists c \in \theta) \ (\hat{\alpha} \geqq c \text{ and } \alpha_0 = 1)\}.$$

That is, θ is the set of commodity bundles of unit labor value and θ^* is the collection of processes in $\bar{P}$ which generate the bundles in θ, using one unit of direct labor input. An additional assumption we now require on P is:

Assumption NFL (no free lunch). Any semipositive net output vector from activities in P requires labor input:

$$\alpha \in P, \quad \hat{\alpha} \geq 0 \Rightarrow \alpha_0 > 0.$$

Under the NFL assumption and the convexity of $\bar{P}$, a standard argument shows that θ is bounded; it is also closed, and hence compact. Thus pc achieves a maximum and minimum value on θ.

Let $\tilde{c} \in \theta$ be such that $p\tilde{c}$ is maximal over θ:

$$p\tilde{c} \geqq pc, \quad \forall c \in \theta$$

and $\underset{\sim}{c} \in \theta$ such that:

$$p\underset{\sim}{c} \leqq pc, \quad \forall c \in \theta.$$

Since θ is the set of commodity bundles of labor value unity, $\tilde{c}$ is that bundle which maximizes price per unit of labor value. Purchasing $\tilde{c}$ is the least efficient way of commanding labor value through the goods one buys. Hence, if our agent ν spends all his revenue on a bundle proportional to $\tilde{c}$, and still commands more than one unit of labor, he is an exploiter.

Thus, ν is an exploiter if and only if:

$$\pi^{\max} W^{\nu} + 1 > p\tilde{c}. \tag{2}$$

This says he can purchase more than one unit of bundle $\tilde{c}$, and hence command more than one unit of labor, even when he commands embodied labor in the least efficient way. Note the use of ALE: we need to know there is enough of every good produced that ν can spend his money on goods in the required proportions. As long as ν can spend all his revenue on any one good, he can also spend all his revenue on a bundle of goods in any given proportions; consequently he could spend it all purchasing some multiple of $\tilde{c}$ or $\underset{\sim}{c}$. In like manner, ν is exploited if and only if:

$$\pi^{\max} W^{\nu} + 1 < p\underset{\sim}{c}. \tag{3}$$

Thus:

$$\nu \text{ is an exploiter} \Leftrightarrow W^\nu > (p\tilde{c} - 1)/\pi^{\max}. \tag{2'}$$

$$\nu \text{ is exploited} \Leftrightarrow W^\nu < (p\underset{\sim}{c} - 1)/\pi^{\max}. \tag{3'}$$

We have just proved the analog of Theorem 4.3.

D. The CECP

Theorem 5.3 (CECP). Let $(p, 1)$ be a reproducible solution and let ALE hold. Then:

(A) Every member of C^H is an exploiter.
(B) Every member of $C^S \cup C^P$ is exploited.

Proof. The proof follows the same format as Theorem 4.7. We must simply compare the wealth characterization of exploitation from inequalities (2′) and (3′) with the wealth characterization of class membership from inequality (1).

We show the first statement of the theorem; the proof of the second is identical. To verify the first statement, it is necessary and sufficient to show, by Theorem 5.2 and (2′), that:

$$W^\nu > \max_{\beta \in \overline{P}} \left(\frac{p\underline{\beta}}{\beta_0}\right) \Rightarrow W^\nu > (p\tilde{c} - 1)/\pi^{\max}$$

or

$$\max_{\beta \in \overline{P}} \left(\frac{p\underline{\beta}}{\beta_0}\right) \geqq (p\tilde{c} - 1)/\pi^{\max}. \tag{4}$$

Since $\overline{P}$ is a cone, we may normalize the left hand side of (4) by taking that action $\beta \in \overline{P}$ for which $\beta_0 = 1$ (that is, the maximal ratio $p\beta/\beta_0$ is surely achieved at such an action, among others). But then (4) reads:

$$\max_{\beta \in \Gamma} p\beta \geqq (p\tilde{c} - 1)/\pi^{\max} \tag{5}$$

where

$$\Gamma \equiv \{\beta \in \overline{P} | \beta_0 = 1\} \supseteq \theta^*. \tag{6}$$

In general, θ^* is a proper subset of Γ since the elements of Γ need not produce nonnegative net output vectors, while the elements of θ^* do. From (6) we have:

$$\max_{\beta \in \Gamma} p\underline{\beta} \geqq \max_{\beta \in \theta^*} p\underline{\beta}. \tag{7}$$

We proceed to show:

$$\max_{\beta \in \theta^*} p\underline{\beta} \geqq (p\tilde{c} - 1)/\pi^{\max}, \tag{8}$$

which, by (7) and (5), will prove the theorem. Notice that $\pi^{\max} p\underline{\beta} \equiv p\hat{\beta} - 1$ for any $\beta \in \overline{P}$, since both sides of this identity express the profits achieved at action $\beta \in \overline{P}$. Hence (8) is equivalent to:

$$\max_{\beta \in \theta^*} (p\hat{\beta} - 1) \geqq (p\tilde{c} - 1). \tag{9}$$

But (9) is true, by definition of θ^* and $\tilde{c}$, since there is an element $\beta \in \theta^*$ for which $\hat{\beta} \geqq \tilde{c}$. QED

It is worthwhile to alert the reader to the criticalness of taking the right definition of labor value, as the key juncture in the proof may have slipped by. If we had adopted Definition 1 of labor value, then the choice of $\tilde{c}$ would have been from a larger set than θ, namely from:

$$\hat{\theta} = \{c \in \mathbb{R}^n_+ | (\exists\ \alpha \in \phi(c))$$
$$(\alpha_0 = 1 \text{ and } \alpha_0 \text{ is minimized over } \phi(c))\}.$$

(Compare this to θ, where α ranges only over $\phi(c; p)$, not $\phi(c)$.) Then the bundle, which we might call $\hat{\tilde{c}}$, maximizing price per unit labor value would be:

$$\hat{\tilde{c}} \in \hat{\theta} \quad \text{such that} \quad p\hat{\tilde{c}} \geqq pc, \quad \forall c \in \hat{\theta}.$$

Then, when we arrive at inequality (9) in the proof, we could not assert that $\hat{\tilde{c}} \in \theta$, and (9) would not necessarily hold. (In fact, counterexamples can be constructed to (9) under the $\hat{\theta}$ specification.) In words, the situation would be this. Consider the *profits* which can be gotten by operating activities requiring one unit of direct labor.

(Profits are $p\hat{\beta} - 1$.) Consider the maximal profits from among those processes with highest profit rate on nonlabor capital (that is, $\pi^{\max}$ processes). Are those profits necessarily greater than profits from operating the process which maximizes price per unit labor value? In general, the answer is no. The process which produces $\hat{c}$ as net output may entail a lower *profit rate on capital* but higher *profits* if the capital outlay for operating that process is sufficiently large.

We now may verify the secondary claim made in the first section, that l.v.(c) may be defined, even more generally, without recourse to labor minimization. The proof of Theorem 5.3 only requires that, however $\tilde{c}$ is defined, it is true that there is an activity $\beta \in \theta^*$ for which $\hat{\beta} \geqq \tilde{c}$. But labor minimization plays no role in defining θ^*. So long as $\tilde{c}$ can be produced by *some* profit-maximizing production activity requiring unit labor (that is, $\hat{\beta} \geqq \tilde{c}$, $\beta_0 = 1$), the theorem follows. Hence, the labor-minimizing approach is only a convenient way of specifying a unique labor value for a commodity bundle; it is not the only possible definition. This will be remarked on further at the end of the next section.

A technical note should be appended here. The CECP is true as well in a model where wages are paid in advance, out of capital, not at the end of the period as in this model. If wages are paid in advance then the appropriate profit rate would be defined on capital inputs plus labor inputs: $\pi(p, \beta) = (p\hat{\beta} - \beta_0)/(p\underline{\beta} + \beta_0)$.

3. The CECP in the von Neumann model: a special case

Since it has been customary to generalize discussions of Marxian value theory to the von Neumann model and not to general convex cone production sets, I provide in this section a proof of the CECP for the special case of the von Neumann activity analysis technology. There is nothing here that is not contained in section 2; in fact, only the main theorem will be proved, not the preliminary results. This section simply translates the argument of section 2 into the von Neumann notation, which may be clarifying for some readers.

Let the von Neumann technology be $(B, A; L)$. There are m processes and n goods. Then producer ν's program, facing prices p and a wage 1, is to choose an action (x^ν, y^ν, z^ν) where x^ν is the m-vector of activity levels which ν operates himself, y^ν is the m-vector of activity levels which ν hires others to operate for him, and z^ν is the scalar amount of time that ν sells his labor power. Producer ν chooses according to this revenue maximization program:

$$\left.\begin{array}{l} \max[(pB - pA)x^\nu] + [pB - (pA + L)]y^\nu + [z^\nu] \\ \text{subject to} \\ pA(x^\nu + y^\nu) \leqq p\omega^\nu \\ Lx^\nu + z^\nu \leqq 1 \\ x^\nu, y^\nu, z^\nu \geqq 0 \end{array}\right\} \quad \text{(P5}')$$

Define the set $\bar{X}$ of activity vectors which are maximally profitable at a given reproducible solution $(p, 1)$. Let π be the profit rate associated with p:

$$pB \leqq (1 + \pi)pA + L.$$

Then $\bar{X} = \{x \in \mathbb{R}^m_+ | pBx = (1 + \pi)pAx + Lx\}$. That is, the only components of a vector $x \in \bar{X}$ that may be positive are those corresponding to processes achieving the maximal profit rate π. Theorem 5.2 now becomes:

Theorem 5.2′. In the von Neumann model, when $\pi > 0$:

$$\nu \in C^H \Leftrightarrow W^\nu > \max_{x \in \bar{X}} \left[\frac{pAx}{Lx}\right]$$

$$\nu \in C^{PB} \Leftrightarrow \min_{x \in \bar{X}} \left[\frac{pAx}{Lx}\right] \leqq W^\nu \leqq \max_{x \in \bar{X}} \left[\frac{pAx}{Lx}\right]$$

$$\nu \in C^S \Leftrightarrow 0 < W^\nu < \min_{x \in \bar{X}} \left[\frac{pAx}{Lx}\right]$$

$$\nu \in C^P \Leftrightarrow 0 = W^\nu$$

We define exploitation as indicated in section 1. Labor value embodied in a commodity vector c is the solution to this program:

$$\begin{array}{l} \text{choose } x' \text{ to } \min Lx \\ \text{such that} \\ (B - A)\, x \geqq c \\ pBx = (1 + \pi)pAx + Lx \\ x \geqq 0 \end{array}$$

Define $\text{l.v.}(c) = Lx'$

or

choose x' to min Lx

such that

$$(B - A)x \geqq c$$
$$x \in \bar{X}.$$

A producer is exploited or exploiter as before. We characterize exploitation status by wealth level as follows. Let θ be the commodity bundles of unit labor value:

$$\theta = \{c \in \mathbb{R}^n_+ | \text{l.v.}(c) = 1\}$$

Let θ^* be the vectors of activity levels which solve the minimization program of Definition 2 for some $c \in \theta$:

$$\theta^* = \{x \in \bar{X} | (\exists c \in \theta)\ (B - A)x \geqq c \quad \text{and} \quad Lx = 1)\}$$

We require the NFL assumption here as well:

$$(B - A)\ x \geq 0 \Rightarrow Lx > 0.$$

With the NFL assumption, we can find a vector $\tilde{c} \in \theta$ which maximizes $p\tilde{c}$ over θ, and another vector $\underset{\sim}{c} \in \theta$ which minimizes $p\underset{\sim}{c}$ over θ. $\tilde{c}$ is that commodity bundle which maximizes price per unit of labor value; purchasing $\tilde{c}$ is the least efficient way of commanding labor value through the goods one buys. This gives rise to the identical characterization of exploitation by wealth:

$$\nu \text{ is an exploiter} \Leftrightarrow W^\nu > (p\tilde{c} - 1)/\pi \tag{2''}$$
$$\nu \text{ is exploited} \Leftrightarrow W^\nu < (p\underset{\sim}{c} - 1)/\pi. \tag{3''}$$

To prove the CECP, it must be shown that two inequalities hold, according to Theorem 5.2′ and (2″). We verify one of them, namely:

$$\max_{x \in \bar{X}} \left[\frac{pAx}{Lx}\right] \geqq (p\tilde{c} - 1)/\pi. \tag{4'}$$

Since $\bar{X}$ is a convex cone, we can normalize the left-hand side of (4′) by examining only processes in $\bar{X}$ for which $Lx = 1$. That is, define

$$\bar{X}' = \{x \in \bar{X} | Lx = 1\}$$

and observe that (4′) can equally well be written:

$$\max_{x \in \bar{X}'} pAx \geqq (p\tilde{c} - 1)/\pi. \tag{5′}$$

Notice by definition that:

$$\bar{X}' \supseteq \theta^* \tag{6′}$$

and in general θ^* is a proper subset of $\bar{X}'$, since for x in $\bar{X}'$, $(B - A)x$ may not be a nonnegative vector. Hence, from (6′),

$$\max_{x \in \bar{X}'} pAx \geqq \max_{x \in \theta^*} pAx. \tag{7′}$$

We proceed to show:

$$\max_{x \in \theta^*} pAx \geqq (p\tilde{c} - 1)/\pi \tag{8′}$$

which, by (7′) and (5′), will prove inequality (4′), which proves the CECP. Notice that $\pi pAx = pBx - pAx - 1$, by definition of p and π. Hence (8′) is equivalent to:

$$\max_{x \in \theta^*} p(B - A)x \geqq p\tilde{c}. \tag{9′}$$

But (9′) is true by the definition of θ^* and $\tilde{c}$, since there is an $x \in \theta^*$ for which $(B - A)x \geqq \tilde{c}$. (4′) is therefore demonstrated.

To see where the argument fails if we adopt the "incorrect" Definition 1 (section 1) of embodied labor value, examine inequality (9′). Under Definition 1, $\tilde{c}$ would be produced by some activity vector $\tilde{x}$ such that

$$(B - A)\tilde{x} \geqq \tilde{c}$$

but it would not be true, in general, that $\tilde{x} \in \theta^*$. Typically, $\tilde{x}$ will involve the operation of some processes that are not maximally profitable, and (9′) therefore will be false.

As in section 2, we now remark that the labor value of c may be defined without recourse to the labor-minimizing program. The proof of the CECP just given only requires that however $\tilde{c}$ is defined, it be true that there is an activity $x \in \theta^*$ for which $(B - A)x \geqq \tilde{c}$. But labor minimization plays no role in defining θ^*. So long as $\tilde{c}$ can be produced by *some* profit-maximizing production activity requiring unit labor (that is, $(B - A)x \geqq \tilde{c}$, $Lx = 1$), the theorem follows.

An application of this fact is as follows. Some researchers have objected to the labor-minimizing definition of labor value on the grounds that it evaluates labor-embodied according to a counterfactual situation (see Flaschel, 1980). For instance, consider the following macroeconomic identity we might like a definition of labor value to preserve:

Total labor employed = Labor value of net product.

This employment identity may fail using the labor-minimizing Definition 2 (and, a fortiori, the false Definition 1), since there may exist a set of profitable processes which could produce the given net product using less labor than was actually employed. It is possible to specify an alternative definition of labor value which does not involve a minimization procedure, but rather evaluates labor content by examining the profitable processes which are actually used to produce the net product in the given equilibrium. We have shown that any such definition will preserve the CECP.

4. Labor embodied as compounded dated labor[8]

It is well known that the vector of labor values in the Leontief model can be thought of as a sum of dated labor times:

$$\Lambda = L(I - A)^{-1} = \sum_{i=0}^{\infty} LA^i. \tag{1}$$

Equilibrium prices are the sum of dated labor, compounded by the appropriate interest factor:

8. This section is the consequence of pursuing a suggestion of R. E. Howe.

$$p = L(I - (1 + \pi)A)^{-1} = \sum_{i=0}^{\infty} L(1 + \pi)^i A^i. \tag{2}$$

(Here, the wage is unity.)

In equations (1) and (2), LA^i is the labor applied to manufacture the inputs i stages ago in the production process. Thus $(1 + \pi)^i LA^i$ is the present value of wages paid i stages ago, compounded by the interest factor $(1 + \pi)^i$. If we sum all compounded dated wage payments, we produce today's prices. The difference between labor values and prices of production is that in the former, dated labor is not compounded by the interest factor. Some writers have referred to the prices of equation (2) as synchronized labor values (see Wolfstetter, 1973, Von Weizsäcker and Samuelson, 1971, and Roemer, 1977, for further discussion).

If there is a positive profit rate, and a planner wishes to economize on labor costs, the appropriate measure of labor value for him to evaluate in considering the merits of a technology is synchronized labor value, not the uncompounded labor value of equation (1). (This is discussed, for instance, in the above-mentioned articles.) This suggests a question concerning our new Definition 2 concept of embodied labor time in the von Neumann model.

We are facing a von Neumann technology (B, A, L). Given a commodity bundle c and certain equilibrium prices $(p, 1; \pi)$, there is a certain embodied labor time for bundle c—let us call it Lx'. If, however, we employed the old Definition 1 of embodied labor time, the labor value of c would, in general, be smaller than Lx'—let us call it Lx^*:

$$Lx^* \leqq Lx'. \tag{3}$$

Recall what is behind the calculations of Lx' and Lx^*. To calculate Lx^*, we solved this program:

$$\left.\begin{array}{l} \quad\text{choose } x^* \text{ to min } Lx \\ \text{such that} \\ \quad (B - A)x \geqq c \\ \quad x \geqq 0 \end{array}\right\} \text{(P*)}$$

To calculate Lx', we solved:

$$\left.\begin{array}{l} \text{choose } x' \text{ to min } Lx \\ \text{such that} \\ (B - A)x \geqq c \\ pBx = (1 + \pi)pAx + Lx \\ x \geqq 0 \end{array}\right\} \quad (\text{P}')$$

When $Lx^* < Lx'$, a different set of processes is operated to optimize (P*) than is operated to optimize (P'). (In particular, some unprofitable process is being used in (P*).) Barring singularities, there will be a square subarray of (B, A) which is operated in P*, call it (B^*, A^*), and another square subarray operated in P', call it (B', A'). The question can now be posed: Although the labor value associated with technology (B', A') for producing c is greater than the labor time associated with producing c using technology (B^*, A^*), can we assert that the "compounded labor time" associated with producing c by using (B', A') is minimal, among all possible ways of producing c as a net output, using the universal technology (B, A)?

The motivation for the question is that we know compounded dated labor time is the correct index of labor efficiency, from the planner's point of view. Hence, if $Lx^* < Lx'$, we wish to show this does not imply that (B^*, A^*) is in some sense a socially preferred set of processes to (B', A'), for producing c. If the labor times are properly compounded for the two sets of processes, then inequality (3) will be reversed.

As this discussion implies, the answer to the question is yes, which we proceed to show. The technology (B, A, L) has m processes and n goods, and we assume $m > n$. The prices and profit rate are defined by:

$$pB \leqq (1 + \pi)pA + L. \tag{4}$$

We need to assume there is a subsystem consisting of at least n processes j for which:

$$pB_j = (1 + \pi)pA_j + L_j. \tag{5}$$

There is, in fact, a good economic assumption which states that at an equilibrium of the von Neumann model, at least as many processes must operate as there are goods, which has been called *indecomposability* (see Roemer, 1980b). If the von Neumann technology (B, A, L) is indecomposable, then given that the vector c can be produced as a net output, there must be a square subarray of (B, A, L) named (B', A', L') such that:

$$(B' - A')x' = c \tag{6a}$$

$$pB' = (1 + \pi)pA' + L'. \tag{6b}$$

From (6b), we can solve for p:

$$p = L'(B' - (1 + \pi)A')^{-1} \tag{7}$$

and so

$$pc = L'(B' - (1 + \pi)A')^{-1}\, c. \tag{8}$$

To see the interpretation of pc as a sum of compounded dated labor times, expand the right-hand side of (8) to yield:

$$pc = \sum_{i=0}^{\infty} L'(1 + \pi)^i (B'^{-1}A')^i (B'^{-1}c), \tag{9}$$

assuming B'^{-1} exists (even though B'^{-1} is not necessarily nonnegative). Let us interpret a typical term $(1 + \pi)^i L'(B'^{-1}A')^i(B'^{-1}c)$ of (9). We wish to produce c as a net output. If the technology (B', A', L') could be operated at an activity vector $B'^{-1}c$, then gross outputs would be $B'(B'^{-1}c)$ or c. $(B'^{-1}A')^i(B'^{-1}c)$ are the gross activity levels i stages back which must operate to produce c today. Hence the term $(1 + \pi)^i L'(B'^{-1}A')^i(B'^{-1}c)$ is precisely the compounded dated labor input from i stages back in the production process, and we see according to (9) that pc is summed compounded dated labor.

This discussion shows that an assumption is needed to be able to speak of compounded dated labor with respect to the production of a vector c by an arbitrary square array $(\hat{B}, \hat{A}, \hat{L})$, namely:

Assumption DL (dated labor). For all i, $(\hat{B}^{-1}A)^i(\hat{B}^{-1}c) \geq 0$.

If Assumption DL fails for $(\hat{B}, \hat{A})$, then it is unclear what dated labor i stages could mean with respect to technology $(\hat{B}, \hat{A})$. We now prove:

Theorem 5.4. Let (B, A, L) be an indecomposable von Neumann technology with a reproducible solution (p, π). Let $c \geq 0$ be a commodity vector whose embodied labor value is Lx', where x' involves operating a profitable (square) subarray (B', A') such that $(B' - A')x' = c$. Then the total dated labor time required to produce c, compounded at interest factor $(1 + \pi)$, is minimal using (B', A'), minimized over all square subarrays of (B, A) which satisfy Assumption DL and can produce c.

This theorem answers our original query. The definition of embodied labor time which has been adopted does minimize appropriately compounded dated labor, among all techniques for which dated labor makes sense. Our definition of embodied labor time corresponds to the planner's choice-of-technique problem.

Proof of Theorem 5.4. Let (B^*, A^*) be any array satisfying Assumption DL which produces c as a net output, $(B^* - A^*)x^* = c$. By indecomposability of (B, A), (B^*, A^*) contains at least n processes, and a nonsingularity assumption will assure us we can always use at most n processes to produce c. Thus, without loss of generality we may assume that B^* and A^* are square $n \times n$ matrices.

By definition of p and π, we have:

$$pB^* \leqq (1 + \pi)pA^* + L^* \tag{10}$$

and so

$$p(B^* - (1 + \pi)A^*) \leqq L^*. \tag{11}$$

By Assumption DL the terms $(1 + \pi)^i(B^{*-1}A^*)^i(B^{*-1}c)$ are all nonnegative vectors; if their sum converges, it is equal to:

$$\sum_{0}^{\infty} (1 + \pi)^i(B^{*-1}A^*)^i(B^{*-1}c) = (B^* - (1 + \pi)A^*)^{-1}\, c, \tag{12}$$

which is therefore a nonnegative vector. Postmultiplying inequality (11) with the vector on the right-hand side of (12) therefore preserves the order of the inequality in (11):

$$pc \leqq L^*(B^* - (1 + \pi)A^*)^{-1}\, c. \tag{13}$$

But, according to (9), inequality (13) is precisely the statement of the theorem, for the left-hand side of (13) is the compounded dated labor for producing c using (B', A'), while the right-hand side is the compounded dated labor involved in producing c using (B^*, A^*).

Finally, if the infinite sum in (12) diverges, then the compounded dated labor used in producing c with (B^*, A^*) is infinite, and is surely larger than pc. QED[9]

In summary, Theorem 5.4 provides yet another piece of evidence that the new definition of embodied labor time, according to program (P′) or Definition 2 of section 1, is superior to the old concept of embodied labor time of Definition 1 or program (P*). The technique which (P′) tells us to use in evaluating socially necessary labor time is that technique which minimizes dated compounded labor times, in the context of the von Neumann model, when the concept of dated labor time is sensible.

9. Notice that the proof does not involve the labor-minimizing aspect of the definition of labor value, but only the fact that the processes (B', A') which are used to evaluate the labor content of a vector c are all profit-maximizing (that is, (6b) is satisfied). Thus our previous remarks apply to Theorem 5.4 as well: labor value need not be defined from a labor-minimizing process for the theorem to be true.

6

Marxian Exploitation and Heterogeneous Labor

In Chapter 5 the CECP was used as a device to increase our understanding of the labor theory of value. By considering more general production sets than the Leontief technology, we gained insight into the correct generalization of the concept of socially necessary labor time to general constant-returns-to-scale technology. The surprise was that labor value must depend on equilibrium prices in the general case. In this chapter I again relax one of the specifications of the model which has been studied, this time to learn something more about the labor theory of exploitation. This marks the beginning of our attempt to understand why the transfer of unpaid labor or surplus value should or might be conceived of as exploitative. Marxists reading these sentences may be somewhat impatient, since for them the identification of the transfer of surplus labor from one class to another may seem self-evidently exploitative. This is, however, not self-evident, as any neoclassical reader will attest to, since what to one appears a transfer of unpaid labor, to the other appears a just return for nonlabor factors contributed to production. Perhaps by the end of this chapter the skeptical Marxist will see there is a real problem, and that one's intuitive notions of exploitation as the transfer of unpaid labor sometimes lead to curious results. In Chapter 7 these difficulties will, it is hoped, be clarified, if not resolved, with the explication of the general definition of exploitation.

To strain the conception of the surplus labor theory of exploitation to the limits, we modify the model of the accumulation economy by perturbing the assumption that each producer is endowed with the same amount of labor power. In the model thus far, producers possessed different amounts of alienable property endowments ω^ν, but all are endowed with one unit of labor power. We now assume that the νth agent is endowed with l^{ν} units of labor power. We still assume that labor power is a homogeneous commodity, but producers have different amounts of it. Some producers work harder or faster than others, or are willing to work more hours in the day. Even without introducing an assumption of heterogeneous labor, this will produce interesting anomalies in the model. One might view the assumption as modeling skills of a very special nature; if truly heterogeneous labor is introduced into the model, it will be shown that the labor theory of exploitation becomes extremely problematic.

The model may equally well be interpreted as one where all producers have the same amount of labor endowment, but they choose to supply different amounts of labor because of different preferences for revenues versus leisure. This second interpretation may give a different flavor to the results concerning exploitation than does the interpretation of differential labor endowments.

Recall that in the model with identical labor endowments for all producers, the CECP related three different characteristics of producers: exploitation status, class position, and wealth. The theorem stated that the rankings of producers according to these three indices (where the ranking according to class position is specified by putting labor hirers on top, and so on) are identical. Thus, exploitation status is a proxy for both class position and wealth. The fact that exploitation status is a proxy for wealth lends an implicit justification to our calling the phenomenon exploitation, since we got the sensible conclusion that the wealthy were the exploiters and the poor were exploited.

What happens in the model with differential labor endowments? We will define a producer's exploitation status in the same way as before: he is exploited if he cannot possibly buy goods with his revenues which embody as much labor as he supplied. As will be seen in the next section, the CECP remains true in this model. What fails, however, is the rank correlation between exploitation and wealth, and therefore class position and wealth. It is possible for some very wealthy producers to be exploited and for some very poor producers to be exploiters. In fact, we will show that exploitation status and class status are correlated with W^{ν}/l^{ν}, the ratio of property wealth to labor endowment, so that a rich producer with a very large "skill" will be exploited, and a poor producer with virtually no skill will be exploiting.

This phenomenon forces us to think more carefully about the labor theory of exploitation. What is its proper scope? Should we or should we not consider these rich, very skilled producers as exploited? After all, they are not able to command through the purchase of goods the labor they expend in production, so their labor is in some sense expropriated by other members of society. But then we are forced to give up the sensible identification of the rich with the exploiting group and the poor with the exploited group. Our class identification still works: proletarians and semiproletarians remain exploited, but some of these semiproletarians may be very wealthy, wealthier than the capitalists—class (+, +, 0). What more basic concept of exploitation can be proposed to indicate a resolution to this riddle?

1. The CECP with differential labor endowment

In this section I prove that the CECP remains true in the model with differential labor endowments, but that both class position and exploitation status are rank-correlated with W^ν/l^ν, not with wealth W^ν. In fact, the proof is immediate. Assume that each agent possesses a positive endowment of labor, l^ν. Define the transformed variables:

$$\bar{x}^\nu = x^\nu/l^\nu, \qquad \bar{y}^\nu = y^\nu/l^\nu, \qquad \bar{z}^\nu = z^\nu/l^\nu.$$

The agent's optimization program (1.1) (Chapter 4) now changes only by replacing inequality (1.1b) with:

$$Lx^\nu + z^\nu \leqq l^\nu \tag{1.1b'}$$

But this program is solved by solving the transformed program:

$$\max(p - pA)\bar{x}^\nu + (p - (pA + wL))\bar{y}^\nu + w\bar{z}^\nu$$

such that

$$\begin{aligned} &pA(\bar{x}^\nu + \bar{y}^\nu) \leqq p\omega^\nu/l^\nu \\ &\quad L\bar{x}^\nu + \bar{z}^\nu \leqq 1 \\ &\quad \bar{x}^\nu, \bar{y}^\nu, \bar{z}^\nu \geqq 0 \end{aligned} \tag{6.1}$$

The optimal solution (x^ν, y^ν, z^ν) is then simply $(l^\nu \bar{x}^\nu, l^\nu \bar{y}^\nu, l^\nu \bar{z}^\nu)$. But program (6.1) is identical in structure to (1.1), with wealth $W^\nu \equiv p\omega^\nu$ of (1.1) replaced by W^ν/l^ν in (6.1). Therefore the class stratification Theorem 4.6 holds in this model, with W^ν replaced by W^ν/l^ν. Similarly, the inequalities of Theorem 4.3 continue to characterize exploitation status, with W^ν replaced by W^ν/l^ν. (An agent is exploited if he cannot feasibly purchase a bundle of goods, with his revenues, embodying as much labor as he supplied in production.) Consequently, the CECP continues to hold, as it was proved using only the inequalities in Theorems 4.3 and 4.6. However, class and exploitation status are now monotonically ranked with the index W^ν/l^ν, not with W^ν as before.

Observe also that the model may be interpreted as applying to a world where agents choose the labor they will supply. Suppose each agent has a utility function over revenue and labor, $u^\nu(\Pi, l)$. His problem is to choose $(x^\nu, y^\nu, z^\nu, l^\nu)$ to maximize $u^\nu(\Pi, l)$ where his revenue Π^ν is the maximand of the program (1.1), with labor constraint $Lx^\nu + z^\nu \leqq l^\nu$. Having found his optimal labor supply l^ν, we may view his class position as being determined by solving the program (6.1), with l^ν fixed at his optimal level.

Before concluding this section, there is an interpretation of the wealth characterization of exploitation status which may be useful in clarifying what Marxian exploitation means in this context. We can rewrite the inequality which characterizes the exploited as:

$$\frac{W^\nu}{l^\nu} < \frac{(p\underset{\sim}{c} - w)}{\pi}$$

where $\underset{\sim}{c}$ is that commodity bundle of unit labor value which is minimal in price. (Recall the notation of Chapter 5, section 2. See inequality (3′) of that section.) But this can be written as:

$$W^\nu < \sum_{i=1}^{\infty} \frac{(p\underset{\sim}{c} - w)l^\nu}{(1 + \pi)^i}.$$

This suggests the following. Suppose producer ν wishes to write a contract purchasing a consumption stream, over his infinite lifetime, in which he receives every period a bundle of goods embodying as much labor as he expended. He is willing to mortgage his entire future earnings to consummate this deal. Thus, in each period he will purchase goods worth $p(l^\nu \underset{\sim}{c})$ and his labor will bring in wl^ν in each period. (l^ν is constant over time.) Thus, the discounted deficit he must cover for a period i in the future is $(p\underset{\sim}{c} - w)l^\nu/(1 + \pi)^i$, and hence the inequality states that ν is not able to consummate this deal today, since his present wealth is not sufficient to cover the present discounted value of his deficits. An exploited agent is one whose wealth is out of line with his labor endowment in this sense: his wealth is not sufficient to allow him to write a contract wherein he purchases an infinite stream of goods embodying, in each period, as much labor as he expended, given that he is willing to mortgage future labor earnings toward the purchases as well. Similarly, an exploiter is one who, when writing such a contract, will always have wealth left over, no matter what bundle of goods he consumes which embodies as much labor as he supplied.

It is not clear why an agent who is exploited in this sense should be considered to be badly off, or why an exploiter is well off. Certainly if we adopt the interpretation of the model in which agents are offering to supply labor in amounts l^ν the inferences are problematical. Any agent with positive wealth can make himself into an exploiter by offering sufficiently little labor.

To review the theorem of this section: when labor power is differentially endowed to agents, the CECP continues to hold, labor hirers are exploiters, and labor sellers are exploited. What fails to hold, however, is the correspondence between wealth and exploitation and therefore between wealth and class status. There may be sellers of labor power—in class (+, 0, +)—who are very rich but are exploited, and hirers of labor power—in class (+, +, 0)—who are relatively poor but are exploiters. The index involving wealth which does correlate with exploitation and class status is W^ν/l^ν. Roughly speaking, then, a producer is an exploiter if his property wealth W^ν is oversized compared to his earning power (given by l^ν), and he is exploited if his property wealth W^ν is undersized compared to his earning power.

2. Heterogeneous labor

In the case of differential labor endowment (or supply) of a homogeneous kind of labor, a natural formal definition of exploitation continues to exist and the CECP continues to hold. There is some question as to the meaning of exploitation in that context. In the case of heterogeneous labor, however, even the formal results dissipate. If labor is heterogeneous, it is unclear how one can define exploitation as the inability to purchase goods embodying as much labor as one supplied—for how can the different kinds of labor embodied in a bundle of goods be added up to arrive at its labor valuation? One possibility is to aggregate the different labors embodied in a bundle by the market wage rates for those labor types. While orthodox discussions of heterogeneous labor and Marxian value theory have shunned such an approach, as it renders labor value dependent on prices, there is no such problem here, as we already know (from Chapter 5) that labor value is a price-dependent concept. Nevertheless, this definition is not formally compelling, because it does not preserve the CECP. More generally, this section will demonstrate that even when a simple class decomposition of society can be arrived at in the case of heterogeneous labor, the classes have no relationship to any wealth variable, that is, the ratio of wealth to earning power (the relevant wage). Since class structure loses any welfare interpretation, there is no point in trying to relate it to any notion of exploitation.

We proceed by supposing that the technology is a convex cone consisting of points $(-\beta_0;\ -\underline{\beta};\ \overline{\beta})$ where β_0 is now a vector of labor inputs in $\mathbb{R}^r_+$, there being r types of labor. $\underline{\beta}$ is the vector of commodity inputs and $\overline{\beta}$ the vector of commodity outputs, both in $\mathbb{R}^n_+$. (The notation is the same as that of the general conical technology of Chapter 5.) The price vector is (p, w) where the wage vector $w \in \mathbb{R}^r_+$. A given person may have ability to provide several kinds of labor; but in optimizing he will only provide one kind, that with the highest wage which he is capable of supplying. (We assume there are no special disutilities associated with supplying any particular kind of labor. Revenue maximization is the only issue.) I will discuss a special case of a general technology to enable a clear class stratification of society. The problems which exist for this special case will only become worse in the general case.

The special assumption is:

Assumption. At equilibrium prices (p, w), for each type r of labor, there is a profit-maximizing activity which employs only r-labor. The set of such process is $\overline{P}^r$.

An optimizing agent will supply one type of labor. (If two types have the same wage, he could offer either or both, but that singularity is of no import.) Designate an optimal solution to an agent's revenue maximizing program schematically as $(+^r, +^{s,t}, 0)$, for example, which means he optimizes by supplying r-labor of his own in his own shop, by hiring others to supply s and t types of labor, and by not selling labor power at all. It is now possible for the class structure to be extremely complex, but with the above assumption we have this simple structure:

Theorem 6.1. An optimizing agent always possesses a solution to his revenue-maximizing program putting him in one of the four disjoint classes, for some r:

$$\begin{array}{ll} (+^r, +^r, 0)\setminus(+^r, 0, 0) & = C^{1,r} \\ (+^r, 0, 0) & - C^{2,r} \\ (+^r, 0, +^r)\setminus(+^r, 0, 0) & = C^{3,r} \\ (0, 0, +^r) & = C^{4,r} \end{array}$$

The theorem allows us to speak of labor hiring and labor selling as characterizations of classes; without it, one would of necessity have many more classes, consisting of agents who simultaneously sell one kind of labor and hire another. (That is, the situation is totally ambiguous.) Hence, the assumption generates a simplicity to the class structure.

The proof is the same as the proofs in Chapters 4 and 5. We need only show an agent can always net out either the hiring or the selling of labor. As before, it is clear the maximal revenue of an agent is $\pi W^\nu + w^r l^\nu$. l^ν is an amount of *time* expended; but different agents have capacity to spend it on different types of labor. For the agent in question, r-labor is his most valuable type. Clearly he has a solution of form $(0, +, +^r)$ when he uses all his capital in any way and makes profits πW^ν by hiring others, and then sells his r-labor to make $w^r l^\nu$. Now according to the assumption, there is a π-process using only r-labor; he could sink his capital entirely into that process in his own shop and hire himself to operate it. If he still has labor time left over, then he continues to sell it. That is, if his own capital can only hire him for time l_1^ν, and $l_1^\nu < l^\nu$, then total revenues will be

$$[\pi W^\nu + w^r l_1^\nu] + w^r[l^\nu - l_1^\nu] = \pi W^\nu + w^r l^\nu.$$

He thus has an optimal solution $(+^r, 0, +^r)$. Similarly, if he has too much capital to occupy his time l^ν, he will be a member of $(+^r, +^r, 0)$. For this demonstration, it is essential to have the assumption.

Note that we cannot say a particular agent is unambiguously a labor hirer or seller; that statement is only unambiguous with respect to his own kind of labor. A producer could be a member of $(+^r, 0, +^r)$ and $(+^r, +^s, 0)$, even with the assumption. If he uses only processes in $\bar{P}^r$ in his own shop, then he has his own r-labor left over after exhausting his capital, which he sells, thus placing him in $(+^r, 0, +^r)$; but, alternatively, he might use processes in his own shop which are less capital intensive (but still profit-maximizing) and employ both r- and s-labor. He can employ all his own r-labor on these processes, with his capital, and also the complementary s-labor, which he hires from outside, thus placing him in $(+^r, +^s, 0)$. Hence, the superscripts in the class definition of Theorem 6.1 are necessary to ensure that the classes C^1 and C^3 are disjoint. Put differently, we cannot assert that an agent is unambiguously a compulsory labor hirer or labor seller, even with the assumption; that statement is only true if we classify him by asking for an optimal solution which uses processes employing only his own most valuable labor type.

What is the relationship of class membership to wealth, or $W^\nu/w^r l^\nu$? In general, there is none, even in this special case. This is seen as follows. By examining the proof of Theorem 5.2, we get this analog:

Theorem 6.2 Let $\bar{P}^r$ be the set of profit-maximizing activities, at prices (p, w), using only r-labor. [By the assumption, $\bar{P}^r \neq \phi$.] Let ν be an agent who optimizes by selling only r-labor, and he sells it in amount l^ν. Then:

$$\nu \in (+^r, +^r, 0)\setminus(+^r, 0, 0) \Leftrightarrow \frac{W^\nu}{w^r l^\nu} > \max_{\beta \in \bar{P}^r} \frac{p\beta}{w^r \beta_0^r}$$

$$\nu \in (+^r, 0, 0) \Leftrightarrow \min_{\beta \in \bar{P}^r} \frac{p\beta}{w^r \beta_0^r} \leqq \frac{W^\nu}{w^r l^\nu} \leqq \max_{\beta \in \bar{P}^r} \frac{p\beta}{w^r \beta_0^r}$$

$$\nu \in (+^r, 0, +^r)\setminus(+^r, 0, 0) \Leftrightarrow 0 < \frac{W^\nu}{w^r l^\nu} < \min_{\beta \in \bar{P}^r} \frac{p\beta}{w^r \beta_0^r}$$

$$\nu \in (0, 0, +^r) \Leftrightarrow W^\nu = 0.$$

The wage rates can be canceled out of these inequalities. To be even more special, and hence simpler, let us assume that everyone works the same unit working day, and w^r is the daily wage for the r type of working day. Then $l^\nu = 1$ for all agents, and an agent offering r-labor will be in the class of r-capitalists, for instance, if and only if:

$$\frac{W^\nu}{w^r} > \max_{\beta \in \bar{P}^r} \frac{p\beta}{w^r \beta_0^r}.$$

Now the problem can be seen. There is no necessary relationship among these maximal and minimal "capital-wages ratios" in the different slices $\bar{P}^r$ of the production set. Let us call $\max_{\beta \in \bar{P}^r} p\beta / w^r \beta_0^r \equiv k^r_{\max}$ and define $k^r_{\min}$ in like manner. Then the class status of an agent selling r-labor depends on the relationship of his wealth-earnings ratio $W^\nu / w^r l^\nu$ to the interval $[k^r_{\min}, k^r_{\max}]$. *There is no reasonable regularity assumption to impose on the relationship among these intervals as r varies.* Consequently, nothing of interest can be inferred about the comparison between two agents ν and μ by knowing their respective class statuses. A person's class position is determined by the relationship of his wealth-earnings ratio to the capital-wages ratio in his slice $\bar{P}^r$, and between slices there is no comparison of interest, that is, no comparison having to do with agents' welfare.

Since class membership is devoid of any reasonable interpretation in terms of wealth or wealth-earnings ratios, there is little point in trying to relate class membership to some (as yet undefined) notion of exploitation.[1] Nevertheless, we can observe that the CECP cannot be preserved by any definition of exploitation which characterizes the exploited as those incapable of commanding as much labor through purchases of goods as they expended in production—if we insist on aggregating the various types of labor embodied in

1. By aggregating labors embodied using market wages, we can define a notion of exploitation as follows. We define a bundle of goods as embodying a unit of labor if it can be produced, net, using profitable processes, by paying total wages of one dollar, but no less. Let $\underset{\sim}{c}$ be the least expensive bundle of unit labor value. (Of course, this is with respect to given prices (p, w).) Let producer ν optimize by earning wages $w^r l^\nu$ and profits πW^ν. Then the cheapest bundle embodying as much labor value as ν expended is $(w^r l^\nu)\underset{\sim}{c}$. Producer ν is exploited if he cannot purchase this bundle with his revenues, that is, if $\pi W^\nu + w^r l^\nu < p(w^r l^\nu)\underset{\sim}{c}$ or $\pi W^\nu / w^r l^\nu < p\underset{\sim}{c} - 1$. It is easily seen this definition is a generalization of our concept of Marxian exploitation in the case of homogeneous labor. However, as shown below, it does not relate to an agent's class position in any regular way.

goods rather than simply looking at one type it embodies, the type the producer in question expended. For any such definition of exploitation will make the exploitation status of a producer depend at most on his wealth W^ν, earnings $w^r l^\nu$, and labor expended l^ν. (Two producers with identical wealth, earnings, and labor must have the same exploitation status.) But class position depends, in addition, on the relationship of these data to the capital-wages ratios in the slice of the production set, $\bar{P}^r$, corresponding to the type of labor the producer uses. Hence there can be no general relationship between exploitation, conceived as described, and class, even in the model we have studied which fulfills the special assumption. In the general case of heterogeneous labor, the situation is even worse, as the class decomposition of society loses its simple form.

The conclusion of this section is not that no suitable generalization of Marxian exploitation exists in the case of heterogeneous labor. (For that discussion, see Chapter 7, section 4.) Rather, it is, first, that class status ceases to be related to any interesting welfare concept with heterogeneous labor, and, second, that the *labor* theory of exploitation ceases to be compelling, even if it can be defined. In Chapter 7 an alternative to the labor theory of exploitation (that is, to Marxian exploitation) will be proposed, which includes the labor theory as a special case when labor is homogeneous and equally endowed among all agents, but which generalizes to the case of heterogeneous labor with no ambiguity. And in Chapter 9, section 4, we complete the argument begun here by claiming that the labor theory of exploitation has cogency as a normative and historically appropriate theory only when labor endowment is homogeneous and equal.

3. The scope of the labor theory of exploitation

Up to this point in the book we have accepted as the definition of exploitation the Marxian concept of the transfer of surplus labor, in the sense it has been modeled. In the subsistence economies of Part I, it was quite reasonable to take the number of hours worked as an index of welfare, since the objective of the producers was to minimize labor time worked. In the accumulation economies of Chapters 4 and 5, where every producer was endowed with the same amount of labor, it was likewise true that a producer's exploitation status was correlated with his wealth; if we take wealth to be an index of welfare, then exploitation status is a measure of welfare. Nevertheless, it is not clear in either the subsistence or the accumulation model why we should choose to categorize producers as belonging to one of two groups, the exploiters or the exploited, according to whether their wealth is below or above a certain critical value. To what ethical conception does the notion that the transference of surplus labor is exploitative correspond? This question is made sharper by the model with differential labor endowments, in which it is no longer even true that exploitation status is a proxy for wealth, or therefore welfare, but rather is correlated to the producer's wealth-earnings ratio W^ν/l^ν. With heterogeneous labor, the CECP ceases to provide any direction as to what the appropriate definition of exploitation is, because class status ceases to be related to wealth and earnings in any global way. (There is a local relationship, with regard to the agent's "production slice" $\bar{P}^r$, in the special case where these slices exist, but that permits no interesting comparison of agents.)

It is perhaps worth remarking that for Marx the problem of differential labor endowments and heterogeneous labor did not appear as severe. Marx considered that the process of proletarianization renders all producers quite homogeneous and that it therefore becomes reasonable to think of labor as homogeneous and uniformly distributed. Perhaps this should be stated more weakly: if one cannot explain capitalist exploitation under the hypothesis of homogeneous and identical labor endowments, then one cannot explain it at all. To understand exploitation under capitalism, therefore, it may be a legitimate abstraction to postulate identical labor endowments. For us, however, this is not the case, as our task is to construct a more general theory of exploitation which is applicable also to socialism, and, as shall be seen, the issue of differential endowments of skills then becomes key. For our purposes, it is therefore legitimate to investigate the scope of the labor theory of exploitation by seeing its implications in a model with differential labor endowments.

A note concerning the terminology used to evaluate the role of a theory of exploitation is necessary before I proceed to describing the general theory of exploitation in Part III. I have spoken of exploitation as associated with welfare, of normative conceptions associated with particular notions of exploitation. There is a tradition within Marxist thought which views exploitation as an objective phenomenon, not associated with any normative position; from that viewpoint it would seem that the position advocated here is incorrect. I will maintain, however, that the position which views exploitation as an entirely objective description of capitalist economic relations is incorrect. The genesis of that position is this: Marx sought to explain profits in a world where markets were competitive and there was no cheating. How could one explain the emergence of a surplus, systematically appropriated by capitalists, when all exchanges were of equivalent value? Marx located the source of profits in the existence of one very special commodity which possessed the seemingly magical property of passing on to goods in the production process more "value" than it itself contained. This commodity was labor power. Thus, profits emerge from surplus value, or the fact that a unit of labor power contributes one unit of (labor) value to commodities on which it is applied in production, although that unit of labor power contains less than one unit of (labor) value itself, and so it trades for less than one unit of value. Hence, the objective nature of the labor theory of exploitation is thought to lie in the objective fact that there happens to be one commodity which embodies less value than it can produce.

Now it is true that profits are positive only because a unit of labor power embodies less than a unit of labor, but this statement is equally true of corn or steel or energy. One could choose corn as the numeraire for calculating embodied (corn) values of commodities, instead of labor, and one could then notice the remarkable fact that the technology is productive, that is, capable of producing a surplus, if and only if a unit of corn embodies less than one unit of corn value. (An appendix to this chapter demonstrates this theorem.) Hence, positive profits are possible for a technology if and only if each commodity is "exploited" when it is chosen as the numeraire for denominating value.

Thus, it is not uniquely the exploitation of labor which explains profits, and some other reason is needed to justify our analyzing exploitation in terms of what happens to labor instead of in terms of what happens to corn. There certainly are differences between labor power and corn which might cause one still to claim there is an objective reason to choose to think of labor as exploited and not corn. I do not think, however, that this line of reasoning is necessary. The theory of Marxian exploitation is best conceived of as a normative theory.[2] Nevertheless, we will be able to provide an objective rationale for the Marxian choice of labor as the value numeraire, given the Marxian assumptions concerning capitalism (Chapter 9, section 4). What we have been directed to ask by the analysis thus far is: What precisely are the norms which lead us to choose the index of surplus labor transfer as the criterion of exploitation? How universal are these norms? Is there a sense in which history directs us to adopt certain norms as appropriate in a given historical period? These questions occupy us in Part III.

Appendix 6.1. On the exploitation of steel in a productive economy

Marx believed that labor power was the commodity which produced a surplus under capitalism. In this appendix I show that one can define embodied value in terms of any commodity numeraire, with the result that the technology is productive if and only if each commodity is exploited when it is taken as numeraire. Steel is exploited if the steel value embodied in a unit of steel is less than one. Labor power is not special in having this property.

This assertion is proved here for a Leontief technology. Let A be the input-output matrix, L the vector of labor inputs and b the vector of consumption of the worker per unit labor power expended. Labor values are defined in the usual way as

$$\Lambda = L(I - A)^{-1} \tag{1}$$

2. Other authors also believe Marxian exploitation has a strong normative component. A. K. Sen (1973, p. 101) argues that Marx viewed his theory partially as a normative theory. Sen expands upon the labor theory of value as a normative theory in his 1978 paper. G. A. Cohen (1979, p. 341) also asserts the normative content of the Marxian theory of exploitation by identifying exploitation as a kind of injustice, which he acknowledges many Marxists are loath to do.

and the condition for the productiveness of the economy, viewing consumption of the worker as an input into production, is

$$\Lambda b < 1. \tag{2}$$

Inequality (2) means the worker is exploited; this is the necessary and sufficient condition for the profit rate to be positive, a statement known as the Fundamental Marxian Theorem. (For proof, see Roemer, 1981a, chap. 1.) In sum, the positivity of the profit rate means the matrix of augmented input coefficients

$$M \equiv A + bL \tag{3}$$

is a productive matrix.

We now compute values using commodity 1 as the value numeraire (say, steel). For this purpose, display the technology in this way:

$$\begin{array}{c|cccc} a_{11} & a_{12} & \cdots & a_{1n} & b_1 \\ \hline a_{21} & a_{22} & \cdots & a_{2n} & b_2 \\ \vdots & \vdots & & \vdots & \vdots \\ a_{n1} & a_{n2} & & a_{nn} & b_n \\ L_1 & L_2 & \cdots & L_n & 0 \end{array}$$

The jth column of this array lists the inputs of all $(n + 1)$ commodities used as inputs into production of the jth good—and this statement is true also for $j = n + 1$, namely, the commodity labor power. The ith row lists the inputs of ith good into the various processes—and this statement is true also for $i = n + 1$, namely, the input of labor. Notice there is, by convention, no input of labor into the production of labor power. In reality, there is such an input but it is performed in the household and not through the market, so it is not recorded in this tableau. (It is assumed that the worker does not hire others to do his chores.)

Let $\mu = (\mu_1, \mu_2, \ldots, \mu_n, \mu_{n+1})$ be the vector of steel values. μ_{n+1} is the steel value of labor power. Then the usual conception of embodied value implies the following definitional relations:

$$\mu_j = a_{1j} + \sum_2^n \mu_i a_{ij} + \mu_{n+1} L_j \quad \text{for } j = 1, n \tag{4a}$$

$$\mu_{n+1} = b_1 + \sum_2^n \mu_i b_i . \tag{4b}$$

Substitute from (4b) into (4a) to eliminate μ_{n+1}:

$$\mu_j = (a_{1j} + b_1 L_j) + \sum_{i=2}^n \mu_i(a_{ij} + b_i L_j) \tag{5}$$

or

$$\mu_j = \sum_1^n \mu_j(a_{ij} + b_i L_j) + (1 - \mu_1)(a_{1j} + b_1 L_j) \tag{5'}$$

or

$$\mu = \mu M + (1 - \mu_1)M_1 . \tag{6}$$

where M is defined in (3) and $M_{1\cdot}$ is the first row of M.

We wish to show that $\mu_1 < 1$ if and only if M is productive: that is the statement that the steel value of steel is less than one, and hence that steel is exploited.

If M is productive, equation (6) can be solved:

$$\mu = (1 - \mu_1)M_{1\cdot}(I - M)^{-1}. \tag{7}$$

What solutions μ_1 are possible to (7)? If $\mu_1 = 1$, then according to (7), $\mu = 0$, which contradicts the assumption that $\mu_1 = 1$. Hence $\mu_1 \neq 1$, and (7) is equivalent to:

$$\mu/(\mu_1 - 1) = M_{1\cdot}(I - M)^{-1}. \tag{8}$$

If M is productive, then $(I - M)^{-1} \geq 0$, and so $\mu/(1 - \mu_1) \geq 0$. This implies $\mu_1 < 1$. (For $\mu_1 > 1$ would imply $\mu_1/(1 - \mu_1) < 0$.) Hence $\mu_1 < 1$, and a solution $\mu \geq 0$ exists to (8).

Conversely, if a nonnegative vector μ exists solving (6), with $\mu_1 < 1$, then $\mu \leq \mu M$, and hence M is productive.

Part III

Exploitation, Socialism, and Historical Materialism

In Parts I and II variations on the Marxian theme of exploitation, conceived of as the expropriation of surplus value, or what Marxists call unpaid labor, were studied. Up to this point little attempt has been made to justify why one should use the vituperative nomenclature "exploitation" to describe the sort of inequality which emerged in the models of subsistence and accumulation economies of those chapters. A story was told in Chapter 1 indicating why one might wish to call that inequality exploitation. But many neoclassical economists would reply that at a reproducible solution of $\mathscr{E}(p)$ or $\mathscr{E}(p, w)$ or $\mathscr{E}(p, r)$ all producers are gaining from trade, and hence there is no basis for viewing some of them as exploited. Are the exploited producers not better off at a reproducible solution than if they had not entered into trade? The answer is yes, for one possibility is always for a producer not to trade at all, and so if he does trade, he must achieve a better value for the maximand of his program by so doing. In fact, we noted that producers who have no capital at all ($\omega^{\nu} = 0$) can often survive in the economy $\mathscr{E}(p, w)$ by selling their labor power, whereas they clearly could not survive without participation in the economy, given our supposition that the production of goods today requires some stock of inputs produced in the past.

It is thus necessary to propose a general and plausible definition of exploitation which will permit an interpretation of the inegalitarian solutions in $\mathscr{E}(p)$ and $\mathscr{E}(p, w)$ as exploitative. It would be begging the question to define exploitation as the transfer of unpaid labor, for what one observer may consider expropriated labor another will consider an entitled labor transfer. This, indeed, is the heart of the disagreement between Marxian and neoclassical economists concerning the Marxian theory of exploitation. Can a formal construct be proposed which will clarify the basis of the disagreement, a general conception of exploitation which will have as one special case "Marxian exploitation" and as another special case "neoclassical exploitation"?

Chapter 7 provides such a general construct. The bulk of the chapter is occupied with three special applications of the general model, to define *feudal, capitalist,* and *socialist* exploitation. It is shown that Marxian exploitation is equivalent to capitalist exploitation, and that what neoclassical economists conceive of as exploitation is equivalent to feudal exploitation. The definition of socialist exploitation enables a discussion of the question with which this book was introduced: the provision of a materialist definition of exploitation applicable to socialist societies. That discussion will be continued in Chapter 8.

The main purpose of Chapter 7, then, is to place the classical Marxian definition of exploitation in a more general context. The general definition of exploitation is a game-theoretic one and makes no special mention of the labor theory of value. One startling outcome of the analysis is a formulation of Marxian exploitation without reference to the concept of surplus labor. This may strike some readers as discarding the baby with the bath water. The concept that comes to the fore in the general definition of exploitation, in place of labor transfer, is property relations. Contrary to those hypothetical critics, I would reply that property relations is the conception upon which one must focus for a clear, historical taxonomy of exploitation, and that Marx captured one important special case with the surplus labor theory of exploitation. Although for simple models the surplus labor definition of exploitation and the property relations concept are equivalent, for more complicated specifications of production the labor theory of value approach cannot be defined, while the property relations approach remains tractable. Moreover, in some models the labor theory of value approach to exploitation is tractable, but gives the wrong answer concerning the exploitation status of some coalitions. In Chapter 6 we have already seen some problems that arise with the surplus labor theory of exploitation in general models.

The discussion of the general theory of exploitation, and its application to socialist society, will occupy the rest of the book. To present the idea as clearly as possible, I will avoid, in Chapter 7, certain important complications; those will be introduced in Chapters 8 and 9.

Many readers will doubtless pose these complications for themselves.

The plan of Chapter 7 is as follows. In section 1, a definition of exploitation is proposed in which exploitation is related to the concept of the core of a game. This is a formal way of capturing a simple, informal concept of exploitation. In section 2 feudal exploitation is defined and characterized using the game-theoretic notion. Section 3 presents the explicit definition of capitalist exploitation in game-theoretic terms, and it is shown that capitalist exploitation so defined is equivalent to Marxian exploitation in the models we have studied. Section 4 generalizes capitalist exploitation to the case of heterogeneous labor. Section 5 defines socialist exploitation and constructs a model to illustrate the difference between capitalist and socialist exploitation. Section 6 writes down, precisely, the characteristic functions of the games which define the various kinds of exploitation discussed in the chapter. Sections 7 and 8 are more technical than the rest; they resolve certain problems which arise with the exploitation concept in the presence of increasing returns to scale. Section 9 contrasts the property relations and surplus labor definitions of labor.

Outlines of Chapters 8 and 9 are presented at the beginnings of those chapters.

7

A General Definition and Taxonomy of Exploitation

1. Exploitation and alternatives

In virtually every society or economic mechanism, there is inequality. Yet not all inequality is viewed by a society as exploitative. The same form of inequality may be viewed as exploitative and nonexploitative by two people. Certainly, however, the notion of exploitation involves inequality in some way. What forms of inequality does a particular society (or person) view as exploitative? The inequality of master and slave was viewed as just and nonexploitative in ancient society, as was the inequality of lord and serf in feudal society, although today most of us consider both of these relationships exploitative. Similarly, Marxists view the inequality in the capitalist-worker relationship as exploitative, although this inequality is conceived of as nonexploitative by many people in capitalist society today. We wish to propose a theoretical device for clarifying the criteria according to which a type of economic inequality is evaluated as exploitative or not.

What is meant when one says a person or group is exploited in a certain situation? I propose that the concept of exploitation entails these conditions. A coalition S, in a larger society N, is exploited if and only if:

(1) There is an alternative, which we may conceive of as hypothetically feasible, in which S would be better off than in its present situation.

(2) Under this alternative, the complement to S, the coalition $N - S = S'$, would be worse off than at present.

The formal analysis in this chapter will take exploitation to be characterized by (1) and (2), although a third condition is also necessary to rule out certain bizarre examples, namely:

(3) S' is in a relationship of dominance to S.

Precisely how to specify the alternative is left open for the moment. The general claim is that this device can be applied whenever people use the word "exploit" in reference to economic inequality. If two people disagree on whether a group is exploited in some situation, then the device leads us to ask: Are they specifying the alternative for the group differently? Different specifications of the alternative will be proposed which will generate different concepts of exploitation.

What is accomplished by the conditions (1)–(3) above? Condition (1) has an obvious meaning. Condition (2) is necessary for exploitation since it must be the case that the exploited coalition S is exploited by other people, not by nature or technology, for instance. (Thus, exploitation as used here is to be distinguished from the exploitation of natural resources.) Condition (3) is sociological and is not formally modeled in this chapter; "dominance" will not be defined.[1] It will be seen, later on, that (3) is not redundant with (1) and (2), and why it is included.

Formally, we can model (1) and (2) by specifying a game played by coalitions of agents in the economy. To define the game, it is specified what any coalition can achieve on its own, if it "withdraws" from the economy. The alternative to participating in the economy is for a coalition to withdraw, taking its payoff or dowry, under the definition of the game. If a coalition S can do better for its members under the alternative of withdrawing, and if the complementary coalition to it, S', does worse after S's withdrawal, then S is exploited under that particular specification of the rules of the game.

To make this more concrete, consider the usual notion of the core of a private ownership exchange economy. The private ownership core is the set of allocations which no coalition can improve upon by withdrawing under these rules: it can take with it the private endow-

1. Although dominance is not defined, it should at least entail the following: that the coalition S' prevents the alternative from being realized, which gives rise to its exploitation of S. Because I do not pursue the dominance issue and various pathological examples, the account of exploitation here cannot be considered to be exhaustive.

ments of its members. Under these particular withdrawal rules, there is a certain utility frontier available to any coalition, and we could say a coalition is exploited if it is receiving utilities which can be dominated by a vector of utilities achievable by the coalition acting cooperatively on its own, given those withdrawal rules. In addition, for exploitation to occur, it must be the case that the complementary coalition fares worse after the original coalition withdraws with its endowments. More generally, if we adopt a different rule of withdrawal, which is to say a different way of specifying the payoffs achievable by the various coalitions on their own, a different game with a different core will result. Our definition implies this: exploitation occurs, at a given allocation, if that allocation is not in the core of the game defined by the particular withdrawal specification under consideration. That is, a coalition is exploited if and only if it can "block" an allocation, under the rules of the game. This will be proved presently.

This device captures the idea that exploitation involves the possibility of a better alternative. Our proposal for what constitutes feudal exploitation, capitalist exploitation, and socialist exploitation amounts to naming three different specifications of withdrawal rules, three different games. One can then compare different concepts of exploitation by comparing the different rule specifications which define their respective games. A particular concept of exploitation is exhibited in explicit or canonical form, as it were, as the rules of a game.

A formal definition of the concept follows. Let an economy be sustaining an allocation $\{z^1, \ldots, z^N\}$. That is, z^ν is the payoff that the νth agent is receiving. (z^ν can be an amount of money, or a bundle of goods and leisure, or a utility level.) Suppose we specify a game for this economy by stipulating a *characteristic function* v which assigns to every coalition S of agents in the economy a payoff $v(S)$. The value $v(S)$ should, of course, be in the same space as the values z^ν. $v(S)$ is to be thought of as the payoff available to the coalition S if it should choose to exercise its right to withdraw from the parent economy; it is the dowry assigned to it by society as a whole. We do not, of course, assume that institutional arrangements exist in the parent economy for actually giving S an amount $v(S)$ if it should choose to withdraw; for instance, the function v may define what some observer considers the just entitlement to coalitions should be, if they were to opt out of society. Given this structure, we say a coalition S is exploited at an allocation $\{z^1, \ldots, z^N\}$ with respect to alternative v if:[2]

$$\sum_{\nu \in S} z^\nu < v(S) \tag{1}$$

$$\sum_{\nu \in S'} z^\nu > v(S'). \tag{2}$$

We assume at this point that the coalition can distribute the dowry to its members so that each member ν receives a share v^ν such that $z^\nu < v^\nu$, which is certainly algebraically possible if (1) holds. (Thus, there are no considerations of incentives and strategy within the coalition, an important complication avoided in this chapter. Within the coalition there is cooperative behavior.)

Notice that exploitation is defined with respect to a specific conception of an alternative. The actual allocation is $\{z^1, \ldots, z^N\}$; the alternative is defined by the function $v(S)$. There are, of course, both interesting and silly ways of specifying v; our task will be to specify particular functions v which capture intelligible and historically cogent types of exploitation. For instance, one might wish to require of a specification v that it permit the possibility of no exploitation. That is, given v, is there an allocation of the economy at which no agent or coalition is exploited? If not, then v would seem to suggest the impossible, if we take as v's suggested ethical imperative the elimination of its associated form of exploitation. A sufficient condition that v permit a nonexploitative allocation is that the game v have a nonempty core (there should be an allocation $\{z^1, \ldots, z^N\}$ which no coalition S can block, according to (1)). We will see that the different games in characteristic function form v which are proposed in this chapter all have nonempty cores.

We define the *exploiting* coalitions with respect to an alternative v as the complementary coalitions to the exploited coalitions. S is an exploiting coalition if and only if the inequalities (1) and (2) hold, but with the inequality signs reversed in each.

2. From now on, reference to the dominance requirement is omitted. For the body of this chapter, (3) is assumed to hold whenever (1) and (2) do. In the concluding section, some perverse examples are given in which this would not be the case. For all practical purposes, however, (1) and (2) together are a satisfactory definition of exploitation.

We now prove, under reasonable assumptions, that the nonexploitative allocations are precisely the core of the game v:

Theorem 7.1. Let v be a superadditive game, and let the allocation $\{z^1, \ldots, z^N\}$ be Pareto optimal: $v(N) \leqq \Sigma_N z^\nu$. Then a coalition S is exploited if and only if $v(S) > \Sigma_S z^\nu$. Likewise a coalition T is exploiting if and only if $v(T') > \Sigma_{T'} z^\nu$. Hence the core of v is precisely the set of nonexploitative allocations.

Proof. The necessity of the condition holds by definition. To prove sufficiency, suppose S is not exploited but:

$$v(S) > \sum_S z^\nu. \tag{4}$$

Then S's failure to be exploited can only be due to:

$$v(S') \geqq \sum_{S'} z^\nu. \tag{5}$$

Adding (4) and (5) gives

$$v(S) + v(S') > \sum_N z^\nu \geqq v(N). \tag{6}$$

But the superadditivity of v implies $v(S) + v(S') \leqq v(N)$, for any coalition S. Hence S must be exploited if (4) holds.

The second statement follows since the complements of exploiting coalitions are exploited coalitions. QED

We remark further on why condition (2) is required for the definition of exploitation. As mentioned, it is to guarantee that when a coalition is exploited, it is exploited *by someone*. If we require only (1) for S to be exploited, then it would be possible for both S and its complement to be exploited. Symmetrically, if we require only $\Sigma_S z^\nu > v(S)$ for S to be exploiting, then both S and S' could be exploiting. Consider, for instance, an economy with increasing returns to scale, and let $v(S)$ be the income a coalition S would attain by withdrawing with its own assets. Because of the returns to scale, it is likely that both S and S' satisfy $\Sigma_S z^\nu > v(S)$, but we would not wish to consider them to be exploiting coalitions at the allocation $\{z^1, \ldots, z^N\}$. Rather, they are each benefiting from (or exploiting) the scale economies present. (Similarly, an economy with decreasing returns would identify many coalitions and their complements as exploited, if only inequality (1) were insisted upon.) Defining exploitation as consisting of (1) and (2) guarantees that every exploited coalition has as its complement an exploiting coalition, and conversely. Thus, exploitation must involve some coalition's benefiting at another coalition's expense—rather than benefits or expenses accruing from a purely natural or technological phenomenon, such as scale economies.[3]

Because both (1) and (2) are necessary for S to be exploited, it follows that the nonexploitative allocations may include more than the core of the game $v(S)$. If $\Sigma_S z^\nu < v(S)$ but $\Sigma_{S'} z^\nu \leqq v(S')$, then $\{z^1, \ldots, z^N\}$ is not in the core, but neither is S exploited there. This, however, can occur only if the allocation is not Pareto optimal (that is, if $\Sigma_N z^\nu < v(N)$). For Pareto optimal allocations ($\Sigma_N z^\nu = v(N)$) and concepts of exploitation generating superadditive games, the nonexploitative allocations are precisely the core of the game.

Thus, the device for defining exploitation conceives of agents as exploited at a particular allocation, with respect to a particular alternative. The alternative is specified as a characteristic function which defines the entitlements of agents and coalitions of agents. The formulation ignores, for the time being, these sorts of problems: Is realization of payoffs $v(S)$ in some way feasible? What are the costs of coalition formation? How will the coalition S arrange to distribute $v(S)$ among its members?

2. Feudal exploitation

I will not be historically precise concerning the underlying model of feudal economy. Think of agents with various endowments who are engaged in production and consumption under feudal relations. A coalition is feudally exploited if it can improve its lot by withdrawing under these rules: the coalition can take with it its own endowments.

3. My first pass at a definition of exploitation involved requiring only inequality (1). I am indebted to Jon Elster and Serge-Christophe Kolm for criticizing the lack of interaction between agents in that formulation. In the current formulation, interaction is necessary for exploitation to the extent that exploiting and exploited coalitions always appear as complements. Interaction is also assured by the dominance requirement (3).

Thus, feudally nonexploitative allocations are, in fact, precisely the usual private ownership core of the economic game, as conventionally defined, for a private ownership economy. This withdrawal specification, it is claimed, is the correct one for capturing feudal exploitation as it gives the result that serfs are exploited and lords are exploiters, which is the result we wish to capture. Moreover, nonserf proletarians will not be an exploited coalition, under these rules, and so the definition captures *only* feudal exploitation.

To verify this claim, we will make the cavalier assumption that the serf's family plot was part of his own endowment. Clearly demarcated property rights in these plots did not in general exist under feudalism, but history will be simplified, for the sake of making a point, to say that the essence of feudalism was the bondage which required the serf to perform labor on the lord's demesne and corvée labor, *in spite* of his access to the means of subsistence for his family which included the family plot. Thus, a crucial distinction between proletarians and serfs is that the former must exchange their labor to acquire access to their means of sustenance, while the latter must exchange their labor despite their access to the means of sustenance. This distinction accounts for the coerciveness of labor extraction relations under feudalism, as contrasted with the voluntary labor market under capitalism.[4]

Thus, if a group of serfs had been allowed to withdraw from feudal society with their endowments, in which we include the family plots, they would have been better off, having access to the same means of production, but providing no labor for the demesne and corvée. Withdrawal, under these rules, amounts to withdrawal from feudal bondage, and that only. There is, however, a counterargument, which could have been put forth by a feudal ideologue: serfs would not be better off, he might say, by withdrawing with their own endowments, because they receive various benefits from the lord which they cannot produce on their own, the most obvious being military protection. The argument concerning military protection is an important one, and it introduces the difficulties in analyzing exploitation as here defined when nonconvexities are present. These are treated at some length in sections 7 and 8; but the essential point is that when nonconvexities are present, it is not relevant to

4. For discussion see Brenner (1977) and Marx, *Capital,* Volume III (1966, pp. 790–791), in the section on labor rent.

ask whether individuals (or small coalitions) are exploited. (Indeed, if one serf withdraws under rules of the feudal game, he may be worse off, and so will the complementary coalition. Thus, he is not feudally exploited. But see the resolution of the problem in sections 7 and 8.) If sufficiently large coalitions of serfs had withdrawn with their plots, they could have provided for their own defense, and hence have been better off; clearly the complementary coalition would be worse off, not benefiting from the serfs' surplus labor. The serfs as a class were feudally exploited and the lords were feudal exploiters.

Second, the feudal ideologue might assert that the lord possessed certain skills or abilities to organize manor life without which the serfs would have been worse off. This argument is put forth by North and Thomas (1973), who claim that the serfs' demesne and corvée labor was the quid pro quo, and a fair one (or implicitly agreed upon), for access to the benefits of feudal society. The claim is rebutted by Brenner (1976), and will not be further discussed here. The disagreement between North and Thomas and Marxists concerns the proper specification of the characteristic function: that is, what income would the serfs have enjoyed if they had seceded from feudal society, even supposing that the immediate costs of withdrawal need not be counted? This disagreement will occupy us more in Chapter 8, when the concept of socially necessary exploitation is discussed.

To say that serfs would be better off if they withdrew from bondage and preserved their access to technology and land is to invoke a static notion of welfare comparison, which is purposeful at this point. What should be conveyed is that the ex-serfs could enjoy a bundle of leisure and goods which strictly dominated the bundle they received under feudal bondage. If the problem is treated dynamically, one is forced to ask other questions. Suppose, after withdrawal from serfdom, the peasant eventually becomes a proletarian, after being impoverished by his ineffectiveness in competitive agricultural capitalism which develops after feudalism's demise. As a proletarian, is he now better off than he was on the manor?

Disregarding these dynamic issues, the purpose of the definition of feudal exploitation should be clear. The alternative we pose to the feudal allocation of society's income is an allocation which agents could realize for themselves, through cooperative agreement, in an economy where private property is respected, but no ties of bondage or coercive dues arising therefrom exist. Thus, the inequality viewed as feudally exploitative is that inequality which is specifically feudal in origin—as opposed, for instance, to inequality which is capitalist in origin, discussed next.

3. Capitalist exploitation (with identical labor endowments)

To test whether a coalition of agents is capitalistically exploited, a different set of withdrawal rules is specified to define the game. When a coalition withdraws, it takes with it the coalition's per capita share of society's alienable, or transferable, nonhuman property. That is, a coalition can block a particular allocation if that allocation can be improved upon by the coalition, when the initial endowment of alienable assets is an equal-division, egalitarian endowment of property. While the test for feudal exploitation amounts to equalizing every agent's access to personal freedom in constructing the alternative against which a current allocation is judged, the test for capitalist exploitation amounts to equalizing every agent's access to society's alienable property (nonhuman means of production) in constructing the hypothetical alternative. Under feudalism, it is asked how well agents do if relations of feudal bondage are abolished; under capitalism, we ask how they fare if property relations in alienable property are abolished. Given this phrasing of the alternative, it is not surprising that capitalist exploitation, as here defined, is equivalent to the usual Marxian definition of exploitation in terms of socially necessary labor time and surplus value.

I proceed to verify that capitalist exploitation is equivalent to Marxian exploitation by showing this to be the case for the models of Marxian exploitation studied in Parts I and II. To prove the equivalence of the two definitions, it will be shown that the coalitions which are characterized as exploited by one definition (in terms of working longer than socially necessary labor time) are precisely the coalitions which are characterized as exploited by the other definition (in terms of having a superior alternative under the per capita share withdrawal option). First, consider the economy $\mathscr{E}(p)$. The work has already been done, for Theorem 1.8 is precisely the required result. In that theorem a communal game was defined, and it was shown that the core of the communal game consists precisely of the egalitarian allocations and that a coalition can block an inegalitarian allocation if and only if it is Marxian exploited. But the characteristic function of the communal game is precisely the characteristic function we specify for judging capitalist exploitation: each coalition S is assigned its per capita share of society's aggregate stocks, $(|S|/N)\omega$, and then minimizes labor performed subject to the requirements of production.

The same argument for equivalence of Marxian and capitalist exploitation applies to the subsistence economies $\mathscr{E}(p, w)$ and $\mathscr{E}(p, r)$. Furthermore, due to the constant-returns-to-scale technology, it is the case that any Marxian-exploiting coalition is capitalistically exploiting. If a coalition S is working less than its socially necessary labor time, $|S|\Lambda b$, at a reproducible solution in $\mathscr{E}(p)$ or $\mathscr{E}(p, w)$, then, under the rules of the game in which it receives its per capita share of endowments when it withdraws, it will fare worse: for it will have to perform socially necessary labor in amount $|S|\Lambda b$ when it organizes on its own, to reproduce.

This is summarized by:

Theorem 7.2. The core of the communal game in $\mathscr{E}(p)$, $\mathscr{E}(p, w)$, and $\mathscr{E}(p, r)$ is precisely the Marxian nonexploitative allocations. A coalition is Marxian exploited if and only if it is capitalistically exploited.

What is the relationship of Marxian and capitalist exploitation for the accumulation economy of Chapter 4? Due to the presence of the gray area of producers, the two definitions are not quite equivalent. A coalition which is Marxian exploited is necessarily capitalistically exploited, but not quite conversely.

First, we must clarify what it means to be better off under withdrawal from the accumulation economy. Agents in that economy want to maximize revenues, which depend on prices. Therefore, in the subeconomy formed by a withdrawing coalition, we must compare the revenues achievable by them to their revenues in the parent economy. Now if $(p, 1)$ is a price-wage vector which reproduces the parent economy, then it will also reproduce any subeconomy with the same technology which is operated by a coalition S possessing $(|S|/N)\omega$ for its endowments: for such a subeconomy is just a scaled-down version of the parent economy. Let a coalition S be Marxian exploited in the parent economy; recall that $\Pi^\nu(p)$ is the notation for the revenues received by producer ν. By our definition of Marxian exploitation, the coalition's total revenues, $\Sigma_{\nu\in S}\Pi^\nu(p)$, are insufficient to purchase goods embodying as much labor as the coalition expended. Now consider the subeconomy which S operates on its own, with its dowry of $(|S|/N)\omega$. By the national income identity, S in the subeconomy can purchase precisely the net output it produces with its revenues in the subeconomy, and total net output embodies as much labor as the coalition worked. Hence its revenues are greater in the subeconomy. Finally, in like manner it is seen that the complementary coalition to S fares worse by withdrawing with its per capita share of endowments, and so S is capitalistically exploited.

This same point can be seen in another way. It is clear that the total valuation of the coalition's endowment in the parent economy must be less than the value of its assigned endowment under per capita redistribution:

$$\sum_{\nu \in S} p\omega^{\nu} < \frac{|S|}{N} p\omega. \tag{3}$$

To see (3), recall $\Pi^{\nu}(p) = \pi p\omega^{\nu} + 1$ (Theorem 4.1); since S is Marxian exploited, it certainly cannot purchase its per capita share, $|S|/N$, of the net output of society, since that bundle embodies labor time in amount $|S|$. Therefore, the revenue of coalition S must be less than its per capita share of total revenue, or:

$$\frac{\pi \sum_{\nu \in S} p\omega^{\nu} + |S|}{\pi \sum_{\nu \in N} p\omega^{\nu} + N} < \frac{|S|}{N} \tag{4}$$

which implies inequality (3). Consequently, when S withdraws and receives its per capita share of social endowment, $(|S|/N)\omega$, it is initially richer than before and therefore will gain greater revenues than before.

As mentioned, the converse is not quite true. Consider a coalition which is receiving in the original economy total revenues just a little less than its per capita share; that is, assume the coalition's endowment is $(|S|/N)p\omega - \epsilon$, where ϵ is a small positive number. If there is a gray area (that is, if the organic compositions of capital are not all equal), then ϵ can be chosen sufficiently small so that S is not Marxian exploited: although its revenues are less than its proportionate share of revenue would be, they are still sufficient to enable S

to purchase *some* bundle embodying $|S|$ units of labor. Thus, S is not Marxian exploited, although it is capitalistically exploited, because under the withdrawal rules of the game defining capitalist exploitation it would achieve slightly greater revenues, as its original allocation would be worth $(|S|/N)p\omega$, and its complement would fare slightly worse.

This anomaly arises from the very strong criterion for defining Marxian exploitation in the accumulation economy, which gave rise to the gray area. Alternatively, suppose we had defined a coalition S as Marxian exploited if it could not purchase a *special* bundle embodying $|S|$ units of labor time, namely the bundle $(|S|/N)f$, where f is total net output. The reader may check that in this case Marxian and capitalist exploitation would be precisely equivalent. This device is essentially equivalent to assuming the economy produces only one good.

In the test for capitalist exploitation we have hypothetically annihilated the only difference among agents, their differential endowment of produced goods. It is not surprising, then, that the endowment-poor become better off after this annihilation and the endowment-rich worse off. In the most summary form, our specifications of the games which define feudal and capitalist exploitation capture precisely what is meant when we say feudal exploitation is that inequality which comes about because of specifically feudal relations, and capitalist exploitation is that inequality which is the consequence of relations of private property in the produced means of production (capitalist relations of property).

Just as the feudal ideologue argued that, in fact, serfs would not have been better off if they had withdrawn with their own endowments, so a bourgeois ideologue might argue that those who are Marxian exploited (that is, those whose surplus value is appropriated by others) would not, in fact, be better off if they were to withdraw with their per capita share of society's produced goods. The surplus value which workers contribute to the capitalist is, perhaps, a return to a scarce skill possessed by him, necessary for organizing production. In the formal models of Marxian exploitation which have been studied here, this is not an issue, as capitalists are pictured simply as owning resources, rather than as the vessels of entrepreneurial talent. Nevertheless, the bourgeois ideologue's argument is in theory a correct one: if, in fact, equalization of produced assets would not be sufficient to make Marxian exploited workers better off on their own, then they are not capitalistically exploited. This nontrivial bone of contention between Marxist and bourgeois thinkers will be called the subtle disagreement on the existence of capitalist exploitation under capitalism.

There is, however, a less subtle disagreement also. A common neoclassical position is that exploitation cannot be said to exist at a competitive equilibrium, because everyone has gained from trade as much as possible. How can one say μ is exploiting ν if ν has voluntarily entered into trade with μ? Now the models of Marxian exploitation which have been referred to show that *gains from trade and Marxian exploitation are not mutually exclusive.* (The proletarian gains from trading his labor power, since otherwise he cannot reproduce, but his surplus labor time is nevertheless transferred.) What is at issue here is precisely the difference between feudal and capitalist exploitation. The statement that no coalition can gain further from trade amounts to saying that the allocation is in the core of the feudal game: no group of agents, withdrawing with *its endowments,* can trade to a superior allocation for its members. Hence, the neoclassical position says, "There is no feudal exploitation under capitalism," a statement which is true by the well-known fact that competitive equilibria lie in the core of the economy, where the core refers to the game defined by private ownership withdrawal rules.

It is not always obvious whether objections to the Marxian notion of exploitation are of the subtle form (in which case there is a substantial disagreement about the contribution of agents' inalienable assets to production), or of the nonsubtle form (in which case there are two different varieties of exploitation under discussion). In the nonsubtle case, the antagonists are adopting different specifications of the hypothetical alternative which they respectively view as normatively cogent for testing "exploitation." Although, in the case of the nonsubtle disagreement, the difference between the two positions may be unambiguous, that does not mean it is simply resolved; there are still substantial disagreements concerning what kind of property entitlements are acceptable or just. I would argue that the nonsubtle disagreement is quite prevalent. In particular, if both parties to the discussion agree to model agents as differing only in their ownership rights of produced goods, then the disagreement must be of the nonsubtle variety. When the neoclassical party says that the proletarian is not exploited by the capitalist because the latter requires a return to his capital (being, we insist, produced goods, not skills) for whatever reason, what is in fact being said is that ownership rights of produced means of production must be respected, and therefore the test for capitalist exploitation is not appropriate.

To be more precise in discussions of this nature, it is convenient to differentiate between *entrepreneurs* and *coupon-clippers* among the class of capitalists. Entrepreneurs presumably earn a high return to their inalienable endowments, while coupon-clippers earn a return only to their alienable endowments. If we conceive of the capitalist class as predominantly composed of the former, then the statement "exploitation does not exist under capitalism" can be consistently interpreted as referring to *capitalist* exploitation; if the latter, then that statement can only refer to feudal exploitation.

There is, however, one most important piece of circumstantial evidence against the hypothesis that the prevailing disagreement about exploitation under capitalism is of the subtle variety. Prevailing norms of neoclassical (liberal, pluralist) social science respect private property in the means of production. (In contrast, they do not respect relations of personal bondage of either the slave or the feudal type.) Consequently, prevailing liberal philosophy cannot accept the test for capitalist exploitation which has been proposed, for that test nullifies property relations. Note that a proponent of the existence of capitalist exploitation would not judge *all* inequality under capitalism as being of the capitalistically exploiting type but only that part of it which could be eliminated by an egalitarian distribution of endowments of *alienable* resources.

I therefore conclude that a fair summary of prevailing liberal opinion, which argues against applying the term exploitation to the idealized equilibria of a private ownership market economy, is, in terms of this taxonomy, "There is no feudal exploitation under capitalism." This is a true statement, at least of a competitive equilibrium. Marxists would argue, however, that there is capitalist exploitation under capitalism, although—and this is critical—not all inequality would be eliminated by abolishing private ownership of the means of production.

The implicit alternative against which neoclassical economists evaluate allocation is the "free trade" alternative, and agents or coalitions are exploited if they could be doing better under that alternative. The culprits in a neoclassically exploitative allocation are barriers to the competitive operation of markets. We can, indeed, link up another traditional neoclassical notion of exploitation with our characterization of it as feudal exploitation. Ostroy (1980) has shown that in large economies the allocations in the private ownership core of an exchange economy (that is, feudally nonexploitative allocations) are precisely those allocations at which every agent is receiving his marginal product, properly defined. Thus, those allocations where there is an agent receiving less than his marginal product are precisely the allocations which are feudally exploitative, in our nomenclature.

On the other hand, the implicit alternative against which a Marxist evaluates an allocation is not one of free trade, but of "free" alienable property.

We close this section by noting that our specification of the communal game, which defines capitalist exploitation, has the advantage of capturing the Marxian theory of exploitation without reference to the labor theory of value. It is property relations which occupy center stage in the definition, not the transfer of labor. This immediately clarifies the different ethical positions which lie behind neoclassical and Marxist conceptions of exploitation, as they are exhibited transparently in the rules of the game which define the two concepts.

4. Capitalist exploitation (the general case)

As has been argued in Chapter 6, the natural environment in which to define Marxian exploitation is one in which labor is homogeneous and supplied equally by all agents. If labor is homogeneous but differentially supplied, or heterogeneous, questions arise concerning the usefulness of a surplus labor concept of exploitation.

There are two candidates for a definition of capitalist exploitation in the presence of differential or heterogeneous labor. One specifies the alternative as one where coalitions withdraw with their per capita share of alienable endowment; in the other, they withdraw with *per labor* shares of the endowment. In the case of differential but homogeneous labor, per labor shares can be easily defined; with heterogeneous labor, it was proposed that per labor shares could be defined by aggregating labors supplied at the equilibrium wage rates. Since exploitation already depends on prices (Chapter 5), no generality is lost by using market wages at this point.

In the model with differential but homogeneous labor, it can be verified, as in the previous section, that surplus labor exploitation, or Marxian exploitation (of Chapter 6), implies capitalist exploitation, if we take the per labor share withdrawal specification of capitalist exploitation. That is, a coalition S would receive $(\Sigma_S l^\nu/L)\omega$, where $L = \Sigma_N l^\nu$, when it withdraws. (The converse, as in section 3, does not quite hold due to the gray area.) If, however, the per capita withdrawal rule is taken to specify capitalist exploitation, then surplus labor exploitation does not imply capitalist exploitation. Consider, for instance, an agent who is "highly skilled"—that is, supplies a large l^ν. His private endowment ω^ν gives him wealth $p\omega^\nu$ greater than his per capita share of wealth, but less than his per labor share. We can concoct such an arrangement where ν is Marxian exploited (that is, ν is incapable of commanding through his purchases the amount of labor he expended); but if he withdraws with his per capita share of ω he will be even worse off—hence, he is not capitalistically exploited, according to this specification.

I do not argue, however, that this constitutes good reason to choose the per labor withdrawal option as the correct generalization of capitalist exploitation to the general case, precisely because it is not clear that the surplus labor (Marxian) definition of exploitation is the proper generalization to the case of differential or heterogeneous labor. The issue cannot be settled on a formal level. Although the Class Exploitation Correspondence Principle is preserved by adopting the surplus labor definition (and hence the per labor share specification of the alternative) in the case of differential homogeneous labor, that provides no good reason for preferring that definition, since it is not at all clear that a group of wealthy, skilled labor sellers *should* be thought of as exploited, from the historical materialist point of view. And in the heterogeneous labor case, there is no formal reason for preferring the per labor specification over the per capita one, as the CECP fails to hold and class becomes an irrelevant phenomenon.

I will argue in the final chapters that, in fact, the per capita withdrawal specification of the alternative is the proper one, from a historical point of view, in the specification of capitalist exploitation in the general case. What is thereby claimed is this: in testing for the existence of capitalist exploitation, what an agent or coalition is presumed entitled to (that is, what he can withdraw with) is the fruits of his own labor in the form of wages, but *not* the capitalized fruits of those wages in the form of a greater-than-per-capita share of the means of production. In the case of a fixed coefficients technology, the per capita withdrawal specification has a drawback in that the alternative distribution of capital stock is not even efficient. (That is, a person supplying very little labor l^ν will not be able gainfully to employ his per capita share $(1/N)\omega$ of the stock, while an agent supplying large l^ν will still be capital-constrained when he withdraws with his per capita share of stock.) This is, however, a problem special to fixed coefficient technology, which also generated other problems, such as the knife-edge property of Chapter 4. If the technology permits substitution of labor for capital, then in the per capita distribution of capital, all capital can be gainfully employed, and an agent's income will increase strictly with his supply of labor. Thus, the "skilled" will receive an extra remuneration for their effort, but not a doubly extra remuneration, due to their effort and to an increased entitlement of capital which their effort would command them in the per labor distribution of productive assets.

Indeed, we can reopen the discussion of whether entrepreneurs are capitalistically exploiting. Suppose an entrepreneur possesses an especially scarce and important skill and is thereby able to earn large revenues and, moreover, to capitalize them and then to become a coupon-clipper in his old age. According to the per capita definition, he is a capitalist exploiter; according to the per labor definition, he is not. Favoring the per capita definition of capitalist exploitation, I am thus able to make a stronger claim than was asserted in section 3: even if capitalist wealth results from entrepreneurial skill or frugality, it constitutes capitalist exploitation. (Indeed, this is one reason for favoring that definition.) A highly paid technician who does not accumulate capital but spends his income is not a capitalist exploiter, however.

A third possibility for a definition of capitalist exploitation will be mentioned, although I have rejected it. The test for feudal exploitation was to evaluate a coalition's well-being (or income) when it is allowed to exempt itself from ties of feudal bondage only. Similarly, we could take as the proper specification of capitalist exploitation that a coalition's alternative is to exempt itself from ties to alienable property in the means of production. That is, its alternative should be to produce in an environment where it is not capital-constrained. The dowry of alienable property which a coalition receives, upon exercising its withdrawal option to test for capitalist exploitation, is that amount of produced capital which it can gainfully employ, with the skills and labor of its members. We hypothetically allow coalitions to exempt themselves from all capital constraints.

Note that this definition of capitalist exploitation is a generalization of the per labor share withdrawal definition of the differential but homogeneous labor case. Indeed, the formal appeal of the definition is that it does generalize that definition to a general model of production. (In particular, it allows us to handle heterogeneous labor without relying on market wages.) It is an unappealing definition, however, for the same reason—it specializes to the per labor share and not the per capita share specification. Moreover, for some technologies, a coalition might be able gainfully to employ an infinite amount of capital, thereby producing infinite income. (This, for instance, is the case with neoclassical production functions.) In this case, no coalition will ever be judged exploited in any allocation, because even if it would be better off under the specified alternative (of withdrawing with infinite capital), so would be its complement, and hence inequality (2) of the definition of exploitation would fail. Thus, in general, this third definition of capitalist exploitation seems more to capture the fact that coalitions may not be able to exploit sufficient capital, than that they are exploited by other coalitions of people.

With heterogeneous labor I conclude that the proper definition of capitalist exploitation entails a per capita distribution of capital in the hypothetical alternative. The surplus labor theory of exploitation is not the correct generalization of Marxian exploitation from the case of homogeneous and identical labor endowment, it is claimed, even though in the case of homogeneous (but differential) labor endowment, the surplus labor concept can be defined and has, perhaps, a certain formal appeal (cf. the CECP). If this is correct, then the property rights approach to Marxian exploitation becomes not only useful but necessary in the presence of differential skills: the transfer of surplus labor becomes an extremely inconvenient and problematic concept, but the idea of entitlement to output based on per capita distribution of productive assets and current wage earnings is clear. It bears repeating, however, that no formal reason has been provided for preferring the per capita wealth distribution specification. At best, the indication to prefer that definition is historical, in this sense: it is this distribution that socialist societies appear to be trying to effect, rather than the distribution of productive assets in proportion to labor or skill.

5. Socialist exploitation

We now pose the rules of the game which define socialist exploitation. Some endowments were not hypothetically equalized in formulating the rules of the game to test for capitalist exploitation: endowments of inalienable assets, skills. Let us picture an idyllic socialist economy where private property is not held in alienable assets, but inalienable assets are held by individuals. Under market arrangements, those with scarce skills will be better off than the unskilled. This inequality is not capitalist exploitation, however, since there is already equal access to social capital, and so no coalition can improve its position by withdrawing with its per capita share of society's alienable means of production. We may wish to refer to this inequality as socialist exploitation, characterized as follows. Let a coalition withdraw, taking with it its per capita share of *all* endowments, alienable and inalienable. If it can improve the position of its members, and if the complementary coalition is worse off under such an arrangement, then it is socialistically exploited at the allocation in question.

There are, of course, formidable incentive problems with carrying out this procedure, as has been discussed by parties to the Rawlsian debate over talent pooling. (See, for example, Kronman, 1981.) How can talents be pooled without destroying them? I shall discuss this sort of problem in Chapter 8. Although the potential *realization* of the alternative is problematical, as a hypothetical test it can be specified. For the sake of concreteness, a model is now presented.

For simplicity, we make several heroic assumptions. First, we assume a "socialist subsistence" economy. The producers wish to minimize labor time expended subject to producing some common subsistence vector b. This is done in order to show the relationship between socialist exploitation, capitalist exploitation, and Marxian exploitation in the clearest manner, at the level of the model of Chapter 1. This assumption could be dropped, but only at the cost of the more complicated definition of Marxian exploitation, of Chapter 4. As our purpose here is to outline an example, the subsistence simplifying assumption is made.

Assume that there is a single indecomposable, productive Leontief technology (A, L), with $L > 0$, and n sectors, but that each producer has access to only some subset of the n processes. Producer ν has knowledge of sectors indexed by integers in the set $J^\nu \subseteq$

$\{1, \ldots, n\}$. This models the idea that producers have different skills. Note, however, that each producer possesses some socially necessary skill, since the economy is indecomposable. A more general model might posit an activity analysis technology with many processes, and some producers would have knowledge of only inferior processes. Such a model would necessitate a more complicated definition of socially necessary labor time.

We model the socialist nature of the economy by remarking that there is no "wealth constraint," as in the producer's optimization program in capitalist and precapitalist economy. Any inputs he needs are instantly available from the center. Thus, producers are never capital-constrained in this economy. It is perhaps more convenient to think of producer ν as a socialist collective, a worker-managed firm, which has access to the produced means of production. Collectives differ only according to their technological know-how.

The subsistence requirement for each producer (collective) is the vector b. As in the models of Part I, each producer seeks to minimize labor time expended subject to being able to pay for the inputs he procured from the center. His program is:

$$\text{choose } x^\nu \in \mathbb{R}^n_+ \text{ to min } Lx^\nu$$

subject to

$$px^\nu - pA\,x^\nu \geqq pb$$
$$Lx^\nu \leqq 1$$
$$x^\nu_j = 0 \quad \text{for } j \notin J^\nu.$$

The purchases of inputs are pAx^ν and pb is the value of subsistence, so the constraint expresses the fact that the value of gross product is sufficient to pay these two costs. Let $\mathscr{A}^\nu(p)$ be the set of solutions to ν's program.

Definition. A price vector p and activity vectors $x^1, \ldots, x^N$ constitute a *reproducible solution* for the socialist subsistence economy with N producers if:

(1) $x^\nu \in \mathscr{A}^\nu(p)$, for all ν
(2) $x = \Sigma x^\nu$ and $(I - A)x \geqq Nb$.

A reproducible solution allows each producer to optimize, and social *net* output is sufficient to feed everyone. That is, the inputs that are used up (Ax) are replaced.

As in the previous models of this genre, it follows that:

Theorem 7.3. At a reproducible solution aggregate work time is:

$$Lx = NL(I - A)^{-1}b \equiv N\Lambda b$$

where $\Lambda = L(I - A)^{-1}$.

Proof. At a RS, $(I - A)x \geqq Nb$ and so $x \geqq N(I - A)^{-1}b$, implying that $x > 0$ since A is indecomposable, so $(I - A)^{-1} > 0$. This implies that $p \geqq pA$, for a sector j with $p_j - pA_j < 0$ would never operate (examine the producer's program). But $p \geqq pA$ implies $p > 0$ by indecomposability of A, and the fact that A is a productive matrix.

At an individual optimum, $x^\nu \in \mathscr{A}^\nu(p)$, it is clear from the program each producer sets

$$p(I - A)x^\nu = pb,$$

for if $p(I - A)x^\nu > pb$, then ν could reduce his labor time further since $L > 0$. Hence summing these equality constraints over all ν gives:

$$p(I - A)x = Npb. \tag{a}$$

However, $(I - A)x \geqq Nb$ by reproducibility; it follows from (a), and because $p > 0$, that $(I - A)x = Nb$. The result follows. QED

We identify Λb as socially necessary labor time, for reasons with which the reader is familiar. Theorem 7.3 thus informs us that at a RS, society as a whole works socially necessary labor time.

However, it is possible that some producers work longer than Λb and some less than Λb. Such *inegalitarian* reproducible solutions virtually always exist. If

$$Lx^\nu > \Lambda b > Lx^\mu, \tag{b}$$

a Marxist might be tempted to say that ν is exploited and μ is an exploiter. Note that such inegalitarianism is an explicitly social phenomenon, in this sense. Suppose μ has knowledge of the whole matrix (A, L), but ν has knowledge only of certain columns, and they are the only two producers in the economy. Then inequality (b) may very well be the case at a reproducible solution. (In particular, μ can never work longer than ν at a RS.) Now suppose ν leaves the economy. Without ν, μ can reproduce himself, but he must work Λb time to fulfill $(I - A)x \geqq b$ (note that $N = 1$ now). Hence μ becomes worse off with ν's departure. Thus μ is better off because of ν's presence; one might argue that surplus value is being transferred from ν to μ through the exchange mechanism, and be tempted to call such expropriation of surplus value "exploitation."

According to our taxonomic device, this inegalitarianism is not *capitalist* exploitation. Indeed, if ν withdraws in a coalition of one, no matter what alienable assets he is assigned he cannot improve his position. (This is clear, since alienable assets are available in unlimited amount from the center in this economy.) In fact, he cannot even reproduce himself on his own, as he does not have knowledge of the whole technology.

However, this inequality is *socialist* exploitation. How do we formulate the withdrawal rule for a coalition to test for socialist exploitation? We allow the coalition to take with it its per capita share of society's inalienable assets. Precisely, each member of a withdrawing coalition is assigned the ability to operate each individual's technology for $1/N$ of the day. Under this average or composite technology, we easily show:

Theorem 7.4. Let $(p, x^1, \ldots, x^N)$ be a RS. Then μ is socialistically exploited if and only if $Lx^\mu > \Lambda b$.

Proof. Let $Lx^\mu > \Lambda b$. At the RS, $(I - A)x = Nb$, and thus $(1/N)(I - A)x = b$. But this means that μ can produce for himself the net output vector b with the composite technology which he has been assigned, as he has precisely the capabilities of $1/N$ of society in the aggregate. Thus he operates activity levels $(1/N)\Sigma x^\nu$ and reproduces himself, working time $L((1/N)x) = \Lambda b$, thus improving his situation.

The converse is immediate. QED

In fact, the same proof shows a slightly more general proposition: a coalition S of producers is socialistically exploited if and only if

$$\sum_{\nu \in S} Lx^{\nu} > |S|\Lambda b.$$

Similarly, a coalition *J* is socialistically exploiting if and only if

$$\sum_{S} Lx^{\nu} < |S|\Lambda b.$$

Thus, if all individual endowments are of either the alienable or inalienable type, then an allocation is free of socialist exploitation precisely when it is in the equal-division core. Before examining this proposal more critically in Chapter 8, we should note how a certain classical conception of socialism and communism is reflected in this definition. The historical task of the socialist revolution is to bring about a regime where each labors according to his ability and is paid according to his work, while the communist revolution (from socialism) transforms the formula so that each is paid according to his need. Thus, socialist exploitation is to be expected under socialism: the elimination of differential rewards to ability is not socialism's historical task, only the elimination of differential rewards to property ownership. The communist revolution is the one which eliminates socialist exploitation. This is as it should be, following the historical parallels of the demise of feudal exploitation in the capitalist revolution, and of capitalist exploitation in the socialist revolution.

Hence, the rules of the latest game seem to fit classical definitions. The troublesome question is: To what extent can we attribute inequality in real socialist economies to "socialist exploitation"?

6. Formal specifications of exploitation

In this section the game-theoretic definitions of exploitation which have been proposed are written down more precisely.

(i) Marxian exploitation in private ownership subsistence economies

To define exploitation for the economies $\mathscr{E}(p)$, $\mathscr{E}(p, w)$, and $\mathscr{E}(p, r)$ of Chapters 1–3, identify the "income" of a coalition at a reproducible solution as the *negative* of its labor time and set

$$v^1(S) = -|S|\Lambda b, \text{ for every coalition } S.$$

This obviously defines the concept of Marxian exploitation studied for those economies. In this case, we have more structure on the game: we can actually tell a story by which each coalition can achieve the payoff $v^1(S)$ under some concrete alternate form of social organization. Namely, each coalition hypothetically withdraws from the original economy, taking its per capita share of aggregate endowments, $(|S|/N)\omega$, and operates the subeconomy on its own, in a communal way. In this way, every producer will be assigned a work time of Λb.

(ii) Capitalist exploitation in the accumulation economy

This has been discussed briefly in section 3. At given prices $(p, 1)$ which reproduce the accumulation economy, we have specified the alternative which defines whether a coalition is capitalistically exploited as withdrawal from the economy, taking with it endowments $(|S|/N)\omega$, and operating the subeconomy at the original prices, distributing revenues in an egalitarian way. Since revenue as a function of wealth W is $\Pi = \pi W + 1$, for a coalition S we define:

$$v^2(S) = \pi \frac{|S|}{N} p\omega + |S| = |S| \left(\pi \frac{p\omega}{N} + 1 \right).$$

A coalition S is capitalistically exploited if and only if it is receiving less revenue than $v^2(S)$ in the original reproducible solution. Note that $v^2(S)$ is linear homogeneous in the size of the coalition.

(iii) Marxian exploitation in the accumulation economy

For this exploitation concept, we defined a coalition S as exploited if and only if it did not possess enough wealth to purchase some bundle from society's net output which embodied as much labor as it worked. The definition of $v(S)$ is a little more subtle in this case. We define $v^3(S)$ as that amount of revenue which S requires to purchase the least expensive bundle of final output which embodies $|S|$ units of labor. We have actually encountered v^3 before, in the appendix to Chapter 4. Using the notation introduced there:

$$v^3(S) = W_s.$$

Thus, $v^3(S)$ is in fact a function only of size of the coalition $s \equiv |S|$, and we see a graph of $v^3(S)$ in Figure 8. Note that $v^3(S)$ is a concave function which implies that v^3 is a superadditive characteristic function, that is:[5]

$$v^3(S) + v^3(T) \leqq v^3(S \cup T) \quad \text{for } S \cap T = \emptyset \tag{5}$$

The functions v^1 and v^2 defined in paragraphs (i) and (ii) above, were linear homogeneous, and so inequality (5) held always as an equality.

Recall that capitalist exploitation in the accumulation economy does not quite imply Marxian exploitation in the accumulation economy. This is because v^3 and v^2 are not identical functions. Notice that, unlike with the exploitation defined by v^1 and v^2, we do not have a story concerning the concrete alternate organization of a subeconomy which will produce revenues $v^3(S)$ for each coalition S. We have simply pulled $v^3(S)$ out of a hat, as it were, to capture a formal concept of the command over embodied labor time. In the subsistence economies $\mathscr{E}(p)$, $\mathscr{E}(p, w)$, and $\mathscr{E}(p, r)$, "Marxian" exploitation corresponded precisely to our notion of capitalist exploitation; that is, the surplus labor definition is precisely captured by the characteristic function $v^1(S)$, which corresponded to a story about an alternative organization of society.

Given the concrete specification of the alternative accumulation economy, in terms of a redistribution of property rights, which defines capitalist exploitation $v^2(S)$, we are directed to consider capitalist exploitation as a perhaps more appropriate generalization of the Marxian concept of exploitation to an accumulation context than what we have studied as "Marxian" exploitation, specified by $v^3(S)$. The exploitation concept $v^3(S)$ cannot be captured precisely by a redistribution of property. It appears that the definition of exploitation in terms of property rights is not only more general than the surplus labor definition but is a better definition as well, due to the concrete institutional alternative which it poses.

(iv) Subsistence socialist exploitation

This refers to socialist exploitation defined for the model in the previous section. Identifying income as the negative of work

5. In fact, v^3 defines a convex game; convex games are discussed in sections 7 and 8.

time, set:

$$v^4(S) = -|S|\Lambda b.$$

As discussed, this concept of exploitation also corresponds to a precise institutional alternative in property rights, this time to property rights in "ownership" of processes in the technology.

(v) Feudal exploitation

We have not studied an explicit model of feudalism in this book, and therefore will not propose a specific function $v(S)$ to capture feudal exploitation. According to the discussion of section 2, the characteristic function for feudal exploitation is the one for the usual private ownership exchange economy, which defines the payoff to the coalition S as what it could achieve by cooperative arrangements on its own, availing itself of the private endowments of its members.

7. Exploitation with increasing returns to scale

The technologies postulated in the models of previous chapters exhibit constant returns to scale. Suppose, however, the technology is characterized by increasing returns to scale or production indivisibilities. Then, according to the definition provided, no individual will be exploited. For instance, if a single proletarian were to withdraw with his per capita share of alienable, nonhuman assets, he would surely be worse off employing a technology characterized by production indivisibilities, social division of labor, and increasing returns. This problem emerged also in the nonconvexity of military protection which serfs were provided under feudalism. A single serf would appear not to be feudally exploited, since by withdrawing with his own assets he could not provide himself military protection. In this section, a way of discussing exploitation in the presence of increasing returns or indivisibilities is proposed.[6]

Note that although no individual may be exploited in an increasing returns situation, individual exploiters are in general identifiable. If the characteristic function defining exploitation is $v(S)$, then

6. This section and the next are more technical, and may be omitted at first reading.

an individual exploiter is an agent ν for whom:

$$v(\{\nu\}) < z^{\nu} \tag{1}$$

$$v(N - \nu) > \sum_{\mu \in (N-\nu)} z^{\mu} \tag{2}$$

where the allocation in question is $\{z^1, z^2, \ldots, z^N\}$. In general, large coalitions (such as $N - \nu$) will be able fully to exploit the increasing returns, so (2) may hold for certain ν; and, as discussed above, (1) is likely to hold for almost every ν due to increasing returns. Hence the typical situation with increasing returns is one where individual exploiters can be identified, but no agents are individually exploited.

In fact, the analytical apparatus for discussing this problem has already been developed in the appendix to Chapter 4, and the task here will be to show how it can be applied to the problems of an increasing-returns-to-scale economy. Summarizing in advance, the result is this: an agent will be called *vulnerable* if he is a member of a minimal exploited coalition, and *culpable* if he is a member of a minimal exploiting coalition. I propose vulnerability and culpability as the appropriate descriptions of individual agents which generalize the traits of individuals being exploited or exploiting. This section shows that for the class of convex games, with which we can model economies with increasing returns and other forms of positive economic externality, vulnerability and culpability provide a partition of the set of agents into the exploited coalition of all vulnerable agents, the exploiting coalition of all culpable agents, and a third (perhaps empty) coalition of agents who are neither vulnerable nor culpable. In section 8, an attempt is made to justify why one might view this partition as the canonical one in discussing exploitation, by showing that under certain postulates of behavior, it will be the coalition of vulnerable agents $\mathcal{V}$ which sets itself against the coalition of culpable agents $\mathcal{C}$ in the struggle to end exploitation. Thus although no individual may be exploited, we can nevertheless speak of the (nonempty) coalition of vulnerable agents as the canonical exploited coalition when economic externalities are present. No serf is exploited, but all serfs are vulnerable, and the coalition of vulnerable agents is the class of serfs.

Let $v(S)$ be the characteristic function against which we evaluate the exploitation status of agents at allocation $\{z^1, \ldots, z^N\}$. The assumption of increasing returns will be modeled by postulating that $v(S)$ is a *convex game:*

Definition.[7] $v(S)$ is a convex game if and only if, for all coalitions S and T:

$$v(S) + v(T) \leqq v(S \cup T) + v(S \cap T).$$

(With the convention that $v(\emptyset) = 0$, note that a convex game is superadditive.)

The sense in which convexity of v captures the increasing returns property of the economy is seen as follows. Let R and S be any two coalitions. Define the set $T = R - S$. Note that $R - T = R \cap S$ and $S \cup T = S \cup R$. Hence, applying the definition of convexity of v to two sets R and S gives:

$$v(R) + v(S) \leqq v(R - T) + v(S \cup T)$$

or

$$v(R) - v(R - T) \leqq v(S \cup T) - v(S). \tag{3}$$

Noting that T is disjoint from both the sets $R - T$ and S, (3) has the following interpretation. Consider the coalition $R - T$ and the coalition S, which includes $R - T$. The coalitions $R - T$ and S can achieve $v(R - T)$ and $v(S)$, respectively, on their own. If the larger coalition, S, is augmented with new members T, the gain $v(S \cup T) - v(S)$ is greater than if the smaller coalition, $R - T$, is augmented with those same new members T. This is precisely an increasing returns condition. The marginal product of new members is always larger for a big coalition than is the marginal product of those same members to a subset of the coalition.

Indeed, and conversely, if inequality (3) holds for all sets R, S, and T defined by $T = R - S$ then the game is convex. This is immediate, since $S \cup T = S \cup R$ and $R - T = R \cap S$. Hence, the increasing returns condition (3) characterizes convex games.

Definition. Let the minimal exploited sets be called V^t and the minimal exploiting sets be called C^t. An agent is vulnerable if he is a

7. Convex games are studied by Shapley (1971).

member of some V^t and culpable if he is a member of some C^t. Let $\mathcal{V} = \bigcup V^t$ and $\mathcal{C} = \bigcup C^t$. The main result is:

Theorem 7.5.

(a) $\mathcal{V}$ is an exploited set;
(b) $\mathcal{C}$ is an exploiting set;
(c) $\mathcal{V} \cap \mathcal{C} = \emptyset$.

As a preliminary result we prove:

Lemma 7.6. Let v be a convex game and $v(N) \leqq \Sigma_N z^i$ at the allocation $\{z^1, \ldots, z^N\}$. Let R and S be two exploited sets whose intersection $R \cap S$ is not an exploited set. Then $R \cup S$ is an exploited set. (This is the generalization of Lemma A4.3 to the present context.)

Proof. By hypothesis:

$$\sum_R z^i < v(R) \tag{4}$$

$$\sum_S z^i < v(S) \tag{5}$$

and from Theorem 7.1 it follows that:

$$\sum_{R \cap S} z^i \geqq v(R \cap S). \tag{6}$$

From (4)–(6) and the definition of convexity of v:

$$\begin{aligned} \sum_R z^i + \sum_S z^i < v(R) + v(S) &\leqq v(R \cup S) + v(R \cap S) \\ &\leqq v(R \cup S) + \sum_{R \cap S} z^i \end{aligned} \tag{7}$$

and hence:

$$\sum_{R \cup S} z^i \equiv \sum_R z^i + \sum_S z^i - \sum_{R \cap S} z^i < v(R \cup S) \tag{8}$$

which implies, by Theorem 7.1, that $R \cup S$ is exploited. QED

A corollary to Lemma 7.6 is:

Corollary 7.7. Let v be a convex game and $v(N) \leqq \Sigma_N z^i$. Let R and S be two exploited coalitions whose union $R \cup S$ is not exploited. Then $R \cap S$ is exploited.

Proof. Immediate.

Next, consider the *maximal exploited* sets W^τ. Note:

Lemma 7.8. The complement of a maximal exploited set is a minimal exploiting set.

Proof. This follows from the fact that exploiting sets are precisely the complements of exploited sets. By definition, $(W^\tau)'$ is an exploiting set. If it were not minimal, then some strictly included set is exploiting, which means some strictly inclusive set of W^τ is exploited, contradicting the maximality of W^τ in the class of exploited sets. QED

Proof of Theorem 7.5, parts (a) and (b).

Part (a): Enumerate the minimal exploited sets $V^1, V^2, \ldots$. Inductive application of Lemma 7.5 proves the claim. That is, $V^1 \cup V^2$ is exploited; $(V^1 \cup V^2) \cup V^3$ is exploited; and so on. At each stage, the minimality of V^i as an exploited set is used.

Part (b): By Lemma 7.8, the complements of the C^t are precisely the sets W^τ. By De Morgan's Laws, $\mathscr{C} = \cup C^t = (\cap W^\tau)'$. By induction on $W^1, W^2, \ldots$ Corollary 7.7 proves that $(\cap W^\tau)$ is an exploited set: $W^1 \cap W^2$ is exploited; $(W^1 \cap W^2) \cap W^3$ is exploited; at each stage, the maximality of W^τ as an exploited set is employed. Hence $(\cap W^\tau)'$ is an exploiting set and part (b) follows. QED

Finally:

Lemma 7.9. $\mathscr{V} \subseteq \mathscr{W}$ where $\mathscr{V} = \cup V^t$ and $\mathscr{W} = \cap W^\tau$.

Proof. It is required to show $\forall t, \tau, V^t \subseteq W^\tau$. Suppose there is a pair t, τ for which $V^t \not\subseteq W^\tau$. Then $W^\tau \cap V^t$ is not an exploited set, since it is a proper subset of V^t, and V^t is a minimal exploited set. Hence, by Lemma 7.6, $W^\tau \cup V^t$ is an exploited set, which contradicts the maximality of W^τ in the class of exploited sets. QED

Proof of Theorem 7.5, part (c). We have shown that $\mathscr{C} = \mathscr{W}'$. Hence $\mathscr{V} \subseteq \mathscr{W}$ implies $\mathscr{V} \cap \mathscr{C} = \emptyset$. QED Theorem 7.5

We can introduce the group of strongly neutral agents:

Definition. An agent is *strongly neutral* if he is neither vulnerable nor culpable. The set of strongly neutral agents is $\mathscr{S}$.

Thus, in the increasing returns economy, society is broken down into three disjoint groups: the vulnerable, the culpable, and the strongly neutral. I have argued above that usually the culpable agents will also be individual exploiters, although the vulnerable agents will not be individually exploited. Nevertheless, in the increasing returns economy, it is proposed that the sensible generalization of the concept of individual exploitation is vulnerability. The result which allows this claim is that no agent is both vulnerable and culpable. Hence the identification of the status of an individual with respect to the "welfare" concept is unambiguous. Although individual serfs may not have been better off under the alternative proposed in characterizing feudal exploitation, they certainly were vulnerable, since every serf (I claim) was the member of some minimal exploited coalition. The same holds for individual proletarians with respect to the definition of capitalist exploitation in an economy with increasing returns.

The collection of all vulnerable agents, $\mathscr{V}$, is proposed as *the* canonical exploited class in the economy. (It is therefore important to show that $\mathscr{V}$ is itself an exploited set.) Similarly, $\mathscr{C}$ is the canonical class of exploiters. There may be, in addition, strongly neutral agents who are members of neither of these classes. (In the economies of Parts I and II, these agents must be members of the petty bourgeoisie, (+, 0, 0).) It should also be remarked that so long as there is at least one exploited coalition in the economy, then there is a minimal exploited set, and hence vulnerable agents; in addition, the complement of that one exploited coalition is an exploiting coalition, and so there is a minimal exploiting coalition and hence culpable agents. Thus, as long as exploitation exists, in the sense of there existing some exploited coalition, then the classification of society into $\mathscr{V} \cup \mathscr{C} \cup \mathscr{S}$ is nonvacuous (neither $\mathscr{V}$ nor $\mathscr{C}$ is empty).

The proposal of this section can be summarized as follows. The correct general question to ask, when evaluating the exploitation status of an agent, is: Is he vulnerable or culpable or strongly neutral? In economies where the payoffs in the hypothetical alternative enjoy constant returns to scale, the minimal exploited coalitions all consist of single agents, and hence vulnerable agents and exploited agents are the same individuals.[8] (This was true of the subsistence economies of Part I with respect to Marxian exploitation.) In those cases, it is therefore sufficient to ask if an agent is exploited or exploiting. In economies with increasing returns to scale, however, the more general question concerning vulnerability and culpability must be asked.

Finally, it must be said that the assumption that a game be convex is a strong one. One might argue that a weaker characterization of increasing returns is desirable; but then, of course, the truth of the main result, Theorem 7.5, will be problematical. An additional advantage of convex games is that they always possess nonempty cores (see Shapley, 1971). Thus, nonexploitative allocations are guaranteed to exist, and so the ethical imperative associated with the exploitation notion is not vacuous.

Despite the strength of the convexity assumption, I would argue that it does capture our intuitive notion of increasing returns in many instances. Suppose, for example, that all agents have identical skills but different endowments of alienable assets, and the technology enjoys increasing returns. We are examining capitalist exploitation, and hence define the alternative $v(S)$ by examining the output of coalitions endowed with their per capita shares of alienable assets. That game will be convex, as can be seen by considering the characterization of inequality (3) of this section.

It is possible, however, to construct reasonable economic games with nonempty cores, but which are not convex, and in which some agents are vulnerable *and* culpable, thereby indicating an ambiguity in the theory as developed here. In fact, such an example has appeared in Chapter 1, section 4: reference is made to the economy with three agents, containing two blocking coalitions at the reproducible solution. The game $v(S)$ will be to test for *feudal* exploitation. Thus, the payoff to a coalition is determined by how well it can fare by withdrawing with its own assets. Since the objective function is

8. One can have increasing returns to scale in the absence of production; scale economies here refers to returns to scale in the size of coalitions. For example, in a pure exchange economy, there are generally returns to scale in the size of coalitions. (That is, there are gains to be had from trade.)

to minimize time worked, let the payoff be the negative of time worked. Let $\lambda \equiv \Lambda b$; then the payoff structure for that example is:

$$v(1, 2, 3) = -3\lambda$$
$$v(1, 2) = v(1, 3) = v(2, 3) = -2\lambda$$
$$v(2) = v(3) = -\lambda$$
$$v(1) = -M \ll -\lambda.$$

This asserts that every coalition except {1} is viable, and since {1} cannot reproduce himself, he suffers some large disutility, $-M$. At the reproducible solution constructed in Chapter 1, the coalitions {1, 2} and {1, 3} are minimal *feudally* exploited coalitions. Consequently all agents are feudally vulnerable. However, agents 3 and 2 are each feudally culpable. Notice that v is superadditive but not convex, since $v(1, 2) + v(1, 3) > v(1) + v(1, 2, 3)$. The feudal core is nonempty, as it contains the feasible allocation $(-\lambda, -\lambda, -\lambda)$. Note that Appendix 2.2 shows that this "feudal" exploitation exists because of the incomplete set of markets in $\mathscr{E}(p)$.

8. The canonical exploited coalition and class struggle[9]

In Section 7 it has been argued that when returns to scale are increasing, the game-theoretic definition of exploitation appears not to be satisfactory in the sense that there may be no exploited individuals. Who, then, do we identify as the agents bearing the brunt of exploitation? In general, every agent is a member of some exploited coalition (even the richest), and so being a member of an exploited coalition is surely too weak as a criterion to identify the agents with whom we should sympathize. It has been proposed that vulnerability and culpability are appropriate generalizations of the conditions of being individually exploited and exploiting, respectively. Thus far the motivation for the significance of vulnerability and culpability has been only heuristic. It has been suggested that the set of vulnerable agents $\mathscr{V}$ is, in some sense, the canonical exploited set, whose members we should consider to be bearing the brunt of exploitation at the allocation in question: yet this suggestion is only heuristic in that no behavioral justification has been provided to mo-

9. I thank Lloyd Shapley for very useful discussions pertaining to this material.

tivate the claim. By behavioral justification, I mean this: can we propose a procedure by which agents would coalesce to demand their "just" entitlements (under the alternative specified by the characteristic function v), resulting in the formation of the coalition $\mathscr{V}$ as *the* one which would cooperatively assert its claim? If so, some explanation based on rational behavior could be offered for considering the coalition then formed as the canonical exploited coalition. Put differently, where will the barricades form in class struggle? Which agents will be on one side and which on the other, in the struggle to end exploitation?

This section studies this problem, and will specify a behavior of coalition formation under which a unique coalition emerges to claim its payoff $v(S)$, from an initial situation where the allocation is $\langle z^1, \ldots, z^N \rangle = \zeta$. We will expect to "observe" class struggle taking place between two coalitions: on the one hand, an exploited coalition Ω nested somewhere between $\mathscr{V}$ and $\mathscr{V} \cup \mathscr{S}$, and on the other hand its complement, which includes $\mathscr{C}$ and perhaps some members of $\mathscr{S}$.

A refinement of the concept of an exploiting coalition is defined next. We will call a subcoalition R of S to be *parasitic* in S, if the gain to $S - R$ from taking its payoff $v(S - R)$ is greater than the gain to S. That is:

Definition. Let $R \subseteq S$. The allocation ζ and game v are given. R is *parasitic* in S if and only if:

$$v(S - R) - \sum_{S-R} z^\nu > v(S) - \sum_{S} z^\nu.$$

We think of coalitions evaluating the gain they get from taking their payoff $v(S)$ over their income in the current allocation. If R is parasitic in S, then S would do better to expel R, as $S - R$ gains more than S. Parasiticity will form the basis of our analysis of coalition formation, as follows. Suppose it is announced that exploitation will now be ended. That is, coalitions are hereby allowed to form and come claim their $v(S)$. What coalition(s) will form and step forward to claim their payoff? By definition any exploited coalition will gain by stepping forward. But not all exploited coalitions can step forward, as they are not mutually disjoint. Moreover, some exploited coalitions may contain parasitic subcoalitions, and they arguably would want to eliminate these parasitic subcoalitions, thereby increasing the gain of the remaining members. What we might therefore ask is this: consider the class Γ of exploited coalitions which contain no parasitic subcoalitions. (These will be called *formable* coalitions.) Γ contains all the coalitions which might step forward to claim their payoff $v(S)$. Among these, we can argue the relevant subclass consists of the coalitions which are maximal in Γ (maximal in the set-theoretic sense of having no including coalitions in Γ), for the gain $(v(S) - \Sigma_S z^\nu)$ is maximized for maximal coalitions in Γ. What will be shown below is that for convex games there is a *unique maximal* coalition in Γ, and it is a coalition Ω nested between $\mathcal{V}$ and $\mathcal{V} \cup \mathcal{S}$. Thus, a behavioral justification is provided for considering Ω to be the canonical exploited coalition in the economy. If we consider the process of coalition formation to be the form class struggle takes in the model, then I have argued there is one story, at least, which indicates it is the coalition Ω that will be on one side of the barricade. On the other side will be the complement Ω' which includes $\mathcal{C}$, the set of culpable agents, and some subcoalition of $\mathcal{S}$.

The story told above is not the only reasonable one. One might respond, for example, that coalitions should not form on the basis of maximizing their gain $v(S) - \Sigma_S z^\nu$, but rather to maximize their per capita gain $(1/|S|)\ (v(S) - \Sigma_S z^\nu)$; or more complicated formulas for sharing the surplus could be considered. (Some of these will be briefly commented upon below.) The problem of providing a non-cooperative justification for coalition formation is much deeper than the present discussion. One way in which the above approach of maximizing the gain to coalitions can be justified is this: when coalitions withdraw and take their payoff $v(S)$, they agree to first make each member as well off as he was in the old regime (that is, each receives z^ν out of $v(S)$) and then the surplus is spent on a public good, which the entire coalition can enjoy. This recipe leads to the criterion proposed. Indeed, this is perhaps the recipe that socialist revolutions will adopt in sufficiently rich countries. It is not the private incomes of workers in most industrialized countries which will be increased, but the public services they can enjoy. One can also argue this has been the direction of modern social democratic capitalism.

Definition. A coalition is *formable* if and only if it has no parasitic subcoalitions.

Theorem 7.6. Let Ω be the coalition of agents who belong to some formable coaltion, for a convex game v at a Pareto optimal allocation

$\langle z^1, \ldots, z^N \rangle$, at which exploitation exists. Then:

(A) Ω is a formable coalition, and therefore the unique maximal formable coalition in N;
(B) Ω is an exploited coalition;
(C) $\mathscr{V} \subseteq \Omega \subseteq \mathscr{V} \cup \mathscr{S}$.

First, we establish:

Lemma 7.7. If T is parasitic in S, then T is parasitic in every subcoalition Q with $T \subseteq Q \subseteq S$.

Proof. By parasiticity of T in S:

$$\sum_T z^\nu > v(S) - v(S - T).$$

By convexity of v,

$$v(S) - v(S - T) \geqq v(Q) - v(Q - T)$$

and hence

$$\sum_T z^\nu > v(Q) - v(Q - T),$$

which is the definition of T being parasitic in Q. QED

Proof of Theorem 7.6. Define the excess[10] of a coalition S as

$$e(S) = v(S) - \sum_S z^\nu.$$

(Exploited coalitions are those with positive excess.) It can be immediately verified that $e(S)$ is a convex game:

$$\forall \text{ coalitions } S, T, \quad e(S \cup T) + e(S \cap T) \geqq e(S) + e(T).$$

Consider the class of coalitions which maximize $e(S)$, and among those, let Ω be a maximal coalition. It is claimed that Ω is the unique maximal formable coalition in N. Ω is formable, since if it were not, some subcoalition of it would have greater excess, an impossibility.

10. For much more intricate use of the excess function in game theory, see Maschler, Peleg, and Shapley (1979).

Suppose there were some other formable coalition $T \not\subseteq \Omega$. Then, by convexity of e:

$$e(\Omega \cup T) \geqq e(\Omega) + e(T) - e(\Omega \cap T).$$

But $e(T) - e(\Omega \cap T) \geqq 0$, since T is formable and consequently its subcoalition $\Omega \cap T$ has smaller excess. It follows that:

$$e(\Omega \cup T) \geqq e(\Omega)$$

and therefore $\Omega \cup T$ is a coalition strictly including Ω with excess as large as Ω, which contradicts the choice of Ω. By contradiction, $T \subseteq \Omega$. This proves part (A).

Part (*B*). Since exploitation exists, there is some coalition S for which $e(S) > 0$. Hence $e(\Omega) \geqq e(S) > 0$ and Ω is exploited.

Part (*C*). Every minimal exploited coalition is a subcoalition of Ω, since every minimal exploited coalition is formable. (*Proof.* If a minimal exploited coalition S had a parasitic subcoalition T, then $e(S - T) > e(S)$, and $S - T$ would be a smaller exploited coalition.) Since Ω consists of all agents who belong to formable coalitions, Ω contains $\mathcal{V}$, the union of the minimal exploited coalitions.

To show $\Omega \subseteq \mathcal{V} \cup \mathcal{S}$, we show $\Omega \subseteq W^\tau$, where W^τ is any maximal exploited coalition. It will follow that $\Omega \subseteq \cap W^\tau = \mathcal{V} \cup \mathcal{S}$ (see the proof of Theorem 7.5b, where it is shown that $\cap W^\tau = \mathcal{V} \cup \mathcal{S}$). Suppose, then, that $\Omega \not\subseteq W^\tau$ for some maximal exploited coalition W^τ. Let $T = \Omega - W^\tau$. Then $W^\tau \cup T$ is not exploited, since W^τ is maximal exploited, so

$$e(W^\tau \cup T) \leqq 0.$$

But $e(W^\tau) > 0$, so T is parasitic in $W^\tau \cup T$. However, $\Omega \subseteq W^\tau \cup T$, and so by Lemma 7.7 T is parasitic in Ω, contradicting the formability of Ω. QED

Theorem 7.6 is the basis for viewing Ω as the coalition which erects the barricades to end exploitation, under the "socialist" behavioral rule of coalition formation under which coalitions seek to maximize the absolute excess over current incomes. In fact, examples can be constructed in which Ω will be precisely $\mathcal{V}$, and others in which it will be precisely $\mathcal{V} \cup \mathcal{S}$, so no further restriction on where

Ω lies in the "interval" between $\mathcal{V}$ and $\mathcal{V} \cup \mathcal{S}$ can be made without further conditions.[11]

Finally, the analog to Theorem 7.6 will be proved, when the rule of coalition formation is taken to be: maximize per capita excess, defined as

$$e^{\mu}(S) = \frac{1}{|S|}\left(v(S) - \sum_{S} z^{\nu}\right).$$

That is, we view a coalition as distributing the entire excess to its members on a per capita basis. More generally, let $\mu(S)$ be any positive additive measure on the subcoalitions of N. (That is, $\mu(S) = \Sigma_S \mu(i)$ and $\mu(i) \geq 0$ for all i.)

Define:

$$e^{\mu}(S) = \frac{1}{\mu(S)} e(S).$$

We think of coalitions dividing the excess among their members according to seniority or age or some other measure of the importance of members: in coalition S, agent i receives $z^i + [\mu(i)/\mu(S)]e^{\mu}(S)$, and these payments exhaust the payoff $v(S)$.

Definition. A coalition $S \subseteq T$ is *μ-parasitic* in T if $e^{\mu}(S - T) > e^{\mu}(S)$. A coalition S is *μ-formable* if it has no μ-parasitic subcoalitions.

Under this rule of coalition formation, the coalitions we expect to observe forming are the maximal μ-formable coalitions.

Theorem 7.8. Let v be a convex game and $\zeta = \langle z^1, \ldots, z^N \rangle$ a Pareto optimal allocation at which exploitation exists. Let Ω^{μ} be the coalition consisting of all agents who belong to μ-formable coali-

11. By introducing a concept of "exhaustion of external economies," it can be guaranteed that, under reasonable conditions, $\Omega = \mathcal{V} \cup \mathcal{S}$ always, and furthermore that $\mathcal{E}$ consists precisely of the individual exploiters. This is, perhaps, the nicest situation with the individual exploiters confronting everyone else. Presentation of this material goes beyond the scope of this chapter.

tions. Then $\mathcal{V} \subseteq \Omega^{\mu} \subseteq \mathcal{V} \cup \mathcal{S}$. In general, however, Ω^{μ} is not μ-formable. [That is, several maximal μ-formable coalitions may exist.]

Lemma 7.9. If S is μ-formable, then S is formable.

Proof. The statement that S is μ-formable means that $[1/\mu(S)]e(S) \geqq [1/\mu(T)]e(T)$, for all $T \subseteq S$. This implies that $[\mu(T)/\mu(S)]e(S) \geqq e(T)$, which implies that $e(S) \geqq e(T)$ for all $T \subseteq S$, which means that S is formable. QED

Proof of Theorem 7.8. From Lemma 7.9 it follows that $\Omega^{\mu} \subseteq \Omega$, and hence $\Omega^{\mu} \subseteq \mathcal{V} \cup \mathcal{S}$. $\mathcal{V} \subseteq \Omega^{\mu}$ since every minimal exploited coalition is μ-formable.

To show that there may be several maximal μ-formable coalitions, consider the convex symmetric game with five players defined by:

$$\begin{aligned} v_0 &= 0 \\ v_1 &= 1 \\ v_2 &= 2 \\ v_3 &= 4 \\ v_4 &= 6 \\ v_5 &= 8 \end{aligned}$$

[Notation: $v_3 = 4$ is a shorthand for v(any 3-member coalition) $= 4$.] The allocation is $\langle z^1, \ldots, z^5\rangle = \langle 0, 0, 0, 1, 7\rangle$. It can be computed that (123), (124), (234), and (134) are each maximal μ-formable coalitions, where $\mu(S) = |S|$ is simply the size of the coalition. QED

Thus, in the case of maximizing per capita gain (for instance) over current income, we will expect to observe, in general, competing coalitions forming to demand an end to exploitation, but the union of these coalitions will, as before, be nested between $\mathcal{V}$ and $\mathcal{V} \cup \mathcal{S}$. In no case will any culpable agent be admitted to a μ-formable coalition.

It should be reiterated that this section is only a beginning of a formal approach to the question of coalition formation or class struggle. Not only is the assumption of convexity of v strong, but the rationality of both the "maximize total excess" and "maximize per capita excess" rules can be challenged. Nevertheless, this section and the previous one are offered to show that even when individually exploited agents do not exist because of increasing returns to scale or other sorts of external economies, it is still possible to identify canonical exploited coalitions, and these coalitions are intimately related to the concepts of vulnerability and culpability.

9. Conclusion

A general device has been proposed for defining concepts of exploitation. Exploitation presupposes some alternative allocation implicitly used as a standard against which the existing allocation is evaluated. This idea was formalized in a game-theoretic way, by specifying the alternative as the payoffs defined by the characteristic function of a game. A given coalition is exploited at a given allocation if its payoff under the game is better for its members than what they are achieving. A number of different games were specified, each corresponding to a common informal notion of exploitation. In this way, we described Marxian exploitation (in subsistence and accumulation economies), feudal exploitation, capitalist exploitation, and socialist exploitation.

We can go one step further than specifying coalitions' alternatives simply by a characteristic function $v(S)$. We might choose to require that the alternative be more explicitly delineated, that we be able to proscribe some form of social organization which actually gives rise to the payoffs $v(S)$. This was in fact possible for the definitions of feudal, capitalist, and socialist exploitation. Each alternative consisted of a new delineation of property rights among producers.

Indeed, this approach mandated the conclusion that the definition of capitalist exploitation, in terms of equalizing producers' access to alienable endowments, is superior to the "Marxian" definition of exploitation in terms of surplus value expropriation. For the case of subsistence economies, these two definitions are equivalent in that they identify precisely the same individuals and coalitions as exploited. However, for the accumulation economy, the definitions are slightly different: there may be producers who are in the gray area and are not Marxian exploited but are capitalistically exploited. There is no restructuring of property rights which captures Marxian exploitation in the accumulation economy. In this case, it seemed that the game-theoretic definition of capitalist exploitation is superior, being associated with a concrete specification of the organizational alternative that would lead to producers receiving their entitlements $v(S)$. In the case of differential labor endowments or heterogeneous labor, it has been claimed that the per capita property redistribution conception of exploitation is clearly superior to the surplus labor definition. It might be added that in the extreme case with which Marx was concerned, where there are two classes the proletariat and the capitalists, the distinction between capitalist and Marxian exploitation is unimportant. It is only in the gray area that the two definitions can render different judgments. If an agent only sells labor power at the optimum, then he has no capital at all, and giving him any amount—whether it is his per capita or his per labor share—will improve his situation. From a theoretical point of view, however, the dependence of the Marxian theory of exploitation on a homogeneous and equal labor endowment will be seen to be important (in Chapter 9) in explaining why labor is the *single* best numeraire for the Marxian theory of value.

I have claimed that the property relations approach to Marxian exploitation is superior to the surplus value approach, and the confrontation between the two definitions can be made even sharper. Consider an example based on the model of section 3 of the Introduction. There are two technologies for making corn: the farm, which requires only direct labor, and the factory, which uses labor plus seed corn as capital. To reproduce a worker (which requires one bushel of corn) using the farm requires six days' labor, while using the factory technology only three days' labor is needed, plus some capital. Suppose that the society in question has exactly enough capital for it to reproduce one-half its members using the factory, and that capital stock is distributed in an egalitarian manner among all producers. Suppose producers desire only to subsist. Then each producer will work $4\frac{1}{2}$ days in each week. As was pointed out in the Introduction, there are several ways of achieving this result; the simplest is the autarchic solution where each producer works up his seed corn in the factory in $1\frac{1}{2}$ days, thereby producing one-half his subsistence requirement, and then travels to the farm and produces the other half of his subsistence needs in 3 days' work on the farm. Now consider a second arrangement which achieves the same results, but with a social division of labor. Two-thirds of the society, whom we will call coalition A, will contract to hire the other one-third, coalition B. Each agent in B will work up his own stock of seed corn, plus the stock of two agents in A, his employers. Thus, a typical agent in B works $4\frac{1}{2}$

days a week. He produces $1\frac{1}{2}$ bushels of corn, and pays as profit to his employers $\frac{1}{2}$ bushel ($\frac{1}{4}$ bushel to each of them). Thus, he works precisely $4\frac{1}{2}$ days and receives his subsistence needs of one bushel. Each agent in A works only on the farm, for $4\frac{1}{2}$ days, thus producing $\frac{3}{4}$ bushel of corn there; the other $\frac{1}{4}$ bushel he requires is received as profits from his employee in B. Thus each agent in A works precisely $4\frac{1}{2}$ days and receives his subsistence needs.

Let us now evaluate this outcome in the light of the two definitions of Marxian and capitalist exploitation. Surely in the first, autarchic equilibrium there is no Marxian exploitation—for each producer works only for himself, the original distribution of the means of production is egalitarian, and the result is egalitarian. Each works $4\frac{1}{2}$ days. But in the second arrangement, where some hire others and indeed gain profit from them, the outcome is identical. Each works $4\frac{1}{2}$ days. According to the property relations, game-theoretic definition, there is no capitalist exploitation in the second arrangement, as producers can do no better by withdrawal with their per capita shares of seed corn. But according to the surplus value definition, there is Marxian exploitation in the second arrangement. Some producers are hiring others, and indeed are "expropriating" some of their product. I submit that the property relations approach is clearly the correct one in this case: for if we agree that there is no exploitation in the autarchic equilibrium, then how can there be exploitation in the equilibrium with trade (of labor power), since the final allocation of goods and leisure is identical to the autarchic one and egalitarian? The surplus labor definition fails in this case because it takes too micro an approach; it is confused by the particular markets which are used, and does not evaluate what the alternatives are for producers. In contrast, the game-theoretic definition evaluates only the consequences of the distribution of the means of production and pays no attention to which markets are used to achieve the equilibrium.[12]

To summarize, the property rights, game-theoretic characterization of capitalist exploitation is superior to Marx's classical surplus value definition in at least these ways:

(1) It specifies explicitly what the alternative is against which an allocation is judged exploitative, by specifying a new set of property relations which will eliminate the exploitation in question. By so doing it avoids the confusion which the surplus value definition suf-

12. This example and argument are expanded in Roemer (1983a).

fers from in treating situations such as the one outlined above, where surplus value appears to be expropriated but in reality is not. As well, the clear statement of an alternative regime of property relations makes the game-theoretic definition superior in an ethical theory.

(2) It generalizes in a clear and obvious way to the case of heterogeneous labor, or the case where several nonproduced factors exist, while the surplus value definition has no adequate generalization to these cases.

(3) It enables distinction between different kinds of exploitation, all of which may be undistinguishable from the surplus value point of view. For example, from the surplus value point of view, the "transfer of surplus value" occurring in the model of section 5 appears indistinguishable from the transfer of surplus value under capitalism. With the property relations approach, however, it is clear that the origin of the transfers are entirely different, being in one case due to differential ownership of alienable assets and in the other to differential skill. The second variety is not capitalist exploitation, although that is not evident from the Marxian definition.

Thus Marx captured capitalist exploitation with his surplus value concept, but in some ways his method was inadequate. By embedding Marxian exploitation in a more general theory, we find a more natural way of characterizing it which distinguishes it clearly from feudal and socialist exploitation, as the surplus value definition did not.

We are able to make explicit the different conceptions of property entitlement which lie behind important notions of exploitation. When Marx speaks of the expropriation of unpaid labor, his claim is that all agents are entitled to the fruits of their per capita share of the means of production. When a neoclassicist speaks of exploitation, on the contrary, his claim is that agents are entitled to the fruits of their own private property: they should be free to trade with that property. It is noteworthy that neoclassical exploitation seems appropriately described as feudal exploitation: it accepts as nonexploitative the outcome of a competitive, private ownership economy and identifies exploitation with feudal property relations. Similarly, Marxian exploitation accepts as nonexploitative the "transfer of surplus value" that comes about in a socialist economy (see section 5) in which capitalist relations of private property in alienable assets have been dissolved. One might conceive of a communist as one who will not be satisfied until socialist exploitation is abolished. Hence, the neoclassical notion of exploitation corresponds historically to a revolution (from feudalism to capitalism) which occurred some centuries ago, for the most part, while the Marxian notion seems distinctly more modern, being associated with property forms which have come into existence in the twentieth century. One might wish to conclude from this that neoclassical or feudal exploitation is a somewhat stale ethical conception for the modern world, and I will try to give some theoretical support for that claim, from the point of view of historical materialism, in the final chapter. We have shown that a taxonomy of exploitation can be defined; but which definition *should* we choose as the appropriate one for our normative notion of exploitation at a particular point in history?

Finally, it must be pointed out why the dominance condition (3) of the definition of exploitation is necessary. Consider an invalid who requires very costly care and is supported by society. According to the game-theoretic conditions (1) and (2) of the definition of exploitation, he is a capitalist exploiter. (If he withdrew with his share of the resources he would be worse off and his complement would be better off.) But the dominance requirement fails; in fact, it is the rest of society who dominates him, as they make the decisions regarding his care. As a second example for the necessity of dominance, consider two islands. One is rich in resources, the other poor in resources. Their populations are equally skilled. There is no trade or relationship between the two islands. Yet according to the game-theoretic criteria, the rich island capitalistically exploits the poor one. If, however, we include the dominance requirement, this is not so, as there is no relationship between the two islands. Thus dominance, although not formally modeled here, is needed to rule out these various perverse cases.[13] I maintain, nevertheless, that to model the major distributional issues of an economy, the game-theoretic conditions (1) and (2) are sufficient to characterize exploitation; hence the formal analysis of this chapter.

13. I thank Serge-Christophe Kolm for the challenge of the two islands, and Erik O. Wright for the suggestion to include dominance as a requirement of exploitation. Jon Elster provides additional challenges forthcoming in *Politics and Society* (see Roemer, 1982). Further refinements of the game-theoretic characterization of capitalist exploitation are proposed in Roemer (1983a), which solve the two-island problem without invoking dominance.

8

Exploitation in Existing Socialism

The presentation of the taxonomy of exploitation in Chapter 7 implies that as society evolves from feudal to socialist, successive types of inequality are considered exploitative and are eliminated. Under feudalism, feudal, capitalist, and socialist exploitation all exist (that is, there are coalitions who suffer because of ties of bondage, property relations in alienable, nonhuman assets, and the privatization of skills); under capitalism, capitalist and socialist exploitation exist; under socialism, presumably only socialist exploitation exists. The historical task of each revolution is to eliminate the appropriate form of exploitation. We must now discuss whether this simple picture gives an adequate representation of inequality and exploitation in existing socialism.

One important lesson emerges already: it would be utopian to conceive of socialism as an egalitarian society or even a classless society.[1] The historical task of the socialist revolution is to eliminate that form of exploitation due to differential ownership of alienable assets. From a historical point of view, it is an open question how inegalitarian a society will appear which does this but preserves differential remuneration to skills and other inalienable assets (in which we might include, perhaps, social connections). Indeed, it is a premature theorem to assert that socialism, construed as the regime in which capitalist exploitation is eliminated, will be the society in which "the free development of every individual is a condition of the

1. Being classless, for a society, is a weaker condition than being egalitarian, as we observe from $\mathscr{E}(p)$, which is classless but inegalitarian.

free development of all'' (Marx and Engels, *The Communist Manifesto*). This is perhaps the first major criticism we derive of much current Marxian thinking, which views the elimination of capitalism as the necessary and *sufficient* condition for the complete flowering of individual development. An interesting historical parallel to this utopianism is pointed out by Horvat (1980). He remarks that eighteenth-century French revolutionaries who performed the capitalist revolution conceived of the elimination of the feudal bond as the sufficient condition for the creation of a free and brotherly society. ''Liberté, egalité, fraternité'' would follow necessarily if all citizens were to be treated equally before the law. It is not surprising that the form of inequality which is being eliminated by the revolution of the contemporary era is conceived of as responsible for all the ills of society. What political structures will evolve in consequence of only the more subtle or advanced forms of exploitation in the hierarchy of exploitations cannot easily be predicted.

Capitalist exploitation (or, more precisely, the private ownership of alienable assets which gives rise to it) is viewed by Marxists as *necessary* for many ills which are found in capitalist society: unemployment; recurrent economic crises; decadent culture; nationalism, racism, and sexism; imperialist foreign policy and wars; authoritarian political structures. If capitalist exploitation is eliminated, so must be its consequences. Again our analysis would suggest this is too hasty a conclusion. If, indeed, some forms of inequality and exploitation are preserved after capitalist exploitation is eliminated, one must investigate these new societies to see whether the phenomena listed can evolve in consequence of only the types of exploitation and property relations which exist under socialism. Indeed, a frequent error of modern Marxian thinking is to define socialism by its expected consequences: a state with an imperialist foreign policy cannot be socialist; if two states go to war with each other, at least one is not socialist. The approach suggested here is to define socialist transformation as the elimination of capitalist exploitation, in the precise sense of our definitions, and then to develop a theory concerning what politics can be expected to accompany the remaining forms of property relations and exploitation. I do not mean to imply that the laws of motion of existing socialism can be deduced in vacuo by axiomatic modeling; of course, historical observation is essential to formulate the models properly. Rather, the point is that one should be open-minded concerning what economic and political transformations will accompany the ending of capitalist exploitation only.

In this chapter I apply the taxonomic device for defining forms of exploitation, introduced earlier, to propose various forms of exploitation which are prevalent in existing socialism. It is not within the scope of this book to carry out a careful empirical evaluation of contemporary socialist societies, but the level of empirical concreteness of the present discussion will be somewhat higher than that of the previous chapters. In section 1 the extent of socialist exploitation in existing socialism is discussed, and the concept of socially necessary exploitation is introduced. Section 2 introduces a type of exploitation not discussed previously—status exploitation—and it is argued that such exploitation exists in socialist countries today. Section 3 is a digression on policy, or perhaps ethics. If a form of exploitation is socially necessary, what should one's attitude toward it be? Should its existence be endorsed? (A more protracted ethical discussion is in Chapter 9.) Section 4 discusses capitalist exploitation in socialist countries and evaluates the various arguments which assert that these societies are capitalist, of one form or another. In section 5 the debate concerning the plan versus the market is cast in the language of this theory, insofar as it says something about exploitation.

1. Socialist exploitation under socialism

Certainly the clearest type of inequality which continues to exist after the socialist transformation is differential remuneration to inalienable assets, or skills. (For the moment, let us treat skills as embodied and innate, and not learned through schooling, whose access may be differentially distributed for some other reason; that problem will be dealt with in the next section.) This is what we have defined as socialist exploitation in Chapter 7. From the epithet "each works according to his ability and is paid according to his work," it is clear that the historical task assigned to socialism in Marxian theory is not the elimination of socialist exploitation but only of capitalist exploitation.

Nevertheless, there has been a continuing debate on this issue. The most significant episodes have been experiments in socialist societies with egalitarianism. Prior to the early 1930s there were various egalitarian experiments in the Soviet Union, and in China the Great Proletarian Cultural Revolution stands out as the major episode in which material incentives were castigated. It is now generally (although not universally) accepted that these egalitarian experiments were premature.[2] The elimination of skill wage differentials led to a retardation in development, labor productivity, and material welfare.

This suggests a new definition. Recall that we have defined a coalition as socialistically exploited if it could improve its welfare by withdrawing with its per capita share of society's assets, alienable and inalienable. Suppose, however, it is impossible to realize this alternative because of incentive problems which will accompany the pooling of skills. (The way of pooling skills, in the present case, is to eliminate wage differentials to skilled and unskilled.) If skills are pooled, they will disappear at this stage in the development of social consciousness, or some might say of human nature. We will then say that socialist exploitation is *socially necessary* at this stage in history. Put slightly differently, a form of exploitation is socially necessary if its attempted elimination will alter institutions and incentives in such a way as to make the exploited agents worse off, instead of better off. My claim is that at this stage, socialist exploitation is socially necessary in existing socialist societies.

In defining the social necessity of a form of exploitation, we take more seriously the feasibility of the alternative by which we are evaluating exploitation. The games which were defined in Chapter 7 to capture feudal, capitalist, and socialist exploitation included a strong ceteris paribus clause: the withdrawing coalition would have the capacity to work as hard and avail itself in the alternative of the knowledge which it possessed in the original economy. For this reason, exploitation was defined in reference to hypothetically feasible alternatives, not actually possible ones. If, however, the motivations and incentives necessary for production are themselves a function of extant property relations, then the elimination of those property relations may obviate the achievement of the hypothetical alternative. That is, we take more seriously now the feasibility of cooperation in the coalition S, the possibility of achieving $v(S)$. We continue to define the alternative payoff $v(S)$ as the income the coali-

2. Elster and Hyllund (1980) provide a model which allows a precise discussion of various alternatives for defining premature revolution in the theory of historical materialism.

tion could receive if it were to expend as much labor as it does in the present allocation, that is, assuming no alteration of incentives. We then ask the second-order question of whether this assumption is a good one: if incentives would change so as to make the achievement of $v(S)$ for the exploited coalition S impossible, then its exploitation is socially necessary.

There are difficult issues associated with this concept which will be pursued in Chapter 9. One concerns the relationship between people being "better off" and the conditions for the development of the productive forces. One might argue that in early capitalism, capitalist exploitation was socially necessary, since if private property in the means of production had been eliminated, capitalism could not have played its progressive role of developing the productive forces, thus liberating workers (eventually) from poverty and disease. The logical connection, however, between improving welfare and development of the productive forces is subtle. Another example of socially necessary exploitation of current interest is in the Rawlsian maximin just allocation of income; without the inegalitarianism of that distribution, the poorest would be worse off. (More on this, also, in Chapter 9.)

If one defines a class as a group of agents who relate to the means of production in a similar way, then the possibility of class differentiation arises in a society where only socialist exploitation exists, according to whether one performs skilled or unskilled tasks. To put this more generally, property rights in inalienable assets are respected under socialism, and hence classes are defined with respect to ownership relations to that property. The socialistically exploiting class is the one owning this property, and the socialistically exploited class is the one bereft of it (see, for instance, the model of Chapter 7, section 5). What political implications will flow from this class and exploitation structure must be the subject of another study. The key distinction drawn thus far between the socialist exploitation structure and capitalist exploitation and class is that the former is socially necessary at this stage in history, while the latter is not—at least, that is the predominant Marxian contention. Proletarians can improve their welfare by abolishing relations of private property in the alienable means of production.

If socialist exploitation were the only form of exploitation existing in socialist societies today, one would be justified in concluding, according to this analysis, that these societies are unequivocally socialist. The story is complicated, however, by the presence of other forms of inequality.

2. Status exploitation in existing socialism

In socialist societies, positions exist which entitle their holders to especially high salaries or other forms of privilege and remuneration. Examples are membership in the communist party, offices in the bureaucracy, and certain jobs that require loyalty or are in the public spotlight. If these positions required special skills, then one might be justified in calling the differential remuneration to these positions an aspect of socialist exploitation. This would, however, be twisting the meaning of skill or inalienable asset. Surely some of the extra privileges accruing to this stratum of positions are a return to skill, but some are not. Consider, for instance, the "skill" of holding a position in the KGB: the skill is loyalty, and it is created by the extra remuneration itself. Presumably almost anyone could attain this skill if he were paid the extra remuneration. The same is true of positions in the bureaucracy: there is some extra remuneration to holders of those positions which accrues solely by virtue of the position and not by virtue of the skill necessary to carry out the tasks associated with it. These special payments to positions give rise to *status exploitation.* A coalition will be status-exploited if it could improve the lot of its members by withdrawing with its own assets but exempting itself from the dues to status, and if the complementary coalition thereby fared worse. One might note a parallel: feudal exploitation arose from ties of bondage which followed from the status of the lord and serf, independent of their relations to other forms of property, alienable or inalienable.[3]

Consider this story illustrating status exploitation. There is a population of identical producers. Total output varies with the assigned wage structure. If each producer is paid a wage of one dollar, he will

3. The lord would have been wealthier than the serf even if the two traded on a free market, but that aspect of inequality is capitalist exploitation. I am referring here to that inequality which is specifically feudal. Note, also, feudal exploitation enjoys another similarity with status exploitation, in the cases where the lord received his land grant from the king as a consequence of his status as vassal. In these cases, his landed wealth was a consequence of his status, not the other way around.

produce output worth two dollars. Suppose, however, five percent of the population is chosen for preferential treatment, and they are paid two dollars while everyone else is paid one dollar. The incentive behavior is such that all will now produce three dollars' worth of output. This occurs, perhaps, because status will be reevaluated next year, and if a low-status person does not work hard he will be ineligible for promotion, while if a high-status person does not work hard he will be demoted. (Thus, the increase in output due to status differentiation is, in this case, the outcome of noncooperative behavior among the producers.) Clearly, everyone can be made better off in the economy with status, through investment of the extra surplus, for instance, assuming only a small deterioration in welfare due to the extra labor producers expend. This is an example of status exploitation which is socially necessary. If the status-exploited coalition (of ninety-five percent) were to withdraw and maintain the same productivity as in the differentiated economy (which it is certainly technologically capable of doing, since all producers are identical), but if it abolished the extra one dollar dues to status, then all its members would be made better off. Such an alternative is, however, not realizable, because in the egalitarian coalition the incentive will be absent to produce three dollars' worth of output.

If pure status exploitation is socially necessary, then a criterion is immediately evident for a second-order evaluation of the phenomenon: it is better if positions of status are distributed in a stochastically random manner than if they are not. In our example, the privileged five percent should be randomly chosen, instead of assigning those positions, for instance, to members of the same families generation after generation.[4] The application of this principle is never so clear-cut, since most positions of privileged status are associated with skills to some degree. To the extent that membership in the Party is a signal for a special skill (the ability to lead in the construction of socialism), then positions of membership should not be dis-

4. One might challenge: if the status in the above example is randomly allocated, why should anyone work hard? (Of course if the status is given to the hardest working five percent, the ensuing inequality ceases to be status exploitation, but comprises socialist exploitation.) Suppose the rule is that the five percent with high status will be chosen randomly from among the harder working half of the population. Assuming the agents do not cooperate, then everyone will work hard, and identically so (assuming identical agents), to place themselves in the harder working half. Thus a random selection mechanism can reproduce status exploitation which is socially necessary.

tributed in a stochastically random fashion. To the extent, however, that membership entails only duties which a large fraction of the population are capable of performing, but such membership provides privileged access to educational facilities for one's children which are in short supply, then membership positions should be stochastically distributed.[5]

There are two arguments which can be raised against the practice of status exploitation in existing socialist society. The first is that it is not socially necessary. This argument maintains that status exploitation is a form of corruption, which could be eliminated to the benefit of the nonprivileged group. The second argument is that, although status exploitation is socially necessary at this stage of historical development, it is not randomly distributed.

Why might status exploitation be socially necessary? Perhaps the positions of status are virtually all associated with the nonmarket mechanism of these economies, with its bureaucratic mechanism. For a bureaucracy to perform its function, perhaps it must be privileged. If one eliminates privilege, therefore, one must choose a nonbureaucratic mechanism for running the economy, presumably the market. If the market is used, perhaps capitalism, and thus capitalist exploitation, will regenerate. (Some traders will accumulate alienable assets and use them as means of production, exploiting others in the old fashion.) The workers will be worse off, suffering under the old yoke. Status exploitation is the better alternative.

I do not advocate this position but pose it as a logical possibility. Indeed the notion of socially necessary status exploitation can provide a facile apology for virtually every form of corruption and privilege. The intention of this chapter is surely not to do so, but to provide a framework for decomposing the inequality in socialist countries into its constituent parts in an analytically useful manner.

Although there is considerable discussion in the literature of socialist development concerning the social necessity of socialist ex-

5. Alternatively, why not eliminate privileged access to university positions? First, it is possible that the children of the intelligentsia will do better in university (that is, the positions so allocated will be more efficiently used) than children of workers and peasants, due to social and cultural conditioning. But second, the perquisite of privileged educational access may be the form of income required for the bureaucracy to secure its services. Hence, if status exploitation is socially necessary, so may be privileged educational access. Third, the bureaucracy can be viewed as toll collectors: the bureaucratic stratum has the power to allocate to itself the tolls of privilege.

ploitation (although not in those terms), there is little discussion of the necessity of status exploitation. Perhaps the closest approximation to such a discussion is the debate between advocates of self-management and planning. The former can be thought of as claiming that self-management is an alternative to bureaucracy which shows that status exploitation is socially unnecessary. Thus, while it is clear that the intention of socialism is to eliminate capitalist exploitation but not to eliminate socialist exploitation, the historical imperative of socialism vis-à-vis status exploitation is unclear. I think the social necessity of status exploitation in the current historical period is an open question. Indeed, the very different degrees and forms of privilege to status in different socialist societies (Cuba, China, the U.S.S.R.) call into question the social necessity of any particular magnitude of status exploitation, if not the existence of some degree of it, in any particular society.

Regardless of its social necessity or otherwise, the stochastic randomness of the distribution of status positions can be evaluated. There has been considerable research concerning social mobility in Eastern European countries which can be brought to bear in this evaluation (for instance, Parkin, 1971; Katz, 1973; Matthews, 1978; Yanowitch, 1979). The general picture is that stochastic randomness in assignment of status positions has improved since the time of Stalin. The ability to inherit a position in the privileged stratum is far from secured. Nevertheless, forms of nonrandomness continue to exist, such as anti-Semitism in the Soviet Union. Zaslavsky (1980) maintains that while there was considerable mobility into the high-status positions when the number of those positions was growing, now that the population of those positions is stationary, status is rigidified and "status inheritance is clearly evident in all spheres" (p. 390). Many commentators say that social mobility into positions of status is more considerable in these countries than is mobility into the capitalist class in the United States, although this obviously cannot constitute a final verdict on what degree of stochastic randomness one should consider adequate under socialism.

The relationship between status and socialist exploitations must be noted. Perhaps the most important perquisite of status is the access to positions in schools and universities for the children of the high-status stratum, enabling them to embody skills and thereby benefit from socialist exploitation. Where capital cannot be inherited, one can attempt to pass on either status or skills to one's children. To the extent that education is a signal for skill and that education is an independent criterion for assignment of positions of privileged status, it is perhaps the most important asset with which to equip one's children. If one takes the most radical position for nurture in the nature versus nurture debate, then all skills can be viewed as an embodiment of previous access to status, and hence socialist exploitation is simply the dynamic effect of prior status exploitation. This does not imply that if socialist exploitation is accepted as socially necessary today, status exploitation must also be. A similar parallel between socialist and capitalist exploitation will be explored in section 5 below.

Status exploitation is a problem not only for socialism but also for capitalism. Indeed, the status exploitation of capitalist society may be even more severe than in existing socialism. In large corporations, salary is set on an internal hierarchy and includes a large element of remuneration to status, to secure loyalty to the company, and so on.[6] Perhaps the status exploitation is not so noticeable under capitalism as under socialism because it is small in comparison to the capitalist exploitation which exists; as well, capitalism has no pretentions to egalitarianism and annihilating privilege, as does socialism, and hence capitalist status exploitation is less remarked upon.

Finally, it must be remarked that status exploitation is an elusive category which might be difficult to measure. Perhaps some elusive personal trait is in fact being rewarded by what appear to be dues to status. Doubtless this is the claim of those bureaucracies, capitalist and socialist, which pay what appear to be status differentials. This position holds that what appears to be status exploitation is in reality socialist exploitation, as the differential reward is a payment for some inalienable trait. I think, however, that the distinction between status and skill is sufficiently real and documented to require a special category to describe the former.

6. There is a large literature on internal labor markets under capitalism. See, for instance, Doeringer and Piore (1975).

3. Socially necessary exploitation and policy

If status exploitation is socially necessary and randomly distributed, are there then no grounds for criticizing existing socialism for its practice? First, one must take care to think about this dispassionately, that is, not to assume that status privilege as practiced in socialist countries is socially necessary, and hence that an affirmation of the claim suggested by the question necessarily justifies those practices. More generally: If any form of inequality is socially necessary, are there then no grounds for criticizing it? Rawls would appear to affirm the claim, if one interprets socially necessary inequality in his theory as inequality which increases the welfare of the least well off, for he describes such a regime as *just*. (What stronger endorsement could one give?)

Consider, however, that the social necessity (or otherwise) of a form of inequality is in large part entailed by how the people involved think. It is the "level of social consciousness" which determines whether certain incentives are necessary. If the exploited fight against their exploitation, does that not ipso facto call into question its social necessity? More weakly, even granted that a revolution or rebellion against a form of inequality is doomed to failure, might one not support the rebellion nonetheless, as such experiments are necessary for the development of a level of consciousness which will, eventually, render the inequality unnecessary? It is one thing for a moral philosopher to ask these questions, but for a communist party, critical policy decisions depend on the answers. If the party decides to agitate against, say, status exploitation, it may thereby create the mental and social conditions for its successful demise. Alternatively, the outcome may be its unsuccessful demise (that is, the elimination of the privileges but to the detriment of all). The latter seems to have been the outcome of the Chinese cultural revolution, although that conclusion is not uncontested. The complicating factor is that a decision to call a form of inequality wrong may thereby contribute to making it unnecessary. (The same issue arises for capitalist exploitation in early capitalism, with at least one difference. Marxists generally assert that such exploitation was socially necessary as capitalism was for a period the optimal regime for developing the productive forces and thereby promoting the welfare of the exploited. But would a Marxist have not supported premature revolutionary attempts by workers—more generally, any working-class struggle against capital? I think yes, because of the need for experimentation. The difference with the socialist case is that in early capitalism there was no communist party whose decision was itself a factor in the outcome, and so the policy dimension was absent. This does not solve the moral problem, but it is rendered less important from a practical standpoint.)

What, then, of the policy issue under socialism? It is, I think, possible at once to admit the social necessity of a form of exploitation and to criticize it.[7] Lenin introduced the NEP with the belief that some capitalism (and its concomitant exploitation) was necessary in the U.S.S.R. in the 1920s, but he did not glorify the capitalists. He also argued for the necessity of bureaucracy, authority, and one-man management, while simultaneously advocating the formation of trade unions with which workers could protect themselves against the necessary authority. It is, surely, a difficult tack to both admit the necessity of exploitation and argue for its demise, but I think historical evidence demonstrates the possibility of doing that, and I conclude that the social necessity of a form of exploitation does not entail approving of it.

Although experimentation is necessary for the level of consciousness to develop sufficiently to render a form of inequality socially unnecessary, it is not sufficient, according to historical materialism, for consciousness is corollary to the development of the productive forces. This provides the clue to which form of exploitation a Marxist would agitate against, among those which are socially necessary: the one which is next on the historical agenda for elimination.[8] (Perhaps this is status exploitation, and not socialist exploitation today.) Even if all status exploitation is socially necessary and randomly distributed (surely not the case), current socialist practice must be sharply implicated for not doing this. For the most part, both socialist and status exploitation are uncritically accepted in existing socialism. Worse still, status exploitation is not officially acknowledged to exist; it is claimed, instead, that such privileges are either remuneration to skill or necessary for carrying out the duties of the position, rather than tolls collected by the group in control.

7. Jon Elster strongly disagrees, in personal correspondence, and I thank him for bringing the issue to my attention. A related passage in his work is in Elster (1978, pp. 50–51).

8. Historical agenda, that is, in terms of the possibilities to be opened by the current level of development of the productive forces.

4. Capitalist exploitation in existing socialism

In the U.S.S.R. of the 1920s and China of the 1950s capitalism was encouraged; capitalist exploitation was deemed to be socially necessary for the development of the productive forces. The great industrialization debate in the Soviet Union concerned itself with which group should bear the brunt of capitalist exploitation (the peasants, urban workers), and also what the objective should be (to eliminate the necessity for exploitation as rapidly as possible but at high current costs, or to go more slowly). The eventual collectivization of agriculture could be viewed as feudal exploitation of the peasantry, if it is true that the peasants would have been better off if they could have withdrawn from the economy with just their own assets (including, of course, the land). Even in ideal circumstances the construction of socialism in an underdeveloped country necessitates some capitalist exploitation, if one takes seriously the progressive nature of capitalism when the forces of production are weak; it need hardly be mentioned that the world situation in the 1930s was far from ideal for the Soviet Union. The Bolshevik Party saw itself as engaged in a race against time to develop sufficient infrastructure and military capability to defend the country in war.

The impossibility of eliminating capitalist exploitation in an underdeveloped country does not imply that a Marxist should advocate the postponement of a revolutionary transformation in an underdeveloped country, for perhaps capitalist exploitation can most quickly be eliminated through development of the capital stock under the aegis of central planning rather than capitalism or the semifeudalism of prerevolutionary Russia and China. That necessarily places the leadership of socialist construction in the position of advocating forms of socially necessary exploitation and simultaneously criticizing them. It can account for many aspects of the history of Soviet and Chinese development, including autocratic methods and frequent reversals of policy.

Should existing socialist countries be considered capitalist? Since we have acknowledged the existence of capitalist exploitation in, at least, the early histories of some of these countries, perhaps it would be appropriate to consider the mode of production capitalist, in some measure. It is useful to differentiate three types of claims of this nature which have been put forth: one maintains that the bureaucracy constitutes a new capitalist class, another that the firm managers are the new capitalist class, and a third that what exists is state capitalism, although no precise capitalist class is located.[9]

Many considerations not addressed by the model could fruitfully be brought to bear on the discussion, some of which will now be mentioned. It is, however, the purpose of this chapter to gain insights from the particular abstract simplification embodied in the general theory of exploitation; hence, all the sociological and historical evidence from which one might reach a conclusion on this question, but which evades categorization in our formal structure, will not be discussed. I will argue that it is not useful or correct to view existing socialist societies as capitalist. The principal piece of evidence offered for the opposite position is that although the means of production are publicly owned, they are not controlled by the direct producers, and hence the producers do not gain from public ownership. Or, more strongly, others gain at their expense. What has changed in the transition to existing socialism is the de jure property relations in the means of production, it is claimed, but the de facto alienation of that property from the direct producers remains, and the surplus is not appropriated by them. Which of the three above positions one holds is determined by whether one thinks the bureaucracy appropriates the surplus, or the firm managers, or the state channels the surplus into investment independently of the will of the producers according to some logic of the state as autonomous agent.

From the definitional point of view, some of the most basic traits of capitalism are absent in existing socialism. Labor power is not a commodity, nor are the means of production (except, perhaps, in Yugoslavia). Although labor power is still paid a wage, workers are guaranteed support in existing socialism. A primary defining trait of capitalism is that the proletarian must sell his labor power to survive, and this is not true in the countries under discussion. It is, or has been at various times, a crime not to work in existing socialist countries, but the relationship between the selling of labor power and survival is fundamentally different from under capitalism. Under ex-

9. Goldfield and Rothenberg (1980) catalog the various arguments which assert the regeneration of capitalism in the Soviet Union. They proceed to rebut them, citing much empirical evidence. The literature on this subject is too vast to cite here. The most thorough treatment of the question by an advocate of the capitalist restoration thesis is Bettelheim (1976, 1978). A survey of the literature and critique is provided by Nuti (1979).

isting socialism, workers are guaranteed their means of subsistence by society; in return, society requires them to work.[10] The perverse effects of this relationship of labor power to the wage are incentive problems: absenteeism, drinking on the job, and so on, are held to be consequences of job security in existing socialism. Second, capital cannot be traded (with certain minor exceptions) in existing socialism. If the freedom to hire labor power, the necessity to sell it to survive, and the freedom to trade capital do not exist, it is difficult to call this mode of production capitalist.

Evidence exists on income distribution suggesting different laws of motion in existing socialism than in capitalism. The privileged stratum is far less rich than in any capitalist country. Matthews (1979) estimates that a family in the Soviet elite stratum lives about as well as the average American family. This includes nonmonetary remuneration. Hence, if the elite is a capitalist class, it appropriates the surplus in a much more modest way than any conventional capitalist class has ever done. Various commentators have concluded that the Soviet income distribution is among the most equal in the world, and has made more rapid progress toward equality than any (Wiles, 1974). Hence, the most stunning aspect of capitalist exploitation, the differential return to property measured in material goods and services, is largely absent in these societies. It would be fallacious to conclude that therefore these countries are not capitalist. (That would, indeed, be an example of the sort of consequential reasoning criticized in the Introduction and earlier in this chapter.) The evidence is only circumstantial.

The general point is this. The usefulness of categorizing certain societies as capitalist is to identify them as sharing certain laws of motion. To identify these economies as capitalist is to imply that their laws of motion are understood, and that is palpably not the case. What is to be gained by this nomenclature, except cutting off important inquiry concerning how these societies operate?

Some evaluation of whether the privileged stratum in existing socialist societies can be considered a capitalist class will now be at-

10. This distinction must be qualified by the practice of modern social democracies, in which the link between the selling of labor power and the wage has been mollified. I am uncertain to what extent the difference between the labor power-wage relation in existing socialist and social democratic societies holds up. Also, the relatively full employment in socialist societies is more realistically ascribed to structural conditions than to statutory guarantees.

tempted, but more strictly within the terms of the theory of exploitation which is our topic. This evaluation is not straightforward because it is not clear what it would mean for workers under socialism to withdraw with their share of society's alienable property, since supposedly public ownership of the means of production has already given the direct producers everything. The formal model of capitalist exploitation has not captured what appears as the key taxonomic problem in the evaluation of the class nature of existing socialism: How does one judge whether ownership of the means of production is social (in the sense of being administered in the interests of the workers) and not just public? (See, for instance, Brus, 1975, for the distinction between social and public ownership.)

Perhaps the problem can be clarified by contrasting it with the evaluation of forms of exploitation under feudalism. In that case, it is possible to perform a thought experiment where a coalition of serfs exempts itself from feudal bonds, while not exempting itself from bonds of property in alienable assets. Thus, one can judge whether serfs are feudally exploited *independently* of whether they are capitalistically exploited. (They turn out to be exploited in both ways, but that is beside the present point.) However, there is no way of judging by thought experiment whether Soviet workers are status-exploited, independently of whether they are capitalistically exploited, due to the extra remuneration which the privileged stratum receives: for the test wherein they withdraw to exempt themselves from relations of status to the bureaucracy and elite is precisely the same as the test performed to judge whether they would be better off if they had access to their share of the society's capital stock. It is precisely the role of the bureaucracy and the state which obscures the nature of property relations between the means of production and the workers.

I will argue that the privileged position of the bureaucracy is a case of status exploitation rather than capitalist exploitation, despite this ambiguity. To see why, reconsider the definition of capitalist exploitation. Recall that agents in capitalist society are capitalistically exploiting when they are coupon-clippers: it is necessary that their extra revenues are due solely to their ownership of property and not to their possession of some scarce talent such as entrepreneurial ability, in which case we would consider them as benefiting partially from socialist exploitation. Now one could consider these coupon-clippers as enjoying a special status, defined by their possession of property. It so happens that because of the particular economic mechanism which is used to distribute income, those agents enjoying the status of property ownership benefit. Hence, we could say, formally, that capitalist exploitation is a type of status exploitation. Nevertheless, we do not, the reason being that there is a *prior determination of status* in the case of the capitalist property owner —namely, his possession of property. It is his ownership of the means of production which determines his "status," thus giving him a claim on the social output. Similarly, we could pedantically consider the highly skilled to be benefactors of status exploitation, instead of socialist exploitation, by the same argument. Possession of skill entitles one to a certain status which rewards one with a certain superior claim on social output, because of the particular mechanism of income distribution in society. Here, too, there is a prior determination of status. It is the possession of a skill which determines one's status and gives one a claim on the social surplus.

Consider now the socialist bureaucrats. Admit for the sake of argument that they are better off than otherwise because of their position in control of society's capital stock, and to a measure not explained by the skill they possess. (They are, if you will, coupon-clippers.) But there is a key difference between them and capitalists: their status is not determined by their ownership (or control) of the means of production, but rather it is the other way around. There is *no prior determination* of their status as controllers of the social capital. Unlike capitalists, who derive their status from ownership of property, the commissars derive their control of property from their position, their status. It is for this reason that they are properly thought of as benefiting from status exploitation and not capitalist exploitation.

That power attaches itself to positions rather than persons in the Soviet Union has been noted by many observers. Connor (1979) writes that "power can only be acquired by *direct* quest in the U.S.S.R., while it can, in some measure, be bought in the United States . . . There, economic rewards of considerable size will flow *from* power; in the United States, the acquisition of behind-the-scenes power and the power that comes with public office both, generally, require substantial *prior* financial resources" (p. 321). This is precisely the evidence which demonstrates that the phenomenon under discussion is status exploitation, not capitalist exploitation, in the Soviet Union.

As a further illustration, consider a hypothetical society where kings are chosen and given all the capital stock. After the death of the incumbent king, it is decided that the first male child born under the next full moon will be the new king (with some provision made for the disposition of leadership during the infant's maturation). Now our test would indicate the king is capitalistically exploiting the rest of society (assuming he keeps most of the social output). In fact, he is also status-exploiting them; as in the case of the socialist bureaucracy, there is no adequate way of differentiating between the two, at the level of thought experiments in which coalitions withdraw, exempting themselves from relations of property or status. Nevertheless, it is clear that the appropriate category here is status exploitation, since it is his status as firstborn under the new moon which is the ultimate determinant of his good fortune, rather than his ownership of society's capital determining his status. In this case, there is a prior determination of status; one might better call the phenomenon lunar exploitation.

Indeed, a championed aspect of capitalism (and some would say the essence of its political freedom) is that even the most privileged has no claim to status other than through his property. His only gains are noncoercive, purely "economic," unlike oriental despots, feudal lords, socialist bureaucrats, and perhaps lunar kings, whose status has no such objective and limited determinant, and is hence to some extent arbitrary and capricious. This, at least, is the advertisement. In practice, there is status exploitation in existing capitalism, as has been mentioned. The remuneration to many positions is not a competitive one, but contains a component of status dues. Admission to certain universities is not purchased solely with money and talent but also by trading on family background, and so on. It is not clear that status exploitation in existing capitalism is less than in existing socialism, assuming one could measure it.

Despite formal similarities between feudal exploitation and status exploitation under socialism, it would be a mistake to conclude that the presence of status exploitation indicates a reversion to feudalism, to a form of inequality more primitive, less democratic, than capitalist inequality. The dues to status have varied tremendously throughout history, from the ancient Chinese emperor who had buried with him the entire court and thousands of soldiers to usher him commodiously to the next world, to the socialist bureaucrat who has preferential access to a dacha outside Moscow, an automobile, and a good chance at a college education for his child.

The position asserting that some stratum constitutes a capitalist class concentrates on the observation that bureaucrats or plant managers are wealthier than workers. The position that existing socialist countries are state capitalist is distinguished from this in that the wealth of the bureaucracy is not at issue; rather, the state, through a logic of its own, is said to exploit the workers in a capitalist way. Evidence for the state capitalist position is overinvestment: these state apparatuses invest a higher fraction of national product than the workers would, were they in control (Harman, 1975). If the workers were controlling the surplus, they would dispose of it in a different way; hence, the regimes are capitalist. It is not essential to the state capitalist position that the bureaucrats be better off than under true socialism, only that the workers be worse off. Indeed, adhering to the game-theoretic definition of exploitation, we can thereby conclude that the workers are not capitalistically exploited according to this argument, because the second condition fails (that the complementary coalition be worse off under the hypothetical alternative). If workers are exploited, they must be exploited by some other coalition, who must be gaining from their exploitation.

More careful evaluation of the state capitalist position depends partly on how one treats the propensity to overinvest. The least charitable view is that of Harman, who argues that overinvestment is a response to an incentive structure faced by planners: they are personally rewarded for investment and growth of the economy; the motivation of the planner is essentially the same as for the capitalist, to accumulate, although not personally. Thus overinvestment is an undesirable consequence of the aggregation of self-interested behavior of planners. If this is the case, one might argue that the planners are gaining from overinvestment (as contrasted with what their welfare would be with a lower rate of growth). Even then, the arguments presented above indicate that this should be called status exploitation and not capitalist exploitation (cf. lunar exploitation).

On the other hand, others do not agree that the tendency to invest such a large portion of national product is due to planners' self-interested behavior. Nuti (1979) ascribes the pattern instead to their disinterested goals of building the level of infrastructure necessary for communism. Planners have a longer time horizon than workers. If Nuti is correct, then it becomes problematic to decide whether in fact the workers would be better off if they were to "withdraw" and run the economy without planners, using a larger discount rate;

second, it is no longer clear that the planners themselves are gaining by the high investment rate, and thus the complementary coalition is not exploiting. How do we evaluate when the workers are better off—by using their own current preferences for leisure and income, or some other set of preferences (such as the planners')? It is, at very best, highly problematic to call the system state capitalist, under Nuti's description of the cause of overinvestment, according to our definition of exploitation. (Nuti himself does not agree to the state capitalist description.)

Even if Harman's planner-incentive description is correct and it is also unequivocally true that the level of investment is too high, overinvestment would more properly be called status exploitation than capitalist exploitation. Aside from the above arguments, calling the phenomenon state capitalism begs more questions than it answers. First, it must be a capitalism without capitalists (the exploiting coalition does not accumulate wealth); second, the investment behavior is precisely the opposite of what normal capitalist countries have experienced, namely underinvestment. Thus, to the extent that the category is intended to imply that state capitalism is similar to capitalism in its laws of motion, it seems entirely inappropriate.

5. Planning versus syndicalism and the market

Suppose that the syndicalist alternative to existing socialism is to operate the means of production as cooperatives, rather than under central state control. The capital stock would be parceled out on a per capita basis, and individuals would coalesce into cooperatives. This solution would appear to conform more precisely to assigning each producer his per capita share of the capital stock than does the solution of state control, and hence perhaps the syndicalist solution is to be entertained as the proper way of solving the problem of public versus social ownership of the means of production.

Under the syndicalist alternative, differences in skill soon become embodied in differential ownership of alienable assets. Capital, after all, is dead labor. Thus, socialist exploitation in the presence of a market mechanism produces property relations which bring about capitalist exploitation. If the historical task of the socialist transformation is to abolish capitalist exploitation but not socialist exploitation, then some mechanism must be adopted which eclipses the private capitalization of embodied skills in alienable produced assets. Syndicalism allows the high returns to skill to be embodied in capital, while the various centrally planned economies do not.

It has been pointed out that status exploitation under socialism gives rise to privileges which engender socialist exploitation. Socialist exploitation, according to the laws of the market, will give rise to capitalist exploitation.

The distinction between existing socialism and syndicalism relates to the problem raised in Chapter 7 concerning the proper generalization of capitalist exploitation to a model with differential labor or skill endowments. Is the hypothetical alternative to allow coalitions to withdraw with their per capita or per labor share of the capital? The syndicalist proposal comes close to specifying the alternative as one assigning per labor shares of capital to departing coalitions. Even if the original distribution of capital is on a per capita basis under syndicalism, after some time has passed the capital stock distribution will come to approximate a per labor share distribution, since differential labor will be differentially capitalized. Under the centrally planned model, this is not the case. Even if producers are paid different wages for their various skills, these wages cannot be capitalized. Some historical rationale is therefore provided for preferring the per capita specification of capitalist exploitation to the per labor one, to the extent that we treat the experience of existing socialist countries (which are predominantly nonsyndicalist) as experiments in the elimination of capitalist exploitation. That is, we define capitalist exploitation (somewhat circularly) as what they are evidently trying to eliminate.

An insight from this argument concerns the classical Marxian conception that socialism is a social formation in transition between capitalism and communism. Under communism, socialist exploitation is abolished (and presumably status exploitation); every producer works according to his ability and is paid according to his need.[11] The property relations which socialism legitimizes constitute

11. One might define another type of exploitation, called needs exploitation, which is also eliminated under communism. The elimination of status and socialist exploitation will produce an egalitarian income distribution, but communism goes beyond that. See Chapter 9.

an unstable constellation of relations, as legitimate differential remuneration to skill has a tendency, at least in a market economy, to become embodied in illegitimate differential possession of productive assets. Capitalism legitimizes both types of property relations, and communism declares both illegitimate. Socialism is a holding pattern in which the alienable assets are first socialized, because of the relative ease in doing that, compared with what today appears to be the more difficult incentive problem of socializing the returns to inalienable assets.

There are, in addition, arguments of market imperfections which are often given to argue for the necessity of central planning. These have not been discussed as they do not flow particularly from the present theory of exploitation.

On the other hand, the clearest modern argument for syndicalism is associated with the self-management school of socialism. In terms of our discussion, they advocate self-management as the cure for status exploitation under socialism, as well as for the inefficiencies of planning. Branco Horvat (and others) describes the social formation in the Soviet Union as étatist, and draws many parallels between étatism and capitalism (see, for instance, Horvat, 1980). For Horvat, étatism and capitalism are two sides of the same coin, to be contrasted with self-management socialism. From our discussion, this appears to be incorrect. Self-management would seek to abolish status exploitation but at the risk of reproducing capitalist exploitation as skills become embodied in capital controlled by workers' cooperatives; while central planning (or étatism) keeps capitalist exploitation down to that minimum which is socially necessary (in the sense of the NEP), but the tradeoff is a certain degree of status exploitation associated with placing power in a bureaucracy and not the market. In a different context, Marx's remark on the tradeoff between locating social power in the market and in community, which is apt here, was: "Rob the thing [money] of this social power, and you must give it to persons to exercise over other persons" (1973, pp. 157–158).

6. Conclusion

Socialist and status exploitation, but probably not capitalist exploitation, have been located as present in existing socialism. It is not the historical task of the socialist transition to eliminate socialist exploitation. What inequalities exist because of differential remuneration to skills should be expected under socialism. While much criticism has been levied from the "left" against socialist exploitation (the Chinese cultural revolution, egalitarian movements), there is also a current in the literature maintaining that skilled workers are underpaid in existing socialism. Hungarian planners maintain that wage differentials must be widened to compensate workers properly for their skills, and hence to promote productivity. It has been maintained that the economic reform movements in Eastern Europe were attempts to make market forces a determinant of returns to skills, among other things, and thus rectify egalitarian tendencies (Flakierski, 1979). Thus, unskilled workers were purportedly against the reforms and skilled workers and the intelligentsia supported them. It has been maintained that skilled workers in the Soviet Union are underpaid because of the relatively egalitarian pay scale (Zaslavsky, 1979). (In the language here, these arguments assert that existing socialism is trying, perhaps mistakenly, to eliminate socialist exploitation.)

In assessing capitalist exploitation in existing socialism it is useful to divide history into two periods, one in which capitalist exploitation was consciously adopted as policy to develop the productive forces, and a later period when it is not. There may, of course, also be capitalist exploitation in a socialist country with relatively well-developed capital stock. Unemployment is the clearest example of such: for a coalition of unemployed workers could surely be better off if they had access to some capital stock, while the complementary coalition would arguably be worse off. The existence of significant unemployment in Yugoslavia is an indication of capitalist exploitation; one can argue that Yugoslavia has chosen to take its exploitation in that form rather than in the form of status exploitation of the other Eastern European societies.

Status exploitation in existing socialism is the form about which there is the least developed theory. While the general Marxist position is that socialist exploitation is socially necessary at this point of historical development and capitalist exploitation is not, there is no well-developed discussion concerning the social necessity of status exploitation. Indeed, there is not even agreement that it exists. The orthodox position of Eastern European and Soviet communist parties is that all special privileges and income of the elite stratum are either a return to skill or are necessary for the performance of the job. (See Zaslavsky, 1980.) On the other extreme is the position of those who consider these societies capitalist, who argue that status exploitation not only exists but is equivalent to capitalist exploitation. I have argued sharply against the second position, and have discussed the first one by casual observation. The middle position adopted here is that status exploitation does exist and is qualitatively different from capitalist and socialist exploitation. The historical verdict is not yet rendered as to whether it is at this time socially necessary, although there is strong reason to believe that in the absence of a market mechanism it is to some extent.

Whether status exploitation is socially necessary becomes in part a question of whether the market can replace bureaucracy in existing socialism. This has been a long and venerable debate, although classical contributions such as Lange (1938) addressed themselves more directly to questions of efficiency rather than of income distribution. (The two questions are, of course, not unrelated.) Modern writers concerned with the inequities of étatism vary from recommending increased democratization within a framework of central planning (Brus, 1975) to self-management and market socialism (Horvat, 1980; Selucky, 1979). I cannot do justice to this debate here, but I did remark that the major paradox of the introduction of a market mechanism is that socialistically legitimate returns to differential skills can become embodied as differential ownership of capital, thus regenerating capitalist exploitation. It is this unstable aspect of socialism —the acceptance of socialist exploitation but not its dynamic implication of capitalist exploitation—which leads to the problem of how to harness the market to do its good deeds as a decentralizing device under socialism. The participants in the debate are, of course, aware of this problem and most therefore advocate a limited market in which capital cannot be accumulated and investment decisions remain with the center. It is a question to what extent the internal logic of the market permits viability of such a system. Furthermore, even if the market solution were more efficient in the sense of generating greater output than central planning, the market implies its own corollary income distribution, in which some groups, such as the unemployed, may be worse off.

What, then, is the verdict concerning the nature of the mode of production in existing socialism, the forms of exploitation and class which exist? Should we consider these societies to be aberrations from the Marxist dream, brought about by errors of policy at best, tyrannical despots at worst? At the coarsest level, the answer must be no, for the purpose of the socialist transformation is assertedly to eliminate capitalist exploitation, and it has been argued here that has been largely accomplished. Much of the inequality, class phenomena, and political authoritarianism appear to have a logical foundation in our analysis of the problem of socialist transformation in an underdeveloped economy. Given its limited historical task to eliminate inequality flowing from the differential ownership of alienable means of production, it would be utopian (in retrospect at least) to conceive of socialism as the era in which man achieves the unconstrained economic environment necessary for the full flowering of individuality and human potential. Recall the error of the French revolutionaries.

That socialist exploitation remains in existing socialism is no surprise, but that status exploitation seems so prominent was not adequately predicted by the classical theory. Two questions must be posed. First, is status exploitation socially necessary? Second, does the status exploitation in existing socialism render the exploited worse off than they would be as capitalistically exploited proletarians in a capitalist alternative? The relationship between the two questions is this: if the answer to the second is yes, then the answer to the first must be no, since a feasible alternative under existing socialism would be to revert to capitalism. (However, if the answer to the second question is no, the answer to the first is indeterminate.) This is the position of many Western liberals and Marxists and Eastern dissidents—that life in a society with status exploitation is worse than in one with capitalist exploitation. Many, on the other hand, hold either that this is not so, or that if it is, the present features of socialist society so rendering it are not indispensable to socialism, and so a socialist alternative is feasible which is superior to capitalism.

Even if one decided that the present practices in existing socialism of status exploitation were socially necessary (which entails, in particular, that existing socialist society is better than the capitalist alternative), that would not imply that these societies and their authorities should escape uncriticized by Marxists. Myriad political practices exist which are difficult to conceive, even with the most imaginative efforts, as falling within the purview of socially necessary status exploitation.[12] But more basically than that, it is the responsibility of the leadership to discuss openly the nature of status exploitation under socialism, with an intent to eliminating its social necessity, and this surely has not been done. (See the discussion of section 3.) A most telling distinction between Lenin and the post-Lenin leadership is his unscathing and open criticism of contemporary Soviet society, contrasted with their stifling of such criticism. (As was argued earlier in the chapter, the social necessity of a practice does not conflict with a critical stance toward it.) Witness for instance the jailing of Rudolf Bahro in the German Democratic Republic, apparently for his study of these questions (Bahro, 1978).[13] The inadmissibility of scientific criticism of existing socialist societies from within is a most foreboding indication that the elimination of their forms of exploitation, as (and if) they become socially unnecessary, may not be possible without violent revolutionary transformations.

12. Strictly speaking, the discussion here in this chapter applies to economic inequality. What of the abrogation of civil liberties which do not have economic consequences (and would therefore not already be included as status exploitation)? Clearly, one could extend the scope of the exploitation concept to include political repression, as that enters into the determination of individuals' welfare.

13. Besides Bahro's work, two other critical books of recent date, written by Eastern Europeans attempting to analyze the existing socialist mode of production from a Marxist standpoint, are Rakovski (1978) and Konrád and Szelényi (1979). Konrád and Szelényi claim the intelligentsia form the new ruling class, through a combination of socialist and status exploitation.

9

Links with Historical Materialism

In Chapters 7 and 8 a taxonomy of exploitation was defined and applied to analyze inequality in existing socialism. This chapter attempts to relate the theory of historical materialism to the taxonomy of exploitation. There is clearly implied some historical progression in the types of exploitation which societies experience, but until this point that progression has been motivated only heuristically. By invoking historical materialism, the taxonomy of exploitation can graduate from being a description to a theory of historical change.

My approach is to accept the theory of historical materialism as a postulate and to translate its claims into the language of exploitation which has been developed. The theory of historical materialism cannot be developed here, much less subjected to critical appraisal. Fortunately, there has been a renaissance of analytical work on historical materialism recently; worth special mention are the superbly clear account and defense of historical materialism of Cohen (1978) and the criticism of the teleological aspect of the theory presented by Harris (1979). The interchange between Cohen (1980) and Elster (1980a) is also particularly illuminating. That I take historical materialism as a postulate does not imply that I accept all aspects of the theory as correct. Indeed, the intelligence of the modern debate on this question would render such a position premature and dogmatic.[1] Nevertheless, in proposing a general theory of exploitation one is obliged to ask how it relates to the core of Marxist thought, historical

1. Even Cohen does not say he agrees completely with the theory of historical materialism; more cautiously, he says that he has tried to put forth the best case for it. Perhaps the best case is not good enough.

materialism. The rough seams which will appear in trying to match the two theories may provide indications for further criticisms of each.

In section 1 of this chapter the concept of socially necessary exploitation is further refined into statically and dynamically socially necessary exploitation. This allows, in section 2, a characterization of the claim of historical materialism: history progresses by the successive elimination of forms of exploitation as they become socially unnecessary in the dynamic sense. But historical materialism also passes judgment and says that the elimination of those forms of exploitation is good. Why? An explanation concerning the self-actualization of people is proposed. Section 3 discusses the concepts of "return" and "surplus," about which there is disagreement between Marxists and non-Marxists. In section 4, needs are discussed. Communism is supposed to be a system where people are remunerated according to need, but needs have not so far entered into the taxonomy of property relations and exploitation. Section 4 proposes an additional kind of exploitation, needs exploitation, and characterizes communism as the elimination of that form. Further symmetries and asymmetries in the elimination of feudal, capitalist, socialist, and needs exploitation are discussed. In section 5, a question brought up at the end of Chapter 6 is discussed: Why does Marxism choose labor as the value numeraire for its theory of exploitation? The chapter concludes with a short discussion on the sociology of injustice. In this book, there has been no discussion of how people come to think certain forms of inequality are exploitative, and how they come to fight against them. The last section proposes the need for such a theory, in order to explain the mechanism which historical materialism proposes as the engine of history, class struggle. Which groups develop consciousness of themselves as classes, of their position in the exploitation hierarchy?

1. Socially necessary exploitation

From the names given to the various forms of exploitation—feudal, capitalist, socialist—it appears that history, according to the historically materialist conception, necessarily eliminates the various forms of exploitation, in a certain order, until communism is reached, a society which, according to the *Critique of the Gotha Program,* is characterized by "from each according to his ability, to each according to his need." There is a temptation to claim that, in the language of historical materialism, the historical task of a given epoch is to eliminate those forms of exploitation which are socially unnecessary. Yet a more careful reading of historical materialism shows this is not its claim: rather, the historical task of an epoch is to remove fetters on the development of the productive forces, which is not necessarily the same as producing a situation in which the direct producers are "better off," that is, the same as eliminating socially unnecessary exploitation. According to historical materialism, feudal bondage and capitalist private property are eliminated in history as they become fetters on the development of the productive forces; is it clear that that is also the condition which brings about an improvement in the welfare of people?

The models developed here do not deal with this dynamic question of the development of the productive forces. They evaluate the improvement in a person's position in a static and simplistic way, by asking if his "utility function" achieves a higher value under the alternative arrangement. (The implicit utility function in the models of subsistence economies of Part I is the inverse of the amount of time the producer has to work to subsist, and in the accumulation economy of Part II it is the amount of revenue or command over goods which the producer enjoys.) Yet when the mode of production changes, the producers' utility functions do not stay the same. To make welfare comparisons we would be forced to compare proletarians under capitalism to their serf ancestors, or their independent artisan ancestors. To take a utility-based approach to welfare would embroil us in the myriad problems of endogenous preferences and interpersonal/intertemporal comparison of utility. To avoid this, I propose a non-utility-based criterion for welfare improvement, to be justified further in section 2. An individual will be said to be better off in state X than in state Y if he receives more income and at least as much leisure in X as in Y. First, this is a weak criterion, as it does not permit comparison of states in which an individual possesses two bundles of income and leisure which are not comparable as vectors. Nevertheless, it will be argued even this weak criterion takes us a long way in evaluating actual history. Second, it is not asked what type of work an individual performs in X or Y to get his income. For example: one might argue (and many do) that the self-employed shopkeeper who works eighty hours a week for an income of $200 is better off than the factory worker who works sixty hours a week for an income of $210, but I will not. Or, more precisely, I would claim that such examples are of minor significance in the historical picture.

We refine the notion of socially necessary exploitation. It was assumed in the initial definition of exploitation that when a coalition withdraws, the incentive structure which its members face in the alternative economy set up by the coalition does not differ from the incentive structure in the original economy. In general, this is false. Consider proletarians under early capitalism. If they had withdrawn with their per capita share of the produced assets of society, they might very well not have worked long enough to make the income that they had as proletarians; instead they might have chosen to take more leisure and less income. But even if one strengthens the weak criterion for judging welfare improvements that has been proposed, and allows the judgment that these independent producers are better off than the erstwhile proletarians because their leisure-income bundle is superior (even though not strictly dominating), there is a key dynamic consideration. Assuming that capitalist property relations were necessary to bring about accumulation and technical innovation in the early period of capitalism, then the coalition which has withdrawn will soon fall behind the capitalist society because of the absence of incentives to innovate. Even the proletarians under capitalism will eventually enjoy an income-leisure bundle superior to the bundle of independent utopian socialists who have retired into the hills with their share of the capital, assuming enough of the benefits of increased productivity pass down to the proletarians, as has historically been the case. Thus, a more precise phrasing of the criterion is: if by withdrawing with its per capita share of produced assets a coalition would be able to preserve the same incentive structure and improve the lot of its members, then it is capitalistically exploited in the current allocation. If, however, the incentive structure could not be maintained, and as a consequence the coalition would immediately be worse off, then the capitalist exploitation which it endures is *socially necessary in the static sense*. Suppose, however, the coalition would initially be better off after exercising its withdrawal option, even allowing for incentive effects, but then "soon" it would become worse off, due for instance to the lack of incentives to develop the forces of production. In this case, the exploitation is *socially necessary in the dynamic sense*.

There are, in the Marxist reading of history, many examples of the implementation of regimes entailing dynamically socially necessary exploitation, but which brought about an inferior income-leisure bundle for the direct producers, of which two will be mentioned. Marx approved of the British conquest of India, despite the misery it brought to the direct producers, because of its role in developing the productive forces. Thus, the contention is that proletarians in India would have been better off, statically, in the alternative without imperialist interference, but dynamically British imperialist exploitation was socially necessary to bring about the development of the productive forces, eventually improving the income-leisure bundles of the producers (or their children) over what they would have been. (For a discussion of this in an essay not irrelevant to this context, see Brenkert, 1979.) A second example is taken from Brenner's (1976) discussion of the development of capitalism in England as contrasted with France. In England, agrarian capitalists succeeded in breaking the power of the yeoman peasantry, and the productive forces in agriculture were developed under their aegis. In France, the independent peasantry remained strong, did not develop the productive forces, and chose a bundle of leisure and income which was doubtless superior to that of their English counterparts, in the short run.[2] The development of productive forces in agriculture was not synonymous with the improved welfare of the peasantry. Eventually, the British agricultural proletarians were better off (in our sense) than their French counterparts.

Why does Marxism maintain that capitalist exploitation was socially necessary in early capitalism, or, to put it another way, that capitalism was initially a progressive system, an optimal economic structure for encouraging the productive forces at a certain stage in their development?[3] First, it is claimed to be socially necessary only in the dynamic sense: without capitalist property relations, innovation and the development of labor productivity would have stag-

2. Perhaps "doubtless" is not the word, for neoclassical interpreters such as North and Thomas (1973) would say that the English agricultural proletarians voluntarily contracted with their capitalists to enter into relations of wage labor, so that the capitalists would force them to work, prevent them from shirking, thereby improving their welfare. See Brenner (1976) for argumentation against the neoclassical implicit contract interpretation.

3. For discussion of what is meant by an economic structure being optimal for the level of development of productive forces, see Cohen (1978), especially Chapter 6, and Elster and Hyllund (1980).

nated, and workers would eventually have been worse off. Second, and worthy of note, it is *relations* of private property which were socially necessary, not particular individual capitalists. It is not that private property was necessary to coax certain specific individuals in possession of scarce skills to employ them (entrepreneurial ability, inventiveness); rather, it was the *system* of private property in the means of production which stimulated innovation. Many could have played the the role of capitalist, but someone had to. This is not to deny that the skills of capitalists may be somewhat scarce—it is just that they are not that scarce. Within the population of proletarians there are plenty of potential capitalists—that is, persons who are capable of performing that role but who do not, because of their lack of access to the means of production.

There is a difference between the contention that capitalist exploitation exists but is socially necessary, and the bourgeois ideologue's argument that capitalist exploitation does not exist. The bourgeois ideologue is maintaining that capitalists' profits are a return to scarce skills they possess, and hence that the income losses workers would suffer in the coalition, if they withdrew with their per capita share of produced assets, are due not to incentive problems but rather to their lack of access to the skills of capitalists. The bourgeois ideologue claims that the workers under capitalism are experiencing *socialist* exploitation, not capitalist exploitation. This is quite different from maintaining that capitalists possess no skills which do not also exist in the large pool of proletarians (even though they may be scarce), but that the regime of private ownership relations in the means of production produces certain behavior (of competition leading to innovation) which would be absent without those relations. In the second view, it does not matter who the capitalists are, but the workers will be better off if someone is a capitalist. Capitalism is socially necessary; particular capitalists are dispensable.

The social necessity of socialist exploitation in early socialism may appear to differ from this, in that the skills which are specially remunerated are embodied in particular people. Not only may socialist exploitation be necessary, but particular socialist exploiters may be. Viewed dynamically, however, this may not be (and, I believe, is not) the case. If skills are a consequence of nurture only, the result of prior status exploitation, perhaps, then anyone can be the vessel for them, although someone must be. It is, again, not that particular people must be recruited by the offer of a special wage, but rather that the special wage creates a system where a certain fraction of people will train themselves. Once trained, the particular skilled person will be of special value to society, but the same may be true of particular capitalists, like Henry Ford II, who acquire their class status by virtue of birth, but eventually do learn to run capitalist empires.

2. The historical materialist imperative

According to historical materialism, feudal, capitalist, and socialist exploitation all exist under feudalism. At some point feudal relations become a fetter on the development of the productive forces, and they are eliminated by the bourgeois revolution. Feudal exploitation is outlawed under capitalism. Although the proletarians might not immediately appear to be better off than the serfs because of the non-comparability of their income-leisure bundles, one can assert that quite rapidly (in a generation, perhaps) they are better off (in our sense, at least) due to the rapid development of the productive forces and the increase in the real wage.[4] Thus, feudal relations were eliminated when they became *socially unnecessary in the dynamic sense.* Under capitalism, only capitalist and socialist exploitation continue to exist. Capitalist exploitation in the beginning is socially necessary, as discussed; eventually, however, it becomes a fetter on the development of productive forces. Large coalitions of proletarians could be (dynamically) better off by withdrawing with their per capita share of the produced means of production, and organizing themselves in a socialist way, because capitalism no longer performs a progressive innovating function, compared to what society is capable of accomplishing under socialist organization. Capitalist exploitation becomes socially unnecessary, and is eliminated by socialist revolution. Under socialism, capitalist exploitation is outlawed, but social-

4. Lindert and Williamson (1980) claim, on the basis of new statistical evidence, that workers in the cities of mid-nineteenth-century England were better off, in terms of real wages, life expectancy, and other quality-of-life indicators, than rural unskilled laborers of 1780. Their work challenges the conventional Marxist view that the "satanic mills" were an unmitigated disaster for the working class over the period of the industrial revolution. It is nevertheless true that at any *point* in time until the 1880s or so, life expectancy was lower for urban workers than rural workers. They also assert that at any point in time urban workers felt subjectively better off than they had as country dwellers, that is, the higher urban wage compensated for the disamenities of city life.

ist exploitation exists and, most would argue, is socially necessary, at least in the early period.

Historical materialism, in summary, claims that history progresses by the successive elimination of forms of exploitation which are socially unnecessary in the dynamic sense.[5] It is important to reiterate that this does not mean the exploited agents will immediately be better off (in terms of the income-leisure bundle) after the revolution. Nor have I discussed the historical mechanism which might lead to this pattern. The above is a translation of the technological determinist aspect of historical materialist theory into the language of the theory of exploitation.

But historical materialism contains as well, I believe, an ethical imperative, which asserts that it is *good* to eliminate forms of exploitation which are dynamically socially unnecessary (that is, which fetter the development of the productive forces), even when the direct producers may suffer in the short run.[6] Why is this? There are at least two possible paths of argument, one with reference to justice, the other to the self-actualization of man. I will develop the second here, reserving only brief comments for the first.

Why should it be considered good to eliminate forms of property relations which hinder development of the productive forces? Aside from possible considerations of justice, there appear to be two quite different reasons, neither of which is an appeal to egalitarianism as a fundamental goal. Although the successive elimination of exploitations does move society in the egalitarian direction, as it requires the successive removal of categories of property relations (first feudal property, then capitalist property, then socialist property), I do not think it is necessary to make the argument for the moral imperative

5. The precise claim is that history progresses by eliminating property relations which fetter the productive forces, but it is further claimed that the fettering of the productive forces makes the direct producers worse off than they would be with the further development of the productive forces, since enough of the benefits of increased productivity will return to them in the form of better living standards. These two claims together imply the statement to which this note is attached.

6. The language here may be slightly confusing. The elimination of one form of dynamically socially unnecessary exploitation (for example, feudal exploitation) has always entailed the implementation of another form of exploitation which is socially necessary in a dynamic sense (for example, capitalist exploitation). Furthermore, although capitalist exploitation existed under feudalism, the degree of it may sharply increase under capitalism, hence rendering the exploited worse off (perhaps) in the static, immediate sense.

of the theory by an appeal to egalitarianism as an unquestionable good.

The unquestionable good is the *self-actualization of men and of man,* a precise definition of which will not be attempted. A related idea exists not only in Marx but in modern social theorists. Rawls (1971), for example, views primary goods as essentially distinguishable from other goods in that they are necessary for the realization of life plans, an idea similar to self-actualization of men. Sen argues for including the notion of "basic capability equality" in theories of distributive justice.[7]

In the historical period of scarcity (from feudalism to at least the present day), the major block to the self-actualization of men is the constraint they face in providing themselves with material goods needed for survival. Hence, if a coalition is exploited in a socially unnecessary way, its ability to self-actualize (or realize its basic capabilities) can be improved upon. But the Paretian aggregator might reply that by eliminating the exploitation of the underdog, perhaps the basic capabilities of the former exploiters would be infringed upon. I would argue that this has not been the case historically. Typically, distribution has been characterized by a large class of exploited, whose lack of access to income sharply hinders their self-actualization, and a small class of exploiters, who have income far above the level which is necessary to provide them with the opportunities which are available for self-actualization at the current level of development of culture and the productive forces.[8] Elimination of exploitation which is socially unnecessary in the dynamic sense eventually reduces unambiguously the material constraint on people's capacity to self-actualize.

This is the first argument. Notice that there is no essential distinction between the self-actualization of men and Rawls's opportunity for constructing life plans or Sen's basic capability achievement. The

7. "It is arguable that what is missing in all this framework is some notion of 'basic capabilities:' a person being able to do certain basic things. The ability to move about is the relevant one here, but one can consider others, e.g., the ability to meet one's nutritional requirements, the wherewithal to be clothed and sheltered, the power to participate in the social life of the community. The notion of urgency related to this is not fully captured by either utility or primary goods" (Sen, 1980, p. 218).

8. One does not need to be a millionaire to reach the threshold of material constraint on self-actualization which is possible given the current level of development of the productive forces, but requires income only a little more than mine. The ability to self-actualize, unlike neoclassical utility, is a satiable function of income.

second argument, however, distinguishes self-actualization from these other two concepts.

Marx and Engels lauded capitalism not only because it gave the direct producers higher income, but because it broadened their outlook through the introduction of science and culture and the development of the productive forces.[9] The development of the productive forces is the necessary condition for dynamic self-actualization of *man*. Or, more sharply, the development of the productive forces is the proxy for the self-actualization of man. Dynamic self-actualization is to be distinguished from basic capabilities or life plans, because any given person would rather have the resources necessary to realize his life plan or realize his basic capabilities, but no individual cares about being dynamically self-actualized. The dynamic self-actualization of *man* is not something which happens to the individual, but rather to man as he develops over historical time. There is a teleological judgment being made: man who understands how the universe works is more self-actualized than man who does not, and it is *better* to be self-actualized in this sense.[10]

To summarize, the elimination of socially unnecessary exploitation is the relevant evaluative criterion, because, first, during the era of scarcity, it increases the opportunities for short-run self-actualization of *men* by providing the formerly exploited large group with access to the wherewithal for basic living, and second, according to historical materialism, the elimination of dynamically socially unnecessary exploitation is necessary for the development of the productive forces, which is the proxy for self-actualization of *man*.[11]

9. See Cohen (1974) for discussion of this point. For example, a passage from Marx's *Grandrisse:* "Hence the great civilizing influence of capital, its production of a stage of society compared with which all earlier stages appear to be merely *local progress* and idolatry of nature . . . [Its destruction is] . . . permanently revolutionary, tearing down all obstacles that impede the development of the productive forces, the expansion of needs, the diversity of production and the exploitation and exchange of natural and intellectual forces." (Cohen, 1974, p. 250.)

10. Teleological, because the judgment must be based on a belief that thinking and understanding are essential to man. If man understands the universe better, he may be better able to provide for his material needs, but that is the first argument, not to be confused with this one.

It must be admitted the existence of nuclear technology makes this contention problematic. If knowledgeable man destroys nine-tenths of the population with weapons created from that knowledge, is man thereby more self-actualized than prenuclear man?

11. I owe the distinction between the self-actualization of men and of man to G. A. Cohen, although he would perhaps not assign the terms the same meanings.

In contemporary bourgeois society (or, more precisely, among the middle class), an opinion exists asserting that the era of abundance has already arrived—in the terms relevant here, that the constraints on self-actualization are no longer material but are cultural or psychological. This might appear tō nullify the appropriateness of the criterion for self-actualization. I do agree, and did state, that the criterion only applies in the historical period of scarcity, when men's self-actualization is hindered by their access to material goods, given the degree of self-actualization possible during that historical period due to the development of culture at the time. First, it must be observed that such material constraints are still binding on the vast majority of people in the world. Second, it is surely true that such material constraints are not binding on many in the industrialized countries. That, however, is not necessarily an argument for slowing down growth but may be an argument for continuing growth with redistribution to those billions who are severely materially constrained.[12]

But if redistribution is not a useful or feasible option (in the sense of the incentive problems that would accompany it), then according to this argument there would be no imperative (on the growth of self-actualization) for socialist transformations in highly developed capitalist countries with progressive income distribution. There are, however, classical arguments which examine other constraints to self-actualization once the material constraint is no longer binding. First among these is self-actualization through control of one's labor, the contention being that socialism makes possible such control to an extent impossible under capitalism. It was observed in the previous chapter that this is not necessarily the case. Socialism may eliminate capitalist exploitation, but it is not clear that the status exploitation which appears to replace it in existing socialism is a quantitative improvement with regard to self-actualization in societies where the material constraint is no longer binding.

To summarize, the imperative of the theory of historical imperialism is to eliminate forms of exploitation which become socially unnecessary in the dynamic sense. Forms of dynamically socially necessary exploitation continue to exist. The grounds are that the

12. I say "may be" as it is not clear how much redistribution will help, as contrasted with transformations of the mode of production in the less developed economies.

development of the productive forces brings about, if not immediately then soon, increased self-actualization of men by weakening the material constraint on vast numbers of people, and that the development of the productive forces is itself a cause and symptom of the self-actualization of man, for reasons other than material. These arguments do not appeal to egalitarianism, although the path of eliminating exploitation should lead to greater equality, although not necessarily monotonically. (There may be more inequality under capitalism than under feudalism, although the forms of exploitation are fewer.)

These arguments do not locate the historical materialist imperative in considerations of justice. I do not claim that there are no such ethical imperatives; it is rather that I am not prepared to present the argument. The problem can be seen in the debate concerning justice in Marxism. Wood (1972, 1979) presents broad evidence that Marx considered justice to be a superstructural concept, therefore corollary to extant property relations. In this reading, an income distribution is just if it conforms to the laws of society. Income from slavery is just in a slave society and unjust in a capitalist society. Wood (1979) says: "Marx prefers to criticize capitalism directly in terms of this rational content [crisis, anarchy of production, and so on] and sees no point in presenting his criticisms in the mystified form they would assume in a moral ideology." There is a strong undercurrent of adherence to Wood's position in Marxism, which can be seen in the frequent insistence that Marxism criticizes capitalism from an objective rather than normative point of view. Contrarily, Husami (1978), Elster (1980b), and Cohen (1981) maintain Marxism claims that capitalism is unjust, inter alia. (Brenkert, 1979, has another approach; he claims, "Marx's critique cannot be one of justice but can be and is one of freedom.") Cohen (1981) presents the intuitively compelling position that the passion with which Marxism indicts capitalism can only come from a belief in its injustice, and cannot be sustained simply by belief in the thesis that its period of historical usefulness is past. (As I asked in Chapter 8, would Marxists not have supported proletarian revolt even during capitalism's progressive phase? An affirmative answer need not imply that such support indicates Marxists' belief in capitalism's injustice, but it adds evidence to the case.)

Wood's claim is that the Marxian concept of justice provides no effective criterion for criticism of society. If, however, Marxism does entail a less relativist and more powerful concept of justice, the intuitively plausible position, I think it will permit statements such as this: although early capitalism was progressive, and its exploitation was socially necessary, it was unjust. A concept of justice will permit the existence of a necessary evil. I have claimed that historical materialism indicates a direction in history, and an accompanying imperative based on self-actualization, which is not necessarily the same imperative as one based on justice.

Should such a concept of justice exist consonant with historical materialism, it will differ, in particular, from Rawlsian justice in this way. For Rawls, any inequality is just if it maximizes the potential of those most constrained in their possibilities to so achieve life plans. If capitalist relations of property are progressive in the Marxian sense in early capitalism, then early capitalism is just for Rawls. Rawlsian justice is determined by evaluating the allocation in question against currently feasible counterfactuals—feasible in the sense of incentive considerations. A Rawlsian just allocation is, in the present language, one in which the worst-off coalition suffers no socially unnecessary exploitation. The identification of such an allocation with justice flows from the contractarian approach, in which groups in society hypothetically agree to certain forms of organization because they can do no better. (See Howe and Roemer, 1981, for a game-theoretic treatment of Rawlsian justice which makes explicit the specific form of contractarianism in the Rawlsian system.) If a Marxian theory of justice exists which can perform the task mentioned, it cannot be contractarian in this sense.

3. Desert, return, and surplus

The terms *desert, return,* and *surplus* often occupy central roles in theories of distribution and economic justice. In particular, many interpretations of the Marxian theory see Marxism as mandating some distribution either according to deserts or needs. (See Sen, 1973, chap. 4; Elster, 1980b; Husami, 1978.)

When one speaks of the return to a factor, there are two possible meanings: that the remuneration to that factor is a just one (or a deserved one) or that it is a necessary one. If we wish desert and return to connote two different things, then return must be taken to mean *necessary* remuneration. That is, remuneration to a factor is a return if, without that remuneration, production cannot take place, or that factor cannot be reproduced. This is the predominant usage of the term in economic theory. Return is associated with economic *law:* if the payment to factors of their returns is not made, economic law is violated, and the economy cannot function. If the factor capital does not receive its return of profits, then the economy will not reproduce, capital will not reproduce. Wages are the necessary return to labor, profits to capital: such is economic law.

The historical materialist theory outlined implies something quite different. Whether or not profits should be viewed as a return to capital depends on whether capitalist property relations are necessary for the reproduction of physical capital. In early capitalism, as I have argued, profits are properly viewed as a return to capital, in that such remuneration to capital is socially necessary. If the capital stock had been socialized, it would not have been reproduced, at that stage in the development of the productive forces and the consequent possible social organization and consciousness of the workers. In late capitalism, however, profits are no longer properly viewed as a return to capital. Rather, if profits are not returned to capital, then capital will not reproduce itself, *given the constraint* that the capitalist property relations be maintained. It is fallacious to conclude that, therefore, capitalist property relations are necessary. For example, when conservatives argue for a decrease in corporation profit taxes to coax out more creation of capital, liberals reply that lowering the tax rate will not coax out more investment. Marxists, on the other hand, might admit that decreasing taxes will increase investment, but would take this as an indictment of the system of property relations in which such forms of investment stimulus are needed, rather than as a mandate to decrease taxes. Investment "strikes" do not prove the necessity of lowering the tax rate but of socializing capital, if private property in the means of production is no longer socially necessary (in the technical sense we have defined).

Even if profits are a return to capital, it is fallacious to say they are a return to particular capitalists. As has been argued, no individual capitalist need be reproduced to reproduce capital, even when capitalism is socially necessary. This situation differs from the relationship between the worker and his wage, because of the inalienability of labor power from the person. The wage is a return to the worker as well as to labor power.

There are two possible meanings of surplus. The more conventional meaning is this: a surplus is a portion of income which exists beyond what is consumed by the direct producers, at the moment in question. I think, on the contrary, it is more useful to contrast surplus with return, as the above definition does not, as follows: surplus is that part of the economic product which does not have to go to any particular factor for that factor to be reproduced. When capitalism is no longer socially necessary in the dynamic sense, then profits become a surplus. In early capitalism, profits were not a surplus, because it would not have been possible for society to do with them what it pleased, by hypothesis. A surplus is something extra, not in the sense of extra over present consumption, but in the sense that it need not go to any particular factor for economic reproduction. Under this definition, the neoclassical contention that profits are a return and not a surplus is sensible, though (Marxists claim) wrong. The neoclassical argument, as with the tax example, is frequently myopic in taking property relations as fixed. Profits are surely not a surplus, in the second sense, if one refuses to consider the possibility of socialism.

A similar argument can be made with differential remuneration to skill under socialism. When such payments are socially necessary (for those skills to be reproduced), then they are properly viewed as returns to skill. When they are no longer socially necessary, then such remuneration is a surplus rather than a return to skill. Economic law evolves as society evolves.

The term *desert* connotes justice, and since no theory of justice is here proposed, there can be no definition of desert. We can say some things which appear not to be deserts, however, based on the intuitions put forth for necessary features of a historical materialist theory of justice. If early progressive capitalism is unjust (as proposed), then profits, although a return, are not a desert. (Perhaps a clue to justice is that justice must attach itself to judgments of the role of persons, not of things. Even when profits are a return to capital, because they are not a return to capitalists, they cannot be deserved.) It is somewhat more difficult to decide whether a skill remuneration is a desert, at least when such remunerations are socially necessary, if we stipulate, as I did not in previous discussions, that skills are embodied inalienably in individuals, at least at a given moment. Under those conditions, such a payment is a return to skill and to the skilled person, since for that skill to continue to exist (at least in the short run), he must receive the payment. When skill wage differentials become socially unnecessary, they no longer constitute a return to skill, and I would argue, therefore, surely not a desert, as socially unnecessary inequality should not be just (whatever justice means).

4. Needs

To discuss the problem of needs using the framework of the taxonomy of exploitation which has been proposed, imagine the vector of endowments of a person living under feudalism as consisting of four different types of component:

$$\Omega^i = (\phi^i, \pi^i, \sigma^i, \nu^i).$$

Person i has, first, a component ϕ^i which measures his degree of feudal privilege. (We might measure this in such a way that the sum of ϕ^i over all persons i is zero. Positive feudal privilege is the property owned by the lord, and negative feudal privilege is the serf's feudal property.) π^i is the vector of private property in the means of production. σ^i is the vector of labor skills possessed by i, and ν^i is the vector of needs of i. A component in this endowment vector will be positive when the person is well off (as in the feudal component), so the needs component is specified in this fashion: a large negative component of ν^i means person i has a lot of some need. Alternatively stated, the vector ν^i is the freedom from various needs enjoyed by the individual. As in the feudal component, the needs components might be normalized by assigning a person with a normal need a zero endowment of that need type.

This identification of separate components for needs and skills is too facile, in fact, for needs are surely not independent of skills. The form which excessive neediness frequently takes is the inability to work. Needs whose major effect on individual welfare is through the deprivation of skill will already be captured in the vector of skill endowments, and are not independently identified in the needs vector. The needs vector should only list features which are independent of skill: some people may require more income to treat a disease, although the disease does not affect their skill; large family size, though not affecting skill, may require more income. This dichotomy is not always so neat. Nevertheless, a first approximation to the problem of needs can be made in this way.

The taxonomy of exploitation can be stated in this notation. To test whether an agent or coalition S of agents is feudally exploited, it withdraws taking an endowment of vector of the form:

$$\left(0, \sum_S \pi^i, \sum_S \sigma^i, \sum_S \nu^i\right).$$

That is, the coalition is allocated its per capita share of feudal privilege (which is to say none, since by hypothesis the total endowment of feudal privilege is zero), and its own private property of everything else. If it can improve the lot of its members under this allocation, then the coalition was feudally exploited, with the usual ceteris paribus assumption concerning incentives.

To assess whether a coalition is capitalistically exploited, it takes with it, in the hypothetical withdrawal, its per capita share of both feudal privilege and alienable property, that is:

$$\left(0, \frac{S}{N}\sum_N \pi^i, \sum_S \sigma^i, \sum_S \nu^i\right)$$

but keeps its own skills and its own needs. (N stands for the universe of agents and S for the coalition in question. N and S also stand for the cardinalities of these coalitions.) The test is then performed to see whether the coalition can produce an allocation superior for its members to what they were getting in the original economy.

To assess whether a coalition is socialistically exploited, it is hypothetically given endowments in which it receives its per capita share of feudal privilege, alienable property, and skills, but retains its own needs. This will give rise to an egalitarian distribution of income: that is, the egalitarian distribution of income is the one in which socialist exploitation has been eliminated.

We may still consider that the needy are exploited in an egalitarian distribution, and might name this needs exploitation. A coalition is needs exploited if it could improve its lot (from the egalitarian distribution) by withdrawing with its share of all assets and its share of needs. That is, with the endowment vector:

$$\left(0, \frac{S}{N}\sum_{N} \pi^i, \frac{S}{N}\sum_{N} \sigma^i, 0\right).$$

If the coalition can arrange a superior allocation for its members under this allocation of endowments, then it was needs exploited in the egalitarian distribution. To be less abstract, consider a person with high needs, whose ν^i components are therefore negative. When he withdraws with his share of needs (that is, with zero needs), he will be better off than before—because he will have the same income as before (namely, his per capita share of total income, since the distribution of all other assets is egalitarian), but fewer needs than before. Similarly, a person who is less needy than average will be worse off when he withdraws with his share of every component of the endowment, as he will have the same income as in the egalitarian distribution but more needs.

The elimination of needs exploitation requires compensating people for their needs. A distribution in which needs exploitation is absent is one in which the needy receive more income than the needless. Thus, the passage to communism (defined as "from each according to his ability, to each according to his needs") requires the elimination of two kinds of exploitation which exist in early socialism: first, socialist exploitation, and second, needs exploitation. It is generally assumed in the Marxist literature that socialist exploitation will be eliminated first, but there is little reason to suppose this will be so. Modern societies seem more willing to compensate the specially needy than the specially unskilled. Observe also that there is no name for that hypothetical mode of distribution in which socialist exploitation is eliminated but not needs exploitation. (In socialism both forms of exploitation exist and in communism, neither does.)

The theory of historical materialism appears most plausible in explaining the elimination of feudal and capitalist exploitation, that is, in reference to the bourgeois and socialist revolutions. Whether it is useful in the study of other precapitalist modes of production or postsocialist transitions is problematical. (Harris, 1979, argues for its nonapplicability in the former case.) That is: Can it be claimed that property rights in skills, as they exist in socialism in their limited sense (of entitling the skilled to higher income but not to capitalize that income) will eventually come to fetter the development of productive forces, thus "mandating" the abolition of socialist exploitation? What will be the crises of socialism in which such fettering becomes manifest? Or, alternatively, if socialist exploitation is to be eliminated, will that occur as a conscious action of society, to further self-actualization or justice, even though the development of the productive forces is not the issue? The same questions can be put for needs exploitation. These are issues which cannot be seriously discussed with our historical experience. Suffice it to say that historical materialism is a theory which interprets at most two historical transitions, and I can conceive of no argument so convincing to enable us to claim today that the same mechanism will accomplish the elimination of socialist and needs exploitation.[13]

An asymmetry appears to exist in the way society eliminates feudal and capitalist exploitation, contrasted with how one might imagine it will eliminate socialist and needs exploitation. When feudal exploitation is abolished, that form of property is eliminated. When capitalist exploitation is abolished, capitalist property is owned by no one. In contrast, if skills and needs are truly inalienable, then those forms of property cannot be socialized or eliminated: rather, the elimination of the relevant form of exploitation can only occur through compensation of the unskilled or the needy. Entitlements to the fruits of skill (and unneediness) can be changed by society, but the physical possession of those assets and liabilities cannot be (or so it now seems). Some writers take this as evidence that socialist exploitation can never be eliminated, because of problems considered to be intractable in the pooling of talents (see Kronman, 1981), a conclusion which does not follow. Although talents, perhaps, cannot be pooled, it is not necessary to do so to eliminate socialist exploitation, but only to pool income from the exercise of those talents—a difficult problem, but not metaphysically insurmountable.

It may be the case that the elimination of socialist exploitation will be accomplished by the elimination of the socialist forms of property in this way: that all people become equally skilled and hence the socialist property *differential* disappears. Certainly skill differentials under capitalism are highly accentuated from what they

13. Concerning status exploitation, the classical mechanism seems more plausible. To some extent the struggles in Poland, at this writing, are against status exploitation, and are evidence of the crises that exist because of it. Whether the elimination of status exploitation is possible, at this time, without the reintroduction of capitalism is an open question (see Chapter 8).

will be in a society in which special opportunities due to wealth and status have been eliminated. (Or perhaps it is more important to emphasize the inverse, that the alienation and waste of human potential of those lacking wealth and status are eliminated.) To what extent we can each be hunters in the morning (or perform some task of commensurate skill) and critics in the evening, as Marx and Engels propose in *The German Ideology*, has yet to be seen. A similar remark applies to the socialization of needs.

Historical materialism, then, claims that history progresses by successively eliminating the entitlements of individuals to the fruits from various forms of property, in a certain order. The *reason* a property entitlement becomes eliminated is that it comes to fetter the development of the productive forces. The *mechanism* through which the property entitlement in question is abolished is class struggle, where classes are defined with reference to entitlements respecting the income from the property in question. (Why this mechanism develops and succeeds is beyond our scope.) The *good* accomplished in this process is the self-actualization of men and of man; perhaps justice is also approached, although only perfunctory remarks concerning that issue have been made. Whether the *reason* will continue to apply beyond the capitalist era is unclear; whether the argument for the *good* (of self-actualization, though perhaps not of justice) will continue to apply when all societies eliminate the material constraints on immediate survival is also unclear.

5. Why the labor theory of exploitation?

Historical materialism indicates successive concepts of exploitation by which societies judge themselves (that is, according to their laws). Under feudalism, bondage is legitimate; under capitalism, inequalities arising from private property in both alienable and inalienable assets are legitimate but personal bondage is not; under socialism, only inequalities from private property in inalienable assets are legitimate. We will now invoke this characterization to propose why historical materialism directs one to the labor theory of value and exploitation in studying capitalism. We take up the question which was posed, but could not be pursued, at the end of Chapter 6: why is labor the value numeraire in Marxian exploitation?

It is sometimes claimed that the labor theory of exploitation is the proper one, since labor is that sole commodity which, as if magically, produces more value than it embodies. As was pointed out in Chapter 6, this is false: any commodity can be chosen as the value numeraire, and it can be shown that the economic system is productive if and only if that commodity is "exploited," in the sense that one unit of it embodies less than one unit of it. The corn value of a unit of corn in a productive system is less than unity. Thus, this "objective" reason to privilege labor as the value numeraire fails.

An immediate reason to choose labor power as the proper value numeraire would appear to be the following: from a historical materialist perspective, we are interested in studying history as an unfolding series of class struggles. Therefore, we wish to propose a theory of exploitation which illuminates class struggle, which is to say, a theory in which we view the direct producers as exploited, and not the corn. This is an appropriate choice from a scientific point of view if we believe that analyzing history as a series of class struggles will be more enlightening than history as man's conquest of corn, or, more generally, of nature. To the extent that the neoclassical school sees history as the struggle of man against scarcity, rather than man against man, it would prefer the latter approach.[14] Clearly, then, historical materialism directs us to construct a theory which views people as exploited, and not corn, as the most efficacious research program.

Perhaps surprisingly, the argument is not yet finished. The decision that the theory should classify certain people as exploited, instead of certain things, does not immediately imply that labor must be taken as the value numeraire. To see this, recall the definition of exploitation which was studied in Part II. A producer is said to be labor exploited if the labor value he could command with his revenues is less than the labor he contributes in production. Suppose oil were the value numeraire (and labor is viewed as a produced commodity). The analog is to say that a producer is "oil exploited" if the oil value he could command, through purchase of packages of produced goods with his revenues from production, is less than the oil he contributed to production. This decomposes society into people

14. History is both, of course. The struggle of man against man comes about as a consequence of scarcity. Historical materialism maintains that the most useful level of abstraction highlights class struggle, rather than the less proximate natural scarcity.

who are oil exploited and people who are oil exploiters, since the total oil value of commodities produced is equal to the amount of oil used in production. Thus, we do not need to choose labor as the value numeraire to produce a theory of *society* being divided into exploiters and exploited. We could view the exploitation of people in terms of their relationship to oil.

What fails, however, with the description of people as oil exploited is the correspondence between a producer's exploitation status and his wealth. This is because producers possess *different endowments* of oil. It was shown in Chapter 6, in the model where producers were assumed to own different amounts of labor, that the Class Exploitation Correspondence Principle continued to hold, but the ranking of classes and exploitation status against wealth was no longer monotonic. There could be rich exploited producers (who contributed a lot of labor to production) and poor exploiters (who had very little labor to contribute). Of course, the same is true if oil is the value numeraire, as long as producers do not all contribute the same amount of oil to production. Thus, if we wish to produce a description of value transfers, hence exploitation, which will capture the workers as exploited and the capitalists as exploiters, *we must choose as the value numeraire a commodity which is uniformly distributed throughout the population.* The only such commodity is labor power: for, first, the workers own nothing but labor power under capitalism; and, second, the process of proletarianization allows us to treat all labor as abstract labor and hence labor power is uniformly distributed throughout the population, and capitalist inequality is not due to special skills of capitalists. (Both these points are claimed by Marxism as historical observations prior to, not following from, the labor theory of exploitation.)

Our conclusion that labor is the one appropriate numeraire for denominating value, as it alone entails a theory of exploitation which classifies proletarians as exploited and capitalists as exploiters, may seem to be excessively formal. We can, however, explain in more conventional terms why labor is the necessary choice. The choice is due to the inalienability of labor. Capitalism dispossesses proletarians of every alienable productive asset, but leaves them "free" to sell their labor power. It is not simply a formal coincidence that under capitalism all producers possess one unit of an asset, which happens to be labor power, and that is the only productive asset which is uniformly distributed: this, indeed, is the Marxian *characterization* of capitalism.

The labor theory of exploitation is only appropriate for capitalism if we adopt the assumption that endowments of labor are equal (or approximately so) as a characterization of capitalism. Under capitalism, we argue that this is an appropriate abstraction, since capitalist exploitation focuses on inequality due to differential *alienable* assets. For example, the rich, highly skilled producer of Chapter 6 who turns out to be "exploited" according to the labor theory of exploitation is not *capitalistically* exploited. The appropriate classification of producers who possess differential skills or labor endowment into capitalistically exploited and capitalistically exploiting is not given by the labor theory of exploitation, but by the game-theoretic criterion of withdrawing with a per capita share of alienable assets. These two definitions of exploitation differ once differential labor is postulated.

The argument can be summarized in a slightly different way. I have argued that the correct general characterization of capitalist exploitation is in terms of the game where coalitions withdraw with their per capita share of the alienable productive assets. More informally, the inequality which is struggled over under capitalism is that inequality due to differential ownership of alienable productive assets. Among the various commodity-value theories of exploitation, only one produces a decomposition of society into exploiters and exploited which agrees with the decomposition of society according to the definition of capitalist exploitation (that is, the asset-poor and the asset-rich), and that is the labor theory of exploitation. Furthermore, this holds precisely because labor is an equally distributed endowment, and the only equally distributed endowment. If we do not assume equal labor endowment, then not even the labor theory of exploitation gives a correct decomposition of society into capitalistically exploited and exploiting. One has no choice, in such a case, but to use the game-theoretic definition (which, I have claimed, has other merits compared to the labor theory in any case).

Hence, an application of the historical materialist hypothesis to the taxonomy of exploitation provides an answer to the question of why it is appropriate to formulate a labor theory of exploitation for capitalism. It is not because labor is the sole source of profit. It is certainly not because labor is scarce in an economic sense, since the claim that the real wage is bid down to a level sufficiently low to enable positive profits to exist depends on the relative abundance of labor to capital, on the existence of an industrial reserve army.[15] It is rather because the labor theory of exploitation, unlike any other commodity theory of exploitation, presents the focus of class antagonism (that is, the division of society into exploiters and exploited) as the actual one in capitalist society, between capitalists and workers. (Or, if we wish to be more detailed, it provides the four- or five-class decomposition of the exploitation hierarchy, studied in Parts I and II, which has been important in Marxian historical analysis.) And this is so under the assumption that the labor endowment is equally distributed. By its identification of exploiters and exploited, it also points to the claimed historical task of the capitalist era, namely the elimination of capitalist exploitation, which means also the elimination of the labor theory of exploitation as appropriate.

Notice the structure of this argument: we demonstrate that the labor theory of exploitation is appropriate for capitalism as a consequence of the historical observation that class struggle between capitalists and workers is what must be focused on. Thus the choice of labor as value numeraire is an example of how a model is chosen to capture a historical observation. In language I have used elsewhere (Roemer, 1981, introduction), the historical materialist *theory* directs attention to the class struggle of workers against capitalists in a particular mode of production, and a *model* is chosen (the labor theory of exploitation) to portray that theory. The labor theory is not to be justified independently of the historical materialist vision of history—but, given that vision, it is necessarily chosen. History viewed as a class struggle must come logically prior to the labor theory of exploitation. For a neoclassical or "natural scarcity" view of history, the model of the labor theory of exploitation is inappropriate.

An important conclusion follows: Marxists cannot hope to con-

15. I say scarce in an *economic* sense, since there is a sense of *personal* scarcity of labor as time and life duration which can also be held to account for its choice as the value numeraire. This account is rooted in the theory of alienation—namely that the creative capacity to labor/transform nature for the satisfaction of needs is an essential property of human beings. The appropriation of labor thus has special meaning. Laboring activity is time and life has duration, and the appropriation of labor therefore appropriates a part of life-as-duration, an act no person has a right to perform over another, even though his private property may make such an exchange possible. I do not think this Hegelian argument conflicts with mine, although neither is it necessary to it. I am grateful to Erik Wright for this point, and the wording of part of this note.

vince others of the validity of the labor theory of exploitation, on its own terms, as an objective theory. Acceptance of the model of Marxian exploitation is predicated on accepting observations that capitalism is characterized by class struggle between workers and capitalists, for it is that perception which the model is constructed to portray. Therefore, fruitful debate must concern the conflicting historical interpretations, rather than their *corollary* theories of value, which it is a mystification to regard as autonomous.

6. A sociology of injustice

Nothing has been said concerning how people think, in various societies, about the forms of inequality which exist. The theory of exploitation, as proposed, claims to illuminate historical development without reference to the perceptions of people making the history. Historical materialism should imply a corollary sociology of moral beliefs or injustice, in which exploited classes come to think of themselves as exploited and hence rebel against their exploitation.[16] Perhaps the exploited learn to classify feudal bondage as exploitative under feudalism, but not capitalist inequality; capitalist inequality becomes viewed as exploitative under capitalism, but not inequality due to skill differentials; and so on. Each mode of production might inculcate the beliefs in the exploited class which are necessary for it to perform its "historical task." Or perhaps the exploited are less discriminating in the kinds of inequality they struggle against (think of the egalitarian experiments which have appeared throughout history), but the only kind of inequality which can be successfully eliminated at a given point in time is the one which is not then socially necessary.

Indeed, why call the inequality due to differential ownership of alienable productive assets capitalist exploitation, when it is socially necessary? Why not call it capitalist inequality, and reserve the term exploitation for those forms of inequality which have become socially unnecessary? (Then, we would say proletarians are not capitalistically exploited under early capitalism.) Does my terminology not simply replace "inequality" with "exploitation," thus excising what

16. Questions such as these are investigated by Moore (1978), although not from a historical materialist perspective.

should be an important linguistic distinction? I have not previously raised this question, because the proper response requires, I think, a sociology of injustice which has not been developed.[17] The answer tentatively proposed here is that people in a society come to *view* certain forms of inequality as exploitative when the possibility, and eventually the necessity, arises to eliminate them. This occurs before those forms of inequality become socially unnecessary. The choice to describe early capitalist inequality as exploitative is made to respect the nascent moral beliefs of the proletarians, who come to view such inequality as exploitative. The bourgeois revolutionaries of 1789 would speak of feudal exploitation but capitalist inequality; the proletarian revolutionaries of 1848 would speak of capitalist exploitation, even before it became socially unnecessary; the proletarian revolutionaries of 1917 would speak of capitalist exploitation and socialist inequality; and there are those in current socialist society (witness the recent history of China) who would refer to the phenomenon as socialist exploitation, even before the differential remuneration of skills has become socially unnecessary in the dynamic sense. Paying such respect to the participators in class struggles of the time is not done here out of sentimentality, but to suggest the link, which must be made, between the theory of exploitation and the theory of class struggle.

That is, the theory of exploitation presented here is a development of only one facet of historical materialism—what is called, by both friend and foe, its technological determinism. The other facet, neglected here, is the mechanism historical materialism proposes to realize its determinist prediction, class struggle of the exploited against the exploiters. It is the sociology of injustice which must provide the link between these two facets of the Marxian theory of history.

17. The sociology of injustice or moral belief is not necessarily the same as the theory of justice (which may exist) to which I referred above.

References

Bahro, Rudolph. 1978. *The Alternative in Eastern Europe.* London: New Left Books.

Bettelheim, C. 1976. *Class Struggles in the USSR: First Period 1917–1923.* New York: Monthly Review Press.

——— 1978. *Class Struggles in the USSR: Second Period 1923–1930.* New York: Monthly Review Press.

Braverman, Harry. 1974. *Labor and Monopoly Capital: The Degradation of Work in the Twentieth Century.* New York: Monthly Review Press.

Brenkert, George G. 1979. Freedom and Private Property in Marx. *Philosophy and Public Affairs,* 8, no. 2.

Brenner, Robert. 1976. Agrarian Class Structure and Economic Development in Pre-industrial Europe. *Past and Present,* 70.

——— 1977. The Origins of Capitalist Development: A Critique of Neo-Smithian Marxism. *New Left Review,* 104.

Brus, Wlodzimierz. 1975. *Socialist Ownership and Political Systems.* London: Routledge and Kegan Paul.

Cohen, G. A. 1974. Marx's Dialectic of Labor. *Philosophy and Public Affairs,* 3.

——— 1978. *Karl Marx's Theory of History: A Defence.* Princeton, N.J.: Princeton University Press.

——— 1979. The Labor Theory of Value and the Concept of Exploitation. *Philosophy and Public Affairs,* 8.

——— 1980. Functional Explanation: Reply to Elster. *Political Studies,* 28.

——— 1981. Freedom, Justice and Capitalism. Isaac Deutscher Memorial Lecture. *New Left Review.*

Connor, Walter D. 1979. *Socialism, Politics, and Equality: Hierarchy and Change in Eastern Europe and the USSR.* New York: Columbia University Press.

Doeringer, P., and M. Piore. 1975. *Internal Labor Markets and Manpower Analysis.* Lexington, Mass.: D. C. Heath.

Elster, Jon. 1978. *Logic and Society.* New York: John Wiley.

——— 1980a. Cohen on Marx's Theory of History. *Political Studies,* 28.

——— 1980b. Exploitation and the Theory of Justice. Oslo: Historisk Institutt, University of Oslo (unpublished paper).

Elster, Jon, and Aanund Hyland. 1980. The Contradiction between Forces and Relations of Production. Oslo: Historisk Institutt, University of Oslo (unpublished paper).

Flakierski, Henryk. 1979. Economic Reform and Income Distribution in Hungary. *Cambridge Journal of Economics,* 3.

Flaschel, Peter. 1980. Labour Value, Exchange Value and the Measurement of Labor Productivity in a Marxian Model of Reproduction. Berlin: Institut für Wirtschaftstheorie, Free University of Berlin (unpublished paper).

Goldfield, Michael, and Melvin Rothenberg. 1980. *The Myth of Capitalism Reborn: A Marxist Critique of Theories of Capitalist Restoration in the USSR.* San Francisco, Calif.: Soviet Union Study Project, Line of March Publications.

Harman, C. 1975. *Bureaucracy and Revolution in Eastern Europe.* London: Pluto Press.

Harris, Marvin. 1979. *Cultural Materialism.* New York: Random House.

Horvat, Branco. 1980. *On the Political Economy of Socialism.* Belgrad: Institute of Economic Studies.

Howe, Roger E., and John E. Roemer. 1981. Rawlsian Justice as the Core of a Game. *American Economic Review,* 71, no. 5.

Husami, Ziyad. 1978. Marx on Distributive Justice. *Philosophy and Public Affairs,* 7.

Katz, Zev. 1973. *Patterns of Social Mobility in the USSR.* Cambridge, Mass.: MIT (unpublished paper).

Konrád, George, and Ivan Szelényi. 1979. *The Intellectuals on the Road to Class Power.* New York: Harcourt, Brace, Jovanovich.

Kronman, Anthony. 1981. Talent Pooling. *Human Rights: Nomos,* 23, New York: New York University Press.

Lakatos, Imre. 1976. *Proofs and Refutations.* New York: Cambridge University Press.

Lange, Oskar. 1938. *On the Economic Theory of Socialism.* New York: McGraw Hill.

Lenin, V. I. 1974. *The Development of Capitalism in Russia* (1899). Moscow: Progress Publishers.

Lindert, Peter, and Jeffrey Williamson. 1980. English Workers' Living Standards during the Industrial Revolution: A New Look. Davis: University of California, Department of Economics Working Paper No. 144.

Mao Tse-Tung. 1965. Analysis of the Classes in Chinese Society (1926). In *Selected Works of Mao Tse-Tung.* Peking: Foreign Language Press.

Marx, Karl. 1966. *Capital,* Volume III. Moscow: Progress Publishers.

——— 1973. *Grundrisse.* London: Allen Lane.

Maschler, M., B. Peleg, and L. S. Shapley. 1979. Geometric Properties of the Kernel, Nucleolus, and Related Solution Concepts. *Mathematics of Operations Research,* 4.

Matthews, Mervyn. 1978. *Privilege in the Soviet Union.* London: George Allen & Unwin.

Moore, Barrington, Jr. 1978. *Injustice: The Social Bases of Obedience and Revolt.* White Plains, N.Y.: Myron Sharpe.

Morishima, Michio. 1973. *Marx's Economics.* Cambridge: Cambridge University Press.

——— 1974. Marx in the Light of Modern Economic Theory. *Econometrica,* 42.

North, Douglass, and Robert Thomas. 1973. *The Rise of the Western World.* Cambridge: Cambridge University Press.

Nuti, D. M. 1979. The Contradictions of Socialist Economies: A Marxian Interpretation. In *The Socialist Register,* ed. R. Miliband and J. Saville. New York: Monthly Review Press.

Ostroy, Joseph. 1980. The No-Surplus Condition as a Characterization of Perfectly Competitive Equilibrium. *Journal of Economic Theory,* 22.

Parkin, Frank. 1971. *Class Inequality and Political Order: Social Stratification in Capitalist and Communist Societies.* New York: Praeger.

Pryor, Frederick. 1977. *The Origins of the Economy: A Comparative Study of Distribution in Primitive and Peasant Economies.* New York: Academic Press.

Rakovski, Marc. 1978. *Towards an East European Marxism.* London: St. Martin's Press.

Rawls, John. 1971. *A Theory of Justice.* Cambridge, Mass.: Harvard University Press.

Roemer, J. E. 1977. Technical Change and the "Tendency of the Rate of Profit to Fall." *Journal of Economic Theory,* 16.

——— 1980a. A General Equilibrium Approach to Marxian Economics. *Econometrica,* 48.

——— 1980b. Innovation, Rates of Profit, and Uniqueness of von Neumann Prices. *Journal of Economic Theory,* 22.

——— 1981. *Analytical Foundations of Marxian Economic Theory.* New York: Cambridge University Press.

——— 1982. New Directions in the Marxian Theory of Exploitation and Class. *Politics and Society.*

——— 1983a. Property Relations vs. Surplus Value in Marxian Exploitation. *Philosophy and Public Affairs.*

——— 1983b. Unequal Exchange, Labor Migration, and International Capital Flows: A Theoretical Synthesis. In *Marxism, Central Planning, and the Soviet Economy: Economic Essays in Honor of Alexander Erlich,* ed. Padma Desai. Cambridge, Mass.: MIT Press.

Selucký, Radoslav. 1979. *Marxism, Socialism, Freedom.* New York: St. Martin's Press.

Sen, Amartya K. 1973. *On Economic Inequality.* Oxford: Oxford University Press.

——— 1978. On the Labour Theory of Value: Some Methodological Issues. *Cambridge Journal of Economics,* 2: 175–190.

——— 1980. Equality of What? In *The Tanner Lecture on Human Values,* ed.

Sterling McMurrin. Salt Lake City and New York: University of Utah Press and Cambridge University Press.
Shapley, Lloyd. 1971. Cores of Convex Games. *International Journal of Game Theory.*
Steedman, Ian. 1977. *Marx after Sraffa.* London: New Left Books.
Von Weizsäcker, C. C., and P. Samuelson. 1971. A New Labor Theory of Value for Rational Planning through Use of the Bourgeois Profit Rate. *Proceedings of the National Academy of Science,* 68.
Wiles, P. 1974. *Distribution of Income: East and West.* Amsterdam: North Holland Press.
Wolfstetter, Elmar. 1973. Surplus Labour, Synchronized Labour Costs and Marx's Labour Theory of Value. *Economic Journal,* 83.
Wood, Allen. 1972. The Marxian Critique of Justice. *Philosophy and Public Affairs,* 1.
——— 1979. Marx on Right and Justice: A Reply to Husami. *Philosophy and Public Affairs,* 8.
Yanowitch, Murray. 1979. *Social and Economic Inequality in the Soviet Union.* New York: Myron Sharpe.
Zaslavsky, Victor. 1979–80. The Regime and the Working Class in the USSR. *Telos,* 42.
——— 1980. Socioeconomic Inequality and Changes in Soviet Ideology. *Theory and Society,* 9, No. 2.

Index